1 50

L. Ray Marston,
409 Daniel St.,
Champaign,
Illinois

Story of the Nations

A Series of Historical Studies intended to present in graphic narratives the stories of the different nations that have attained prominence in history.

In the story form the current of each national life is distinctly indicated, and its picturesque and noteworthy periods and episodes are presented for the reader in their philosophical relations to each other as well as to universal history.

12°, Illustrated, cloth, each   . net $1.50
Half Leather, each . . . net $1.75

FOR FULL LIST SEE END OF THIS VOLUME.

SIEGE OF CONSTANTINOPLE.

THE STORY OF THE NATIONS

TURKEY

BY

STANLEY LANE-POOLE

AUTHOR OF "THE MOORS IN SPAIN," "THE BARBARY
CORSAIRS," "SALADIN," ETC.

ASSISTED BY

F. J. W. GIBB AND ARTHUR GILMAN

NEW YORK
G. P. PUTNAM'S SONS
LONDON: T. FISHER UNWIN

The Knickerbocker Press, New York

PREFACE.

THE history of Turkey has yet to be written. The standard authority is Von Hammer's *Geschichte des Osmanischen Reiches,* of which there is a French translation, and from which many books have been compiled in many languages. In English, Von Hammer found an able condenser in Sir Edward Creasy, whose *History of the Ottoman Turks* is the best concise work we possess on the subject. Von Hammer, however, is not always accurate, despite his laborious research, and he is generally dull. A Turkish scholar, possessed of a sense of literary form, who would take the Austrian's facts, collate them with the native annalists and historiographers, and present them with all the advantages of skilful arrangement and charm of style, would render a real service to historical literature.

The present volume, however, makes no pretensions to fill the gap. All that is here attempted is to draw the main outlines of Turkish history in bold strokes, and thus try to leave a connected impression on the reader's mind. In so small a compass it is impossible to be detailed. Those who desire more than can here be given should turn to Sir E. Creasy, or to the Vte. A. de la Jonquière's *Histoire de l'Empire Ottoman,* in Duruy's series ; and thence, if still ambitious, to Von Hammer. In these pages clearness and brevity have been the main considerations ; and, while striving to escape the charge of prolixity, I have carefully avoided the sin of moralizing. Many instructive morals have been drawn from the past and present state of Turkey ; but these appear to depend so much for their point and application upon the political bias of the writer that, on the whole, they are best omitted. We have all heard about the " sick man " and the " armed camp : " but, if we are Conservatives, we palliate the disease, and call the encampment an innocent review ; if we are Radicals, we send for the undertaker for the one, and call for the expulsion of the other, that it may no longer menace the peace of Europe. Between these extremes, the reader may take his choice.

The naval history of Turkey, a subject of peculiar interest, has been barely touched upon here, because it is so closely interwoven with the exploits of the Barbary buccaneers, that it will be more satisfactorily traced in the *Story of the Corsairs,* which I am writing for the same series. Another subject which has been omitted is the history of Egypt under Turkish rule : for this belongs to the special volume on Modern Egypt, now in preparation.

I owe special thanks to Mr. E. J. W. Gibb, not only for the chapters on " Ottoman Literature," " Stambol," and " Ottoman Administration," for which he is almost entirely responsible, but also for many suggestions and additions in other parts of the book, the whole of which has had the advantage of his revision. Mr. Gilman has also contributed to a part of the subject which was less familiar to Mr. Gibb and myself ; and I am indebted for valuable assistance to Mr. H. H. Howorth, M.P., and to Mr. W. R. Morfill, whose advice has been followed in the systematic spelling of Russian names.

STANLEY LANE-POOLE.

BIRLING, SUSSEX,
   January 17, 1888.

CONTENTS.

I.

II.

III.

LIST OF ILLUSTRATIONS.

Some of the above are copied from a curious work of P. Coeck, *Les Moeurs*, etc., *des Turcz* (1553), which Sir W. Stirling Maxwell edited in 1873 under the title of *The Turks in* 1533. The original is in the British Museum. Others are reproductions of some of the cuts in the *Recueil de cent estampes gravées sur les tableaux peints d'après nature en* 1707 *et* 1708, *par les ordres de M. de Ferriol, ambassadeur du roi à la Porte* (1714).

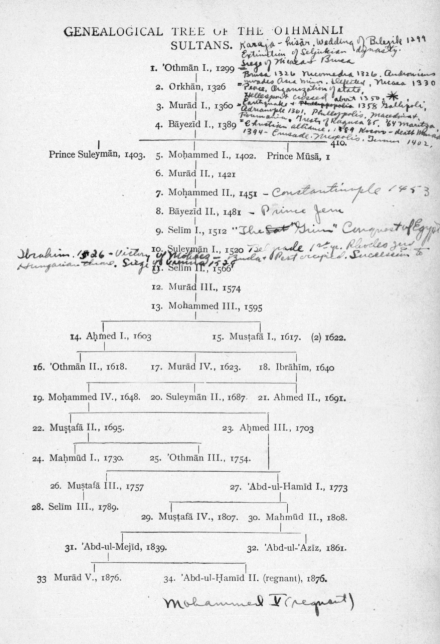

GENEALOGICAL TREE OF THE OTHMÁNLI
SULTANS.

1. 'Othmán I., 1299

2. Orkhán, 1326

3. Murád I., 1360

4. Báyezíd I., 1389

Prince Suleymán, 1403.   5. Mohammed I., 1402.   Prince Músá, 1

6. Murád II., 1421

7. Mohammed II., 1451

8. Báyezíd II., 1481

9. Selím I., 1512

10. Suleymán I., 1520

11. Selím II., 1566

12. Murád III., 1574

13. Mohammed III., 1595

14. Ahmed I., 1603   15. Mustafá I., 1617.   (2) 1622.

16. 'Othmán II., 1618.   17. Murád IV., 1623.   18. Ibráhím, 1640

19. Mohammed IV., 1648.   20. Suleymán II., 1687.   21. Ahmed II., 1691.

22. Mustafá II., 1695.   23. Ahmed III., 1703

24. Mahmúd I., 1730.   25. 'Othmán III., 1754.

26. Mustafá III., 1757   27. 'Abd-ul-Hamíd I., 1773

28. Selím III., 1789.

29. Mustafá IV., 1807.   30. Mahmúd II., 1808.

31. 'Abd-ul-Mejíd, 1839.   32. 'Abd-ul-'Azíz, 1861.

33 Murád V., 1876.   34. 'Abd-ul-Hamíd II. (regnant), 1876.

THE STORY OF TURKEY.

I.

THE KING'S FRONT.
(1250–1326.)

THE thirteenth century was an eventful epoch for
all Europe. The overshadowing power of the Empire
was waning, separate states were springing up in
Italy and Germany, and the growth of civil liberty
was bringing its fruit in the enlargement of ideas and
the founding of universities. In England, the Nor-
man and Saxon were at last one people, and the
business of the nation was to strengthen the bond
which united them ; Magna Charta was signed, and
the first Parliament was summoned. In the East the
long struggle for the Holy City had ended in the dis-
comfiture of the Christians, and the last of the Crusades
was led by Saint Louis against the Mamlūks of Egypt,
where the king and his army were taken captive.
What was lost in the East was gained in the West :
Ferdinand of Castile was winning city after city
from the Moors in Spain, who were now fortifying

themselves in their last stronghold at Granada, where they held out for two centuries more. Sicily, which had once been a favourite province of the Saracens, was the scene of a series of tragedies: Manfred was killed by Count Charles of Anjou, whose tyranny led to the fatal "Vespers" and the foundation of the Kingdom of the Two Sicilies. All Europe was heated with the strong wine of political change.

In this same eventful century Asia was passing through a still more sudden and subversive revolution. The Mongolian hordes of Chingiz Khān had been let loose from their plains of Central Asia, and, like the bursting of long pent up waters, had poured in a swift whirling flood over all the countries of the East, and carried ruin and devastation whithersoever they went. Chingiz himself died in the earlier part of the century, but his sons and grandsons proved themselves worthy disciples of their terrible sire. The famous Khalifate of Baghdad, which during half a millennium had been the inheritor of the most sacred traditions of Islam, now fell for ever before the on-slaught of Hulāgu Khān. The fair provinces which had owned the victorious sway of Saladin and his house, and were now the appanage of those gallant Mamlūk chiefs whose wealth and taste placed Cairo and Damascus on the pinnacle of renown, were menaced and partly overrun by the barbarian; and the mountain passes of Anatolia, which for generations had suffered no sovereign tread save that of the Sel-jūk Sultan of Iconium, now shook under the tramp of the Tartar's horse. A Mongol army even pene-trated Europe as far as Germany, ravaged Hungary, routed the Teutonic knights at Liegnitz, and then contentedly returned to their Eastern deserts, as though contemptuous of the attractions of Europe.

It was fortunate that the Mongols were possessed by the migratory spirit too strongly to think of settling in cities and founding empires ; the wave of barbarism flowed, but happily it also ebbed. In the far East its influence was more enduring ; the descendants of Chingiz were for many generations Yuen emperors of China, Khans of Turkistan, chiefs of the Golden Horde, of the Crimea, and of Kazan, whence for centuries they dominated and curbed the rising power of Russia. All these dynasties reigned in the domain of barbarism : they left no lasting impress on the civilized lands of the Khalifate, where Arab, Persian, and Turk had each in turn put forth the best of his genius, and had assimilated and developed what elements of philosophy, art, and science, had come within his reach.

To trace the pedigree of the Ottoman Turks we must look back into remote antiquity. In the early history of Central and Eastern Asia everything is more or less conjecture, but this at least is certain, that among the numerous nomad tribes who roamed the plains of Sungaria and the great desert of Gobi, and from time to time broke loose in one of those great waves of migration which paralyzed the peoples of Europe and of Western Asia, there were two races which alternately filled the *rôle* of " the scourges of God," the Mongols and the Turks. The Mongols first appear on the scene under the name of Hiong Nu as dominat...g the nomad world in the days of

the Chinese dynasty of the Han, and dominating
especially the two great branches of the Turkish
race known as Uighurs and Turks properly so called.
The Uighurs eventually became free from this domination, and under the names of Yueh chi and
White Huns broke in pieces the Greek kingdom
of Bactria, and founded a famous empire, with its
capital at Balkh, which became the scourge of the
Sassanians on the one hand, and filled a more remarkable place in Indian history than is generally
suspected on the other. The power of the Hiong
Nu was destroyed by the Chinese ; it revived again
presently under the Jouan-Jouan, who were masters of
all the steppes from the Volga eastwards. A revolt
took place against the Jouan-Jouan in the beginning of
the sixth century when the Turks *eo nomine* are for
the first time heard of in history. They founded an
empire which stretched from the borders of Manchuria
to the Carpathians, and commanded also Transoxiana and the country as far as the Indus. Their
power south of the Sihun or Jaxartes was sapped and
eventually destroyed by the Arabs, who founded the
Samani dynasty ; but the Turks remained masters of
the steppes, and supplied the Samanis, and even the
Khalifs, with mercenary troops whose leaders presently supplanted their masters and founded a famous
Turkish dynasty at Ghazni, while somewhat later
fresh hordes under their own leaders planted themselves in Khorasan and created the splendid empire
of the Seljūks, who from the eleventh to the thirteenth
century governed the greater part of the Khalifs'
dominions in Asia, and advanced the Mohammedan

rule into the mountain ranges of Anatolia, and thus prepared the way for the Ottomans, their successors. By this time the empire of the Khalifs was full of Turks. They were introduced first as captives, whose fair beauty speedily commended itself to the Arab princes, and whose martial vigour marked them out as a fit body-guard for the Khalif against his unruly subjects in Persia. First as slaves, then as a military aristocracy, and then as Seljūkian Sultans, the Turks pressed forwards and absorbed all the power which had once belonged to Arab and Persian, from the river Oxus to the borders of Egypt and the Asiatic frontier of the Byzantine Empire.

The Seljūks of Khorasan and Persia were displaced by their own vassals, the Shahs of Khuwarezm or Khiva, who were supported by hordes of the Kankalis from the country north of the Sea of Aral, and who were the ancestors of the modern Turko-mans. The Shahs of Khuwarezm step by step succeeded to the dominion of their late masters, and at one time, at the beginning of the thirteenth century, threatened to gather under their authority the whole Asiatic empire of Islam. But when they were about to realize their utmost dreams of supre-macy a sudden blow crushed them, and the king-dom of Khuwarezm was blotted out from the list of principalities and powers. The resources of the steppes of Tartary were not yet exhausted : there were still whole nations of barbarians ready to emerge from obscurity, and swoop down upon the rich territories of the earlier emigrants. This time it was the Mongol race that Asia again poured forth to terrify the West.

Chingiz Khan, as has been said, surrounded by a family of born soldiers, and followed by hordes of nomads like the sands of the sea without number, overran the dominions of the Khuwarezm Shah, and sweeping over the empire of the Khalifate and of the Seljūks appeared ready and able to make a *tabula rasa* of all existing authority. His armies even spread into Europe, and but for the valour of the Teutonic Knights might have arrested for awhile the dawning civilization of the West. Of this tremendous invasion the only trace which remains in Europe is to be found in Russia, whose history was shaped and whose political and moral characteristics are largely traceable to the long domination of the Tartars.

The Turks, however, remained masters of the west of Asia, and the Mongol tide only swept them further south and west on its boisterous crest. Driven from Khuwarezm on the downfall of that kingdom, they fled south. Some of them took a prominent part in Persian and Syrian history in the fourteenth and fifteenth century under the names of Turkomans of the White and the Black Sheep. Others wandered further south and came into conflict with the Mamluk Sultans of Egypt, who were also members of the great Turkish family; and when they were beaten back, turned north and joined their kinsmen of the race of Seljūk in Asia Minor. One of these tribes who had been set wandering by the rude shock of the Mongol invasion, and who eventually came to join the Turks of Anatolia in the curious manner we have related after the battle of Angora, was that of Ertoghrul, which afterwards became famous under the victorious name of the Ottomans. When they joined their kinsmen in Lesser Asia almost all the Mohammedan world was in the hands of the nomad tribes of the steppes. Turks ruled in Asia Minor, Turks governed Egypt, Turks held minor authority under the Mongols in Syria and Mesopotamia, while the descendants of Chingiz had succeeded to the dominion of the Khalifs in Persia, had assumed all the dignity of sovereignty in the wild regions of the Volga and the Ural Mountains, in the lands of the Oxus, and the deserts of Tartary, had spread across Central Asia and had founded an empire in China, and were preparing to establish the long line of Mongol emperors in Hindustan whom we know by the name of the Great Moguls.[1]

It was reserved for the Turkish race to be lord of the countries bordering the Mediterranean Sea. The Turks were there before the Mongols, and the Turks are there still. The Mamlūks of Egypt, mainly of Turkish blood, withstood the Mongol tide which was breaking upon their marches ; the Turkish Sultans of Iconium, of the lineage of Seljūk, breasted for awhile the swelling surge of barbarism ; and their successors, the Turks of Othmān's line, drove the Mongols inch by inch out of the Lesser Asia, and taking to themselves the whole of the eastern and southern coasts of the Mediterranean, and turning the Black Sea into a Turkish lake, tamed and bitted the descendants of the great Chingiz himself in the Crimea. The

---

[1] I am indebted to our greatest authority on the history of the Mongol and Turkish races, Mr. II. II. Howorth, M.P., for valuable suggestions on the migrations of the Turkish tribes.

Ottoman Turk now sits in the seat of Hulāgu at
Baghdad ; he has long owned the territories of the
Seljūks, the empire of Saladin, and the slim river
valley of the Mamlūks. The dominion of the Saracens, which the Mongols in vain essayed to grasp,
passed into the hands of the Turks, and the stock to
whom this wide empire still belongs, shorn as it is of
its ancient renown, had its origin in the throes of the
Mongol invasion ; the struggle between the invaders
and the old masters of Anatolia was commemorated
by the birth of the Ottoman Turk.

The thirteenth century had run half its course
when Kay-Kubād, the Seljūk Sultan of Iconium, was
one day hard beset near Angora by a Mongol
army. The enemy was rapidly gaining the mastery,
when suddenly the fortune of the day was reversed.
A small body of unknown horsemen charged upon
the foe, and Victory declared for the Seljūk. The
cavaliers who had thus opportunely come to the
rescue knew not whom they had assisted, nor did the
Seljūks recognize their allies. The meeting was one
of those remarkable accidents which sometimes shape
the future of nations. Ertoghrul, son of Suleymān—
a member of the Oghuz family of Turks, which the
Mongol avalanche had dislodged from its old camping
grounds in Khorasan and had pressed in a westerly
direction—was journeying from the Euphrates' banks,
where he had halted awhile, to the more peaceful seclusion of Anatolia, when he unexpectedly came upon
the battlefield of Angora. With the nomad's love of a
scrimmage, and the warrior's sympathy for the weaker
side, he led his four hundred riders pell-mell into the

fray and won the day. He little thought that by his impulsive and chivalrous act he had taken the first step towards founding an empire that was destined to endure in undiminished glory for three centuries, and which even now, when more than six hundred years have elapsed and many a fair province has been wrested or inveigled out of its grasp, still stands lord over wide lands, and holds the allegiance of many peoples of divers races and tongues. From Ertoghrul to the reigning Sultan of Turkey, thirty-five princes in the male line have ruled the Ottoman Empire without a break in the succession. There is no such example of the continuous authority of a single family in the history of Europe.

The Seljūk Sultan was not slow to reward his unexpected allies. The strangers were granted their wish and established themselves in the dominions of Kay-Kubād ; their summer camp was on the Ermeni mountains, which form the southern rampart of the Roman province of Bithynia, wherein were the great Greek cities of Brusa and Nicaea ; and in winter they drove their flocks from the southern slopes to the valley of the Sangarius (Sakariya), where the city of Sugut, which the Greeks called Thebasion, was given them as their capital. Behind was Angora, where they had made their first appearance on a great battlefield ; in front of them lay Brusa, near which they soon displayed again their valour and generalship against a combined army of Greeks and Mongols. Skilfully manoeuvring a body of light horse in the van of the battle, Ertoghrul contrived so to mask the Sultan's main attack that after three days and nights of sore fighting the Seljūks triumphed over their adversaries and drove them headlong to the sea coast. This defence of the Pass of Ermeni brought high renown to the leader of the Turks, who had fought all through the battle in front of the Sultan's guard, and Ertoghrul was given in perpetuity the district of Eskishehr (the Dorylaeum of the ancients), which, in memory of his foremost position in the engagement, received a new name, and was henceforth known as Sultanöni, "the King's Front," as it is in the present day.

Sultanöni was a precious and responsible charge to the new-comers. It formed the barrier between the dominions of the Christian and those of the Moslem on the Bithynian marches. Hence could the soldiers of Islam best wage the Sacred War against the enfeebled outworks of the Eastern Empire. The vantage ground of Sultanöni furnished the Ottomans with the needful $\pi o \hat{v} \ \sigma \tau \hat{\omega}$ whence to subdue the vast empire which long owned their sway. Pasturing their herds on the slopes of Ermeni and Temnos, or in the plains watered by the Sakariya, the strangers grew in number, wealth, and strength ; and though it was not at once nor without many a struggle that they imposed their authority upon the semi-independent chiefs of the district, yet they were already masters in name of a rich and fertile land and of populous and wealthy cities : Eskishehr, with its gardens and vineyards, its baths and hostelries ; Sugut, Ertoghrul's capital, where his grave is still shown ; and other strong places, besides hamlets, formed part of the district in which the cradle of the Ottoman Empire was first securely set.

ROCK MONASTERY, ANATOLIA.

At Sugut in 1258 was born Othmān,[1] son of Ertoghrul, from whom, since he was the first ruler of the
line who ventured to assert his absolute independence,
his descendants took the name of Othmānlīs, or as we
call them " Ottomans." It was their special and proud
title, and until lately they never degraded themselves
by the appellation of " Turk." Othmān was worthy
to be the eponymous hero of a warlike race. Long
years of peace, during which his father strengthened
the hold of the clan upon the province entrusted to
his rule, gave the son time to prepare for the epoch
of conquest which crowned his later years. The first
important event in Othmān's life was as domestic as
it was natural : he fell in love. At the little village
of Itburuni, near Eskishehr, dwelt a learned doctor
of the law, Edebali, with whom Othmān loved to
converse, not the less because the good man had a
daughter fair to see, whom some called Māl Khatun,
" Lady Treasure," and others Kamarīya, " Moon-
bright," from her surpassing beauty. But the family
of Othmān was as yet new to the country, and its
authority was not recognized by the surrounding
chieftains of the Anatolian aristocracy. Other
young men of higher rank might bring their court
to the fair damsel, and her father discouraged
the suit of the son of Ertoghrul. At last he was
convinced by an argument which has ever been
potent among the superstitious peoples of the East .
a dream dispelled his doubts. One night Othmān
as he slumbered thought he saw himself and the old
man his host stretched upon the ground, and from

---

[1] Pronounced, in Turkish, Osman.

Edebali's breast there seemed to rise a moon, which waxing to the full, approached the prostrate form of Othmān and finally sank to rest in his bosom Thereat from out his loins sprang forth a tree, which grew taller and taller, and raised its head, and spread out its branches, till the boughs overshadowed the earth and the seas. Under the canopy of leaves towered four mighty mountains, Caucasus and Atlas, Taurus and Haemus, which held up the leafy vault like four great tent poles, and from their sides flowed royal rivers, Nile and Danube, Tigris and Euphrates. Ships sailed upon the waters, harvests waved upon the fields, the rose and the cypress, flower and fruit, delighted the eye, and on the boughs birds sang their glad music. Cities raised domes and minarets towards the green canopy; temples and obelisks, towers and fortresses, lifted their high heads, and on their pinnacles shone the golden Crescent. And behold, as he looked, a great wind arose and dashed the Crescent against the Crown of Constantine, that imperial city which stood at the meeting of two seas and two continents, like a diamond between sapphires and emeralds, the centre jewel of the ring of empire.[1] Othmān was about to place the dazzling ring upon his finger, when he awoke. He told Māl Khatun's father what he had seen, and, convinced of the great future that was thus foretold for the offspring of Othmān and the Moon-faced damsel, Edebali consented to their union. Their son Orkhan was born in 1288 and Ertoghrul died the same year, leaving Othmān head of the clan and lord of Eskishehr, to which the

[1] Von Hammer, "Geschichte des Osmanischen Reichs," i. 66-7.

Seljūk Sultan added in 1289 Karaja hisār (Melangeia).
Othmān's first care was to build a mosque at Eskishehr, and to appoint the necessary officers for the
administration of the law and the performance of the
ritual of Islam. Firm and impartial justice formed
the forefront of his policy, and largely contributed
to the spread of his authority. All these peaceful
occupations, however, were soon set aside for the
fascinations of war. There had been a time when
the clansmen were content to feed their flocks on the
hillside, to gather their honey and weave their carpets,
and lead the simple unambitious life of the shep-
herd ; but soon they left these familiar paths for new
and daring ascents. One by one they reduced the
smaller chieftains of the province to obedience ; one
after the other they captured the outlying forts of the
Greek Empire, till their power extended to Yenishehr,
and they were thus almost within sight of Bruṣa and
Nicaea, the two chief cities of the Greeks in Asia.
The acquisition of so important a situation as
Yenishehr was the result of craft outwitting craft.
A wedding at Bilejik in 1299 was selected as a
rendezvous for a number of Othmān's rivals, who
plotted to capture him and put an end to his power.
Warned of the conspiracy, forty women of the Ottoman clan were admitted on a pretext to the castle,
where preparations were being made for the wedding.
When both garrison and guests were absorbed in the
ceremonies, the forty women cast away their disguise
and proved to be none other than forty of Othmān's
bravest warriors. They speedily possessed themselves of the fort and the bride, a beautiful young

Greek named Nenuphar ("Lotus-bloom"), afterwards
the mother of Murād I. Before the ruse got wind,
Othmān swept like the lightning upon Yarhisār,
and seized it, while another band of his followers took
possession of Aynegöl. Thus he extended the dominion
of the Ottomans from the Ermeni range to Mount
Olympus. The Turk now set his capital at Yenishehr,
which he used as a stepping-stone to Brusa and
thence eventually to Constantinople. Even with this
addition, however, the Ottoman territory corresponded
only to one of the seventeen sub-divisions of Rūm,
which was itself but one of the twenty-five provinces
into which the great empire of Suleymān the Magnificent was in later times divided.[1]

More than half a century had passed since the
Ottoman Turks first settled in Sultanöni, yet their
borders were still narrow. When the wave of advance
was once undulating, however, it proceeded with accelerated speed. Like the circling ripple that springs up
in a pool when a stone is dropped into its midst, the
sway of the Turk spread in ever-enlarging rings.
A powerful impulse was given to their progress
by the extinction of the Seljūk dynasty at the end
of the thirteenth century. Ten several states, of
which Sultanöni was one, succeeded to the authority
of the Seljūks and divided their territory among
them. Henceforward there was no supreme and
sovereign power to repress the ambitions of the
Turks,—only rivals who could be fought and subdued
with no disloyalty to the king who had first given
them a hospitable welcome to his dominions. All

[1] Von Hammer, i. 75.

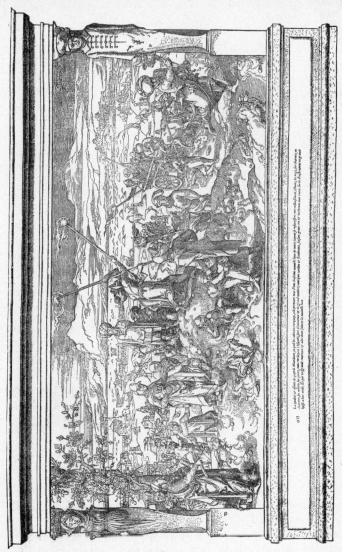

La goalloi xi eßano la part di Mordono, jovel lo ordoano tro parto, pla primara vna e l'una frestiano ouando hana da vantro auand y tridanoffino un viheobedan et obanti, la vega e dar haruro, un chafono la baßmo fatto por groffo, non von vir ye balhumo ona i onno forza d'affrigono ing omido buffa a loa moda. Et por triffamodi vanturo et aloi otono fatoni la vanola hinu

617

A TURKISH MERRY-MAKING.

these states were eventually swallowed up in the
empire of the House of Othmān, but this did not
happen till many years after its founder's death.
The prince of Karaman was the strongest of the ten,
and many long wars were fought with him before his
lands were annexed to the Turkish dominions. In
the early days of which we are writing, the Kara-
manian state was too powerful for the Ottoman to
attempt an advance in this direction ; and the chief
extension of their territory in the beginning of the
fourteenth century was towards Europe, where the
feeble representatives of the once mighty Emperors of
the East offered an easy prey to the hardy warriors of
Sultanöni. From his stronghold at Yenishehr, Othmān sent out expeditions against the nearest Greek
towns, and captured many fortresses before the armies
of the emperor moved out against him. When at
length he met the Byzantine army at Baphoeum, he
put it to utter rout and ravaged the whole of Bithynia,
so that the Greeks dared not venture outside the walls
of Nicaea.[1] Encouraged by such successes Othmān
pushed his forces nearer the sea, and emulated the
example of the princes of Aydin and Saru-Khan,
whose fleets had ravaged the Greek islands and thus
inaugurated the terrible scourge of the Corsair.
Gradually he hemmed in the second city of the
empire, Nicaea ; slowly he brought up his armies
against Brusa, and erected two forts over against
the city, whence for ten years he pressed the
siege. "The method employed by the Ottomans to
gain possession of the large, populous, and well-

---

[1] Finlay, "History of Greece," iii. 387.

fortified cities, inhabited by the wealthy but unwarlike Greeks, was not unlike that employed by the Dorians in the early ages of Greece. Indeed it is almost the only way by which the courage and perseverance of a small force can conquer art and numbers. Instead of attempting to form a regular blockade of the city against which they directed their operations, and thereby compelling the inhabitants to exert all their unbroken power to deliver themselves from the attack, the Ottoman Turks established strong posts in the vicinity of the city, ravaged the fields, carried off cattle and slaves, and interrupted the commercial communications of the inhabitants. The devastation of the country and the insecurity of the roads gradually raised the price of provisions and caused emigration and famine. In this way Nicaea, the cradle of the Greek Church, and which had been for two generations the capital of the Greek Empire, was closely blockaded."[1] Meanwhile Othmān's flying cavalry ravaged the country as far as the Bosphorus and Black Sea : the Emperor, standing on the towers of his palace at Constantinople, could see the flames of the burning villages across the Bosphorus ; the Turk's vessels harried the coast ; the whole country trembled before his unwearied and ubiquitous onslaught. He had laid his plans well, and the ten years leaguer of Brusa produced its result. The great city capitulated in 1326; Orkhan planted the Ottoman flag on its walls, and hastened to Sugut in time to tell the good news to his father. Othmān lived to hear of the victory, and then died contented, at the age of seventy, after a

[1] Finlay, iii. 423–4.

BRUSA.

reign of twenty-six years. His last wish was to be buried at Brusa, the new capital of the growing state ; and thither was he reverently borne, and there did his sepulchre stand to the present century. His sword is still preserved at Constantinople, and each successive Sultan of his posterity is solemnly invested with the founder's blade by way of coronation.

, The Turks with reason hold Othmān to be their first Sultan. Ertoghrul indeed established the clan in Asia Minor, but he did not achieve independence or raise his dignity to more than that of a petty prince. Othmān was the first to dream of empire, and though he did not wholly realize his dream, and view the proud city of Constantine at his feet, he pushed his conquests to the very verge of the Hellespont, set his son upon the throne at Brusa, and prepared the way for the immediate conquest of Nicaea and Nicomedia and the firm establishment of the Turkish sway upon the shores of the Bosphorus He inaugurated the career of victory which his descendants completed ; his wars against Greeks and Mongols, and the Turkish emīrs who had succeeded the Seljūks, set an example which his son and grandson knew how to follow ; and Othmān's commanding influence was felt long after his death.

Personally, like the first Khalifs of the Arabs, he was simple and primitive in his tastes and habits. He left neither silver nor gold behind him ; but only a salt-bowl—symbol of hospitality,—a spoon, a braided coat and white linen turban, his standards, a fine stud of horses, a yoke of oxen, and some flocks of sheep, whose descendants still browse upon the pastures of Brusa. Simple as was his dress, his figure was imposing. Like Artaxerxes "Longimanus," his arms reached below his knees, his thighs were those of a horseman, and his prominent nose, black hair and beard, and swarthy hue, procured him the name of "Black Othmān," for black is a colour of honour in the East, and indicates strength of character as well as bodily vigour and energy. Black Othmān transmitted his physical characteristics to several generations of his successors, and for at least three hundred years there sat no Sultan on the Ottoman throne who was not distinguished for personal courage. Bravery is the heritage of the Turk.

II.

ACROSS THE HELLESPONT.
(1326–1380.)

WHEN Orkhan came to the throne, one of the chief strongholds of the Greeks in Asia had fallen: the rest were not slow to succumb to the young vigour of the Turks. Nicomedia followed Brusa in the same year (1326). The Emperor Andronicus marched in 1329 against the invaders, but was wounded, and his camp at Pelecanon fell into the hands of Orkhan; Nicaea surrendered in 1330, and in 1336 Pergamon, the capital of Mysia, was taken from the prince of Karasi and added to the Ottoman realm. The people of Nicaea were permitted to emigrate and take with them all their goods, archives, and relics, and such moderation greatly strengthened the position of the conqueror. The little clan of shepherds, who had been graciously permitted to settle in the kingdom of the Seljūks, had now possessed themselves, in two generations, of the whole of the north-west corner of Asia Minor, where they commanded the eastern shore of the Bosphorus. Here for the moment they were content to rest. The Greek emperor was glad to make peace, and the Turks were anxious to gain

time to organize their new dominions and prepare
for the great struggle which they knew was before
them.

For twenty years tranquility reigned undisturbed
throughout the land of the Turks, and during these
twenty years Orkhan and his elder brother Alā-ud-
dīn, the first Turkish Vezīr,[1] laboured at the organization of the State and the army.   The insignia of
sovereignty were now assumed : Orkhan issued money
in his own name as independent Sultan.   But
the assumption of royal dignity could be but an
empty form unless means were taken to defend it
against the hostile forces that lay all around.   To
this end Alā-ud-dīn, who was the true founder of
the Ottoman Empire in so far as it depended
upon military organization, began to reform the
army.   Instead of leading their mounted followers
in the old manner of the clan, when the chief sent
messages through the villages to summon his kindred
and liegemen to the fight (where they rode in a serried
wall, without infantry support), and afterwards let
them depart to their homes, the Ottoman Sultans in
future would have permanent regiments to trust to—
the first standing army of modern times.   Instead of
volunteers there was now to be a paid army.   This
was the natural result of the change which had taken
place in the Ottoman State.   It was no longer a question
of leading four hundred clansmen to battle ; the Ottomans now included a vast number of the Seljūks and
other Turkish tribes, who yearly flocked from a dis-

---

[1] Vezīr means "burden bearer," he who carries the burden of State
affairs : hence, Prime Minister.

tance to their standards in hope of victorious spoil, or from a knowledge of the superior order and security of life under the Ottoman rule. The Ottomans had already become a very mixed race ; and the armies that were soon to subdue a large part of Europe were composed chiefly of the tribes of Asia Minor, though the true Ottomans retained the high commands and formed a sort of aristocracy at the head. To organize these miscellaneous followers, a corps of regular infantry, called Piyadé, was first embodied and well paid, and given lands on condition of armed service and repair of the military roads ; then, with a view to holding these in check, a rival body was formed by enrolling a thousand of the finest boys from among the families of the Christians conquered in the campaigns against the Greeks. Every year for three centuries a thousand Christian children were thus devoted to the service of the Ottoman power ; when there were not enough prisoners captured during the year, the number was made up from the Christian subjects of the Sultan ; but after 1648 the children of the soldiers themselves were drawn upon to recruit the force.

Thus was formed the famous corps of the Janissaries, or "New Troops," which for centuries constituted the flower of the Ottoman armies, and eventually obtained such preponderating influence in the state, and abused it so wantonly, that they had to be summarily exterminated in the present century by Sultan Mahmūd II. The children who were taken from their parents to be enrolled as Janissaries were generally quite young ; they were of course compelled to become Moslems, and their training for a life of arms was carefully regulated. Their discipline was severe, and fortitude and endurance were inculcated with Spartan rigour ; but zeal and aptitude were invariably rewarded, and the Janissaries were sure of rapid promotion and royal favour. "Cut off from all ties of country, kith, and kin, but with high pay and privileges, with ample opportunities for military advancement, and for the gratification of the violent, the sensual, and the sordid, passions of their animal natures amid the customary atrocities of successful warfare, this military brotherhood grew up to be the strongest and fiercest instrument of imperial ambition, which remorseless fanaticism, prompted by the most subtle statecraft, ever devised upon earth." [1]

Orkhan led his thousand boys before a saintly dervish, and asked him to bless them, and give them a name ; whereupon Hajji Bektash flung the sleeve of his robe over the head of the leading youth and said "Be the name of this new host *Yeni Cheri*. May God the Lord make their faces white, their arms strong, their swords keen, their arrows deadly, and give them the victory ! " This is the origin of the white woollen dervish's cap, with the sleeve-like pendant behind, which always formed part of the uniform of the Janissaries.

Besides the Piyadé and Janissaries, the Ottoman army included a body of irregular light infantry, who were employed as skirmishers, and used to receive the first fury of the enemy, before the Janissaries were ordered to advance over their bodies to the attack ; and also six squadrons of Horse Guards, numbering at

<hr />

[1] Sir E. Creasy, " History of the Ottoman Turks," 15.

JANISSARIES AND MUSICIANS.

first 2,400, but afterwards many more. One of these squadrons received the well-known name of Sipāhīs, which is the same word as the Indian "sepoys." The feudal system was extended to the cavalry ; some cohorts were settled on lands which they held on condition of military service. There was also a corps of irregular cavalry, called Akinji, or Raiders, who were unpaid, and depended for their living on plunder and booty.

At the head of an army such as this, well disciplined, highly paid, and devoted to a sovereign who knew how to lead them where honours and rewards were to be won, Orkhan was now able to survey the kingdoms around him, and to weigh the chances of the coming struggle. Behind were the small but not yet innocuous states which had sprung up on the decay of the Seljūk power ; they were Turks, and therefore, in some sort, kinsmen ; they were good fighters, and, above all, they were poor. The Sultan was not attracted by the prospect of conquest without spoils, nor was it until many years later that Bāyezīd made a sweep of the petty principalities of Asia Minor. A much more valuable prize lay in front. The wealthy provinces of the Byzantine Empire, already falling to pieces, divided by strife among their rulers, were before Orkhan's eyes. As he stood on the shore of the Bosphorus he could see the domes and palaces of Constantinople. This was a quarry well worthy of pursuit, and the Ottoman directed his first attack against the effete empire of the Palaeologi.

He had already prepared the way by moral force. The firm and equitable government of the Turk had

produced a strong impression upon the Greeks of
Asia, who found themselves better off, more lightly
taxed, and far more efficiently protected, than they
had been under the rule of the Byzantine emperor,
whose persistent and perfidious intrigues, joined to
the insensate jealousies of the nobles, and the demands
of such foreign mercenaries as Roger de Flor and his
Catalans, put any approach to good and impartial
government out of the question.   The civil wars between the rival emperors had reduced the empire
to a mere shadow of its former extent.   " Many
provinces were lost for ever, and the Greek race
was expelled from many districts.   The property
of the Greeks was plundered, their landed estates
were confiscated, and even their families were often
reduced to slavery. . . . The landed property and the
military power, with the social influence they conferred, passed into the hands of the Serbians, the
Albanians, the Genoese, and the Ottoman Turks ;
and after the middle of the fourteenth century we
find foreign names occupying an important place in
the history of Macedonia, Epirus, and Greece, and
Serbian and Albanian chiefs attaining a position of
almost entire independence. . . . In Asia the empire
retained little more than Skutari and a few forts ; in
Thrace, it was bounded by a line drawn from the
Gulf of Burgas carried north of Adrianople to Cavala
on the Aegean ; in Macedonia, it retained Thessalonica and the adjoining peninsulas, but the Serbians
completely hemmed in this fragment on the land side ;
it also held portions of Thessaly and Epirus, and the
Peloponnesus.   The remaining fragments of the em-

pire consisted of a few islands in the Aegean Sea
which had escaped the domination of the Venetians
the Genoese, and the Knights of St. John ; and of the
cities of Philadelphia and Phocaea, which still recognized the suzerainty of Constantinople, though surrounded by the territories of the emirs of Aydin and
Saru-Khan. Such were the relics of the Byzantine
Empire, which were now burdened with the maintenance of two emperors, three empresses, and an
augmented list of despots, sebastocrators, and salaried
courtiers." [1]

In all these twenty years of peace there had been
a friendly understanding between Orkhan and the
Emperors Andronicus and Cantacuzenus, and the latter
had—with that curious contempt for the decencies
of family relations which characterized the Christians
during the whole period of Ottoman triumph —
given his daughter Theodora in marriage to the
sexagenarian Moslem, despite the differences of
creed and age. Cantacuzenus and Anne the Em-
press-Regent stopped at nothing to conciliate the
Ottoman Sultan and win his aid in their domestic
struggles. Their usual fee was to allow the Turk to
ravage one of their provinces, and carry off into
slavery as many Christians as he pleased. Ducas the
historian says that the empress purchased Orkhan's
assistance by allowing him to transport Christians
to Skutari for sale in Asia, "thus rendering the
Asiatic suburb of Constantinople the principal depôt
of the trade in Greek slaves." [2] Orkhan visited his
father-in-law at this convenient mart, which still be-

---

[1] Finlay, iii. 446-8.   [2] Ibid., iii. 443.

longed to the emperor, and there seemed little prospect of a rupture in their amity.

An opportunity however occurred very soon. The struggle which was then going on between the two great maritime powers of the Mediterranean, the Venetians and the Genoese, found a frequent meeting-place on the Bosphorus, where the latter held Galata, a suburb of Constantinople. The Venetians, who were destined for centuries to be the most determined foes of the Turks, had already aroused Orkhan's anger, and he lost no time in giving his support to their rivals. Out of this alliance came the first entrance of the Turk upon European soil. Suleymān Pasha, Orkhan's eldest son, who had already operated with success in the Balkan provinces, crossed the Hellespont on a couple of rafts, with eighty followers, and surprized the castle of Tzympe. In a few days it was garrisoned by three thousand Ottoman soldiers. Cantacuzenus was too busy with the hostility of his son-in-law, John Palaeologus, to resist this unprovoked invasion; he even sought the assistance of the Sultan against his rival. More Turks were accordingly sent over to reinforce Suleymān's command; Palaeologus was beaten; but the Ottomans had won their foothold in Europe. In 1358 an earthquake overthrew the cities of Thrace; houses crumbled to the ground, and even the walls and fortifications fell upon the trembling earth, while the terrified inhabitants fled from their shaking homes. Among the rest, the walls around Gallipoli fell down, the people deserted the city, and over the ruins the Turks marched in. The Emperor in vain protested; Orkhan declared that Providence had opened the city to his troops, and

he could not disregard so clear an instance of divine
interposition. The civil war which still raged left
Cantacuzenus small leisure for attending to anything
but the attacks of Palaeologus. The shore of the
Hellespont was quickly garrisoned with Ottoman
soldiers, and the first fatal step had been permitted
which led to the conquest of the empire, and the
perpetual menace of Europe for several centuries.

Orkhan died in 1359. He had lived to carry his
arms to the confines of Asia Minor, and had even
seen his horse-tails flying on the western shores of
the Hellespont. His son Murād I.,[1] who succeeded
him (for Suleymān, the elder brother, had died before
his father), was to lead the Ottoman armies as far as
the Danube.

A native satirist said of the Greeks : " They are
formed of three parts : their tongue speaks one thing,
their mind meditates another, and their actions accord
with neither." Had there been but the Greek Empire
to subdue, it is possible that the fourteenth century
might have seen the fall of Constantinople. Adrianople (1361) and soon after, Philippopolis succumbed
upon the onslaught of Murād, and Macedonia and
Thrace, or the modern Rumelia, were now Ottoman
provinces. The Republic of Ragusa concluded a commercial treaty with the Ottomans in 1365, by which it
placed itself under their protection ; and it is said that
Murād signed the treaty, for lack of a pen, with his
open hand, over which he had smeared some ink, in

---

[1] Murād is often written Amurath by Europeans. So Bāyezīd
(Bajazet), Suleymān (Soliman), Mohamméd (Mahomet), &c. We
have retained the correct spelling.

the manner of Eastern seals. This veritable sign-manual is believed to be the origin of the *tughra* or Sultan's cipher, which has ever since appeared on the coinage and the official documents of the Turks.

But the Sultan had other foes to reckon with besides worn-out imperialists and time-serving republics. To say nothing of danger from behind, in Asia, there was a belt of warlike peoples beyond the Balkan, who were made of very different stuff from the emasculate Greeks. Behind the empire were ranged the vigorous young Slavonic races of Serbia and Bosnia, the Bulgarians, and the Vlachs, with their traditions of Roman descent, the Skipitars of Albania, a hardy race of mountaineers, and, above all, the Magyars of Hungary, who, with their neighbours the Poles, formed for three centuries the chief bulwark of Christendom against the swelling tide of Mohammedan invasion. In 1364 the first encounter between the northern Christians and the invaders took place on the banks of the Maritza, near Adrianople, whither Louis I., King of Hungary and Poland, and the princes of Bosnia, Serbia, and Wallachia, pushed forward to put an end once for all to the rule of the Ottoman in Europe. Lāla Shāhīn, Murād's commander in chief, could not muster more than half the number of troops that the Christians brought against him; but he took advantage of the state of drunken revelry in which the too confident enemy was plunged to make a sudden night attack, and the army of Hungary, heavy with sleep after its riotous festivities, was suddenly aroused by the beating of the Turkish drums and the shrill music of their

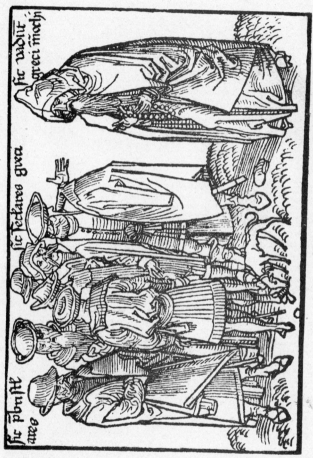

GREEKS.

fifes. The Ottomans were upon them before they
could stand to arms. " They were like wild beasts
scared from their lair," says the Turkish historian,
Sa'd-ud-dīn; "speeding from the field of fight to the
waste of flight, those abjects poured into the stream
Maritza and were drowned." To this day the spot is
called *Sirf Sindughi,* "Serbs' rout."

For the present the Turks were satisfied with repelling the enemy ; but before long they resolved
upon carrying the war into the territories of their
foes. Thus far the Ottomans had only possessed
themselves of less than a quarter of modern Turkey.
Leaving Albania for the present out of the question,
we may compare the eastern and greater part of
Turkey in Europe to a flag bearing a St. George's
cross. From east to west, the range of Haemus, or
the Balkan, divides it into two well-marked divisions,
and the arms which these mountains stretch forth
to the north and south complete the cross. Of
the two upper quarters, that to the west was an-
ciently known as Upper Moesia, and had become the
kingdoms of Serbia and Bosnia ; that to the east was
Lower Moesia, or Bulgaria. The lower squares represent Thrace and Macedonia, and together form what
was known as Rumelia. Of these four portions, the
Ottomans so far possessed only the south-eastern, or
Thrace, the whole of which, with the exception of the
country immediately surrounding Constantinople, now
owned their sway. In 1373, however, by the capture of
Cavala, Serez, and other places, they annexed most
of Macedonia, and pushed their frontier almost up
to the great mountain range which divides Rumelia

from Albania. Two of the four quarters of the square had thus been subdued, and in 1375 the Ottoman armies marched north to reduce the rest. Crossing the Balkan they took Nissa, the birthplace of Constantine the Great and one of the strongest fortresses of the Byzantine Empire. After a siege of twenty-five days the city capitulated, and the Despot of Servia, attacked in the heart of his kingdom, obtained peace on condition of his paying an annual tribute of a thousand pounds of silver, and furnishing a thousand horsemen to the Ottoman armies. The Kral of Bulgaria did not wait to be conquered, but humbly begged for mercy, which was granted on his paying, not tribute, but what he preferred — his daughter. Thus was the greater part of the two northern quarters made tributary to the Sultan. The Greek Emperor, who had not scrupled to become a convert to the Latin Church in order (as he vainly hoped) to secure the aid of the Pope and the Catholic Powers, finding the Ottomans irresistible, declared himself a vassal of Murād.

At the same time a further addition was made, in a peaceful manner, to the Ottoman dominions in Asia. Murād seized the opportunity of a period of tranquility to solemnize the marriage of his son Bāyezīd with the daughter of the prince of Kermiyan, one of the ten states that had grown out of the Seljūk kingdom. The bride brought the greater part of her father's dominions as a dowry to the young Turk, and the province of Kermiyan with its chief cities was thus peacefully added to the Ottoman Empire. The wedding was celebrated at Brusa with the utmost

pomp. Representatives came from the remainder of
the Ten States, the lords of Aydin, of Kastamuni, of
Mentesha, and Karaman, and the rest; and ambassadors arrived from the Sultan of Egypt. They
brought Arab steeds, Greek slave-girls, and the wonderful silk stuffs of Alexandria. Gold plates filled with
gold coins, silver dishes full of silver coins, jewelled
cups and basins, were among the presents, all of
which were given away by the Sultan to his guests.
The keys of the castles of Kermiyan, however, he
accepted from the bride, and with these he did not
part. At the same time Murād purchased from its
ruler the territory of Hamīd, with its cities of
Akshehr, Begshehri, and others, and thus united
under his rule four out of the ten Seljūkian states.
Sultanöni, Karasi, Kermiyan, and Hamīd now formed
part of the Ottoman territory; and ten years later
Bāyezīd overran the whole of the remaining states
and reduced the entire kingdom of the Seljūks.

III.

KOSOVO AND NICOPOLIS.
(1380–1402.)

MEANWHILE the yearly drain of the Christians
to recruit the corps of the Janissaries was exciting
the anger of the princes of the north. The Turks
had indeed reached the Danube ; but they were not
to remain undisturbed in their wide dominion. The
Slavs were not yet subdued. They determined on
another effort to expel the enemy from Europe.
Serbia, Bosnia, and Bulgaria led the crusade ; Albania, Wallachia, Hungary joined ; Poland sent her
contingent. The rest of Europe was too closely
occupied with its own affairs, or too much a prey to
ignoble rulers, to spare any interest for the struggle
that was going on in the Balkan Peninsula. Still
the confederates were able to muster a formidable
array, and their first move was a success. They fell
upon an Ottoman army in Bosnia in 1388, and
killed three-fourths of its twenty thousand men.
Murād was not disposed to sit still under this affront,
and his general, Alī Pasha, forthwith crossed the
Balkan by the Derbend Pass, descended upon
Shumla, seized Tirnova, and brought Sisvan the Kral

of Bulgaria to his knees. Besieged in Nicopolis, the prince surrendered, and Bulgaria was immediately annexed to the Ottoman Empire, of which the Danube now formed the northern frontier.

Lazarus the Serbian, though deprived of his Bulgarian ally, was not yet daunted. He challenged Murád to battle, and the opposing forces met (1389) on the plain of Kosovo by the banks of the river Shinitza. Serbs, Bosnians, Skipitars, Poles, Magyars, and Vlachs were massed on the north side of the stream ; on the south were the Ottomans under Murád himself, supported by his vassals and allies of Europe and Asia. The Sultan spent the night before the battle in prayer for the help of God and a martyr's death, for like all true Moslems he coveted the crowning glory of dying in fight with the Infidels ; and in the morning he saw an answer to his petitions in the rain which laid the clouds of dust that were driving blindingly in the faces of the Turkish troops. When the sky cleared, the two armies came forward and were drawn up in battle array. Lazarus commanded the centre of the Christian line, his nephew Vuk Brankovich the right, and Tvarko the king of Bosnia the left. On the Turkish side, Murád himself was in the centre, his sons Báyezíd and Ya'kúb commanded the right and left wings, and Haydar ranged his artillery on the brow of the hill behind the main body. The battle was long and obstinately contested ; at one time the left wing of the Turks wavered, but its courage was restored by the charge of Báyezíd, whose rapidity of action had earned him the name of *Yildirim*, "Thunderbolt." He raged through the ranks of the enemy, brandishing a mighty iron mace, and felling all who came in his way. With such fury did he renew the fight, that the " Turks, which before as men discouraged fled in the left wing, began now to turn again upon their enemies ; and the Christians, having as they thought already got the victory, were to begin a great battle. In which bloody fight many thousands fell on both sides ; the brightness of the armour and weapons was as it had been the lightning ; the multitude of lances and other horsemen's staves shadowed the light of the sun ; arrows and darts fell so fast that a man would have thought they had poured down from heaven ; the noise of the instruments of war, with the neighing of horses and the outcries of men, were so terrible and great, that the wild beasts of the mountain stood astonied therewith ; and the Turkish histories, to express the terror of the day, vainly say that the angels in heaven, amazed with that hideous noise, for that time forgot the heavenly hymns wherewith they always glorify God. About noontide of the day, the fortune of the Turks prevailing, the Christians began to give ground, and at length betook themselves to plain flight : whom the Turks with all their force pursued and slew them down-right, without number or mercy." [1] The field, says the Turkish chronicler, was like a tulip bed, with its ruddy severed heads and rolling turbans.

But the battle was not to end without an irreparable loss to the Turks. Milosh Kobilovich, a Serbian warrior, made his way to the Sultan's presence, on

[1] Knolles and Rycaut, " The Turkish History," i. 138.

Kossova

pretext of important tidings to be communicated
to his private ear ; and, when he was brought before
him, suddenly plunged his dagger into the Sultan's
body. The assassin was hewn to pieces by the
guard ; but his work had been effectual. Murād
died in his tent, after ordering the charge of his
reserve which completed the victory. With his
dying voice he ordained the execution of Lazarus
the Serbian king, who had been made a prisoner.
Milosh Kobilovich, for this treacherous assassination, has ever since been regarded as a Serbian hero.
As with Harmodius and Aristogiton in ancient Greece,
and Charlotte Corday in modern France, the igno-
miny of betrayal has been absolved by posterity in
consideration of the utility of the result. An assassin
thus becomes a sort of inverted hero.

In consequence of this misfortune, a rule has ever
since been prescribed in Ottoman etiquette that no
stranger shall be presented to the Sultan save led
by two courtiers, who hold him by the arms, and
thus prevent any treacherous attempt. The precaution is no longer insisted on ; but even in the present
century foreign ambassadors were not permitted
to approach the Sultan too closely.

" This [Mūrad or] Amurath was in his superstition
more zealous than any other of the Turkish kings ; a
man of great courage, and in all his attempts fortunate ; he made greater slaughter of his enemies than
both his father and grandfather ; his kingdom in
Asia he greatly enlarged by the sword, marriage, and
purchase ; and, using the discord and cowardice of
the Grecian princes to his profit, subdued a great

part of Thracia, called Rumania, with the territories
thereto adjoining, leaving unto the Emperor of Constantinople little or nothing more in Thracia than
the imperial city itself, with the bare name of an
emperor almost without an empire ; he won a great
part of Bulgaria and entered into Serbia, Bosnia,
and Macedonia ; he was liberal and withal severe,
of his subjects both beloved and feared, a man of
very few words and one that could dissemble deeply.
He was slain when he was three score and eight
years old and had therefore reigned thirty-one, in
the year of our Lord [1389]. His dead body was
by Bajazet conveyed into Asia, and there royally
buried at Brusa in a fair chapel at the west end of
the city, near unto the baths there, where upon his
tomb lieth his soldier's cloak, with a little Turkish
tulipant, much differing from those great turbans
which the Turks now wear. Near unto the same
tomb are placed three lances with three horse-tails
fastened at the upper end of them, which he used
as guidons in his wars." [1] On the plain of Kosovo
three stones still mark the spots where Milosh
Kobilovich thrice freed himself from the onslaught
of the encircling guard, and a chapel shows the place
where Murād fell.

On the battle-field, Bāyezīd, the " Bajazet " of old
Knolles, was saluted Sultan by the army ; and in sight
of the dead body of his father, the new ruler immediately slew his brother Ya'kūb, who had fought
gallantly throughout the day. The murder of their
brothers was henceforward to be a principle of

[1] Knolles, i. p. 139.

A TURKISH FUNERAL.

Ottoman succession. Murád himself had cruelly put to death his son Saveji, when he rebelled against him ; and Báyezíd was equally determined to have no rivals to disturb his state. " Sedition is worse than slaughter," says the Koran, and acting on that adage the Sultans of Turkey for centuries provided against revolution by putting out of the way every male heir who could possibly be a candidate for the throne. The custom was barbarous enough, but it at least procured the desired result ; and for five hundred years the Ottoman Empire has suffered little from civil strife among relations.

Báyezíd soon brought the Serbian war to a close. His armies pushed on to Vidin, and, turning south, took Karatova with its valuable silver mines, and placed a Turkish colony in Uskub. Stephen, the son of Lazarus, was eager to conclude peace, and a treaty was arranged by which the Serbian king agreed, as vassal of the Ottoman, to furnish a contingent to his wars, to give his sister to wife to the Sultan, and to pay a yearly tribute from the proceeds of the silver mines. The Lady Despina soon came to exercise a great influence over her Turkish husband : " Of all his wives he held her dearest, and for her sake restored to her brother Stephen the city and castle of Semendria and Columbarium in Serbia ; she allured him to drink wine, forbidden the Turks by their law, and caused him to delight in sumptuous banquets, which his predecessors never did." [1]

Serbia was now no longer exposed to Ottoman incursions ; but there was not yet peace on the Danube,

[1] Knolles, i. 143.

In the following year, Bāyezīd overran Wallachia, and its prince, Myrché, submitted in 1392, when his province became tributary to the Turks. Recalled to Asia by an attack from the Prince of Karaman, Bāyezīd swept like a whirlwind over the provinces of Asia Minor, and brought all the land to his sway. Master of the whole of the Seljūk kingdom of Rūm, and of most of the country between the Bosphorus and the Danube, he was solemnly invested with the title of "Sultan" by the Abbaside Khalif—who was maintained in puppet state at the Mamlūk Court at Cairo, and exercised what remained of the spiritual authority of the once mighty Khalifs of Damascus and Baghdad.[1] Intoxicated by success, the Sultan now gave himself up to the pleasures of sense ; he drank the forbidden wine, and indulged in the gross vices that have too constantly degraded the rulers of the Ottoman Empire, yet all his sensuality could not quench the general and soldier in him. Hearing that a new and formidable combination was forming against him in Europe, he shook off his sloth and luxury, and crossed the Bosphorus with all the ancient energy which had procured him his title of " Thunderbolt." It is a singular fact, that however indolent and besotted a Turk may appear, you have but to put a sword in his hand, and

---

[1] It is commonly stated that Bāyezīd was the first to adopt this title ; but coins still preserved in the British Museum and elsewhere, prove that both Orkhan and Murād I. styled themselves Sultan on their official currency. Of Othmān there are no coins in existence, and it is probable that the right to coin was first assumed by Orkhan. Bāyezīd's assumption of the title of Sultan was only so far novel that it received the sanction of the titular head of the Mohammedan religion.

he will fire up and fight like a hero. The fighting spirit seems to be inherent in the race.

The league that was gathering against him was indeed enough to dismay any sovereign. Sigismund of Hungary was not the man to sit still after defeat. He had been disgracefully routed in 1392, when he had invaded Bulgaria, and Kosovo and the humiliation of Serbia were events too recent to be easily forgotten. The Hungarians were not, like some of the other adversaries of the Turks, members of what they considered the heretical, or as it styles itself the "Orthodox," Greek Church. So long as the Turks waged war upon such heretics, the Latin Church was content to let them alone. But Hungary was Catholic, and at Sigismund's request the Pope took up the cause, and in 1394 proclaimed a crusade against the Moslems. All the Courts of Europe were besieged with demands for volunteers in the Holy War. France sent a body of men-at-arms under the Count of Nevers to the support of the King of Hungary, and many knights of renown came with their retainers to join in the crusade. They were to defeat the Turks, cross the Hellespont, and rescue the Holy Land from the infidels. Among them were the Count de la Marche, three cousins of the French king, Philippe of Artois, Count of Eu and Constable of France, and many more of the flower of the French chivalry. The Count of Hohenzollern and the Grand Master of the Knights of St. John of Jerusalem came with their followers. The Elector Palatine brought a company of Bavarian knights ; Myrché with his Vlachs and Sisman with his Bulgarians joyfully threw off the

Turkish yoke, broke all their vows, and joined the league.

The allies marched through Serbia, whose king alone remained true to his treaty with Bāyezīd, and his lands were therefore plundered ; they took Vidin and Orsova, and, mustering sixty thousand men, sat down before the strong city of Nicopolis, which, with Vidin, Sistova, and Silistria, formed the four great frontier fortresses on the Danube. They were held by Turkish garrisons, and to re-take them was now the ardent desire of the Christian army. Vidin had already surrendered ; Nicopolis was the next to be attacked. Six days they pressed the siege by land and river, yet the Ottoman governor refused to surrender. The French knights, however, were not disturbed by this obstinacy, which was of the utmost value in detaining the invading army until the Sultan should come up with them ; they ridiculed the mere thought of Bāyezīd's advance, declared that he would not dare to cross the Hellespont, and, betaking themselves to the wine and women that they had brought in shiploads down the Danube, they boasted in their cups that were the sky to fall they would hold it up with their spears.

When scouts brought word that the Sultan was within six hours' march of Nicopolis, the jovial boon-fellows laughed them to scorn, and Marshal Boucicault threatened to have the bearers' ears cut off for raising a false alarm. Bāyezīd heard of these "brave words," and in return swore that he would stable his horse at the high altar of St. Peter's at Rome. He was upon the allies before they could credit their eyes. When the Turkish

NICOPOLIS.

troops were seen advancing in their usual perfect discipline, the young French nobles, full of wine and conceit,
clamoured to begin the fight, and disregarding the counsel of Sigismund, who knew that the practice of the
Turks was to put their worst troops in the van of
battle, the hot-headed Frenchmen charged madly upon
the foe, after first celebrating the occasion by a massacre of Turkish prisoners who had vainly trusted to
their word of honour. Down they charged upon the
Turkish front, and falling like a whirlwind upon the
luckless skirmishers, whom Bāyezīd had thrown forward, cut them in pieces. Hacking right and left, the
chivalry of France rode over their bodies, till they
reached the Janissaries who were drawn up behind
them ; ten thousand of the flower of the Turkish army
fell, before the Janissaries took refuge under cover of
the cavalry. Still unchecked, the triumphant cavaliers
rode pell-mell at the famous squadrons of the Sipāhīs,
and five thousand horsemen went down before their
stormy charge. Right through the third line of the
enemy they rode, exulting in their victory ; and ascending the high ground beyond, where they expected to
see but the flying ruck of the Ottomans—they suddenly
found themselves confronted by a forest of forty thousand lances, the main body of the Turkish army. Then
they remembered, too late, the counsel of Sigismund ;
and seized with panic fear, the knighthood of France
broke up and fled for its very life, pursued by the
horsemen of Asia. Admiral Jean de Vienne, brave
man, bethought him of the shame as he was hurrying
away ; and gathering his twelve knights about him he

[1] See "The Story of Hungary," by Prof. Vámbéry, 183.

cried, "God forbid that we should save our lives at the cost of our honour ;" so they plunged into the thick of the enemy, and died the death of the soldier.

The Christian infantry could not witness this fearful flight without dismay ; the Hungarians and Vlachs on the right and left wings of the main body took to their heels. The centre alone stood firm, where the king's own Magyar followers, the Styrians under Hermann Count of Cilli, and the Bavarians under the Elector, covered the retreat of the French cavaliers, and advanced in serried ranks, twelve thousand strong, against the Turks. Despite their scanty numbers, they drove back the Janissaries and came to close combat with the Sipāhīs, whom they threatened to overthrow, when Stephen of Serbia, faithful to his oath, led his five thousand Slavs upon the Christians and won the day for his master the Sultan. The battle was at an end ; the remnant of the Christian army was cut down round the royal standard, and Sigismund was dragged away from the fatal field by the Count of Cilli and hurried into a boat by which he reached the Venetian fleet which was waiting to coöperate with the army at the mouth of the Danube. Instead of joining in attack, the task of the Venetians was narrowed to saving the few surviving leaders of a vanished host.

Bāyezīd was left victorious on the hard won field. As he rode among the mountains of the slain he wept tears of rage to see how many of his bravest warriors had fallen before the furious onslaught of the French and the steady desperation of Sigismund's attack. He resolved to avenge their death by a fearful retri-

bution upon the captives. Ten thousand prisoners of
war were brought before him the next day, and, after
summoning the Count of Nevers to witness his
vengeance, and permitting him to select twenty-four
knights for ransom, he gave orders that the rest
of the captives should be slaughtered. Company
after company, the stout knights and squires of
France, the soldiers of Germany, of Bavaria, of Styria,
of Hungary, were led before the Sultan, and there, in
the sight of the Count of Nevers and his twenty-
four companions, were pitilessly butchered. One
Schildberger, who was himself present, saved by the
intercession of Bāyazīd's son, and who lived to return to his native Munich after thirty years of captivity, tell us how he saw his comrades massacred in
heaps by the Janissaries and the common executioners;
from daybreak till four in the afternoon the Sultan
sat watching the agonies of his enemies, till at last
his own officers, moved perhaps by pity and disgust,
or else by regret at the loss of so many marketable
slaves, begged him to make an end of the butchery
and send the remainder of the prisoners into captivity.

Thousands however had already paid the penalty
of death, and among them, as Froissart says—

"𝕿𝖍𝖊𝖓 𝖙𝖍𝖊𝖞 𝖜𝖊𝖗𝖊 𝖆𝖑𝖑 𝖇𝖗𝖔𝖚𝖌𝖍𝖙 𝖇𝖊𝖋𝖔𝖗𝖊 𝕷𝖆𝖒𝖔𝖗𝖆=
𝖇𝖆𝖖𝖚𝖞 𝖓𝖆𝖐𝖊𝖉 𝖎𝖓 𝖙𝖍𝖊𝖎𝖗 𝖘𝖍𝖞𝖗𝖙𝖊𝖘, 𝖆𝖓𝖉 𝖍𝖊 𝖇𝖊𝖍𝖊𝖑𝖉𝖊 𝖙𝖍𝖊𝖒
𝖆 𝖑𝖞𝖙𝖊𝖑𝖑 𝖆𝖓𝖉 𝖙𝖍𝖆𝖓 𝖙𝖚𝖗𝖓𝖊𝖉 𝖋𝖗𝖔 𝖙𝖍𝖊𝖒 𝖜𝖆𝖗𝖉𝖊, 𝖆𝖓𝖉 𝖒𝖆𝖉𝖊
𝖆 𝖘𝖞𝖌𝖓𝖊 𝖙𝖍𝖆𝖙 𝖙𝖍𝖊𝖞 𝖘𝖍𝖚𝖑𝖉𝖊 𝖇𝖊 𝖆𝖑𝖑 𝖘𝖑𝖆𝖞𝖓𝖊, 𝖆𝖓𝖉 𝖘𝖔 𝖙𝖍𝖊𝖞
𝖜𝖊𝖗𝖊 𝖇𝖗𝖔𝖚𝖌𝖍𝖙 𝖙𝖍𝖗𝖔𝖚𝖌𝖍 𝖙𝖍𝖊 𝖘𝖆𝖗𝖆𝖟𝖞𝖓𝖘 𝖙𝖍𝖆𝖙 𝖍𝖆𝖉 𝖗𝖊𝖉𝖞
𝖓𝖆𝖐𝖊𝖉 𝖘𝖜𝖔𝖗𝖉𝖊𝖘 𝖎𝖓 𝖙𝖍𝖊𝖎𝖗 𝖍𝖆𝖓𝖉𝖊𝖘, 𝖆𝖓𝖉 𝖘𝖔 𝖘𝖑𝖆𝖞𝖓𝖊 𝖆𝖓𝖉
𝖍𝖊𝖜𝖊𝖓 𝖆𝖑𝖑 𝖙𝖔 𝖕𝖊𝖈𝖊𝖘 𝖜𝖎𝖙𝖍𝖔𝖚𝖙 𝖒𝖊𝖗𝖈𝖞. 𝕿𝖍𝖎𝖘 𝖈𝖗𝖚𝖊𝖑𝖑

iustyce did Lamorabaquy that daye, by the whiche
mo than thre hundred gentlemen of dyvers nacyons
were tourmented and slayne for the love of god, on
whose soules Jesu have mercy."

In the following year the Count of Nevers and the
surviving knights were ransomed. Froissart tells the
story of their leavetaking with the Sultan. When the
Count approached to thank him for his kindness and
courtesy during their captivity, Bāyezīd said, through
an interpreter—

"Johan, I knowe well thou arte a great lorde in
thy countrey, and sonne to a great lorde ; thou art
yonge, and peraduenture shall beare some blame
and shame that this aduenture hath fallen to the
in thy fyrste chyvalry ; and to excuse thyselfe of
this blame and to recouer thyne honour, peraduen=
ture thou wylt assemble a puyssaunce of men, and
come and make warre agaynst me ; if I were in
doute or feare therof, or thou departed I shulde
cause the s̄ ere by thy lawe and faythe that neuer
thou nor none of thy company shulde beare armure
or make warre agaynst me ; but I wyll nother
make the nor none of thy company to make any
suche othe or promesse, but I wyll that whan thou
arte retourned and arte at thy pleasure, rayse what
puyssaunce thou wylte, and spare nat, but come
agaynst me ; thou shalt fynde me alwayes redy
to receyue the and thy company in the felde in
playne batayle ; and this that I say, shewe it to
whome thy lyste, for I am able to do dedes of

armes, and euer redy to conquere further into crystendom. These hygh wordes the erle of Neuers vnderstode well, and so dyd his company; they thought on it after as long as they lyued."

IV.

TĪMŪR THE TARTAR.

(1402.)

THE battle of Nicopolis had placed Bāyezīd at the summit of power. He issued boastful despatches to the chief potentates of the East announcing his triumph, and, in order to convince them of its verity by tangible evidence, he sent them by his messengers presents of Christian slaves taken from the conquered nations. Nothing now could exceed the pride and arrogance of the Turkish Sultan. Lord of the lands of the Greek Empire as far as the Danube, and of Asia to the banks of the Euphrates, he dreamed of world-wide conquest, and even thought of realizing his threat of stabling his charger at the altar of St. Peter's at Rome. Not content while any part of the Eastern Empire remained unsubdued, he carried his arms southward through Thermopylae, which had no Leonidas to contest the pass, and with little opposition established his authority over the Peloponnesus and set up the crescent upon the Acropolis of Athens. The Greek Emperor was already his humble vassal, and had even consented to the building of a mosque in Constantinople, in order to appease the

MANUEL PALAEOLOGUS.

wrath of his imperious suzerain. Saladin the Great and others had extorted similar concessions ; but in the present instance to the mosque was added a Mohammedan college, and a Moslem judge or *Kādi* was appointed to administer the laws of Islam in a quarter specially set apart for Musulmans in the metropolis of Orthodox Christianity.

The Turks had indeed obtained a fatal hold upon the capital of the empire, and now Bāyezīd, not satisfied with the humiliations to which the emperor had submitted, demanded the surrender of the city itself. Manuel scoured Europe in search of allies, but in vain. Even when he descended so low as to beg the assistance of his immemorial rival the Pope, no aid was to be found ; and the Turkish armies, after beleaguering Constantinople for six years, seemed on the point of effecting the conquest, when a new and terrible figure appeared upon the scene, and Bāyezīd was forced to turn his forces elsewhere.

Just at the moment when the Sultan seemed to have attained the pinnacle of his ambition, when his authority was unquestioningly obeyed over the greater part of the Byzantine Empire in Europe and Asia, when the Christian states were regarding him with terror as the scourge of the world, another and a greater scourge came to quell him, and at one stroke all the vast fabric of empire which Bāyezīd had so triumphantly erected was shattered to the ground. This terrible conqueror was Tīmūr the Tartar, or as we call him " Tamerlane."

Tīmūr was of Turkish race, and was born near Samarkand in 1333   He was consequently an old man of nearly seventy when he came to encounter Bāyezīd in 1402. It had taken him many years to establish his authority over a portion of the numerous divisions into which the immense empire of Chingiz Khān had fallen after the death of that stupendous conqueror. Tīmūr was but a petty chief among many others : but at last he won his way, and became ruler of Samarkand and the whole province of Transoxiana, or "Beyond the River" (Mā-warā-n-nahr), as the Arabs called the country north of the Oxus. Once fairly established in this province, Tīmūr began to overrun the surrounding lands, and during thirty years his ruthless armies spread over the provinces of Asia, from Dehli to Damascus, and from the Sea of Aral to the Persian Gulf. The sub-division of the Mohammedan Empire into numerous petty kingdoms rendered it powerless to meet the overwhelming hordes which Tīmūr brought down from Central Asia. One and all, the kings and princes of Persia and Syria succumbed, and Tīmūr carried his banners triumphantly as far as the frontier of Egypt, where the brave Mamlūk Sultans still dared to defy him. He had so far left Bāyezīd unmolested ; partly because he was too powerful to be rashly provoked, and partly because Tīmūr respected the Sultan's valorous deeds against the Christians : for Tīmūr, though a wholesale butcher, was very conscientious in matters of religion, and held that Bāyezīd's fighting for the Faith rightly covered a multitude of sins.

But when two great empires march together, as did those of the Tartar and the Turk, and when each of them has been built up at the expense of a number of petty dynasties, every prince of which naturally sought an asylum at the Court of the rival emperor, the relations of the two Powers are apt to become strained. So it proved in the present case. Bāyezīd had sheltered some of the princes of Mesopotamia whom Tīmūr had overthrown : Tīmūr had welcomed to his Court the petty rulers of Asia Minor whom Bāyezīd had expelled. Of course the refugees on either side, in hope of restoration, lost no opportunity of exciting the jealousy and irritability of the rival tyrants. The result was that, after an interchange of embassies which only embittered the minds of both sovereigns, and in which the Turk displayed more than his wonted insolence, Tīmūr advanced to Sīwās, the ancient Sebaste, in Cappadocia, an important city which had recently acknowledged the authority of the Turk along with most of the towns of Asia Minor, and after a determined siege stormed the place and put the garrison to the sword. Among the rest, Prince Ertoghrul, a son of Bāyezīd was executed (1400).

The Sultan was laying siege to Constantinople when he heard the news of the fall of Sīwās and the death of his son. He hurried over to Asia, at the head of his veteran troops, who had for years borne the brunt of war against the chivalry of Serbia, Hungary, and France, on such fields as Kosovo and Nicopolis ; but when he arrived Tīmūr was gone : he had marched south to menace the Mamlūks of Egypt. It was not till the next year (1402) that the two forces met, and in the interval Bāyezīd had lost prestige with his soldiers. Tīmūr's spies had been at work, sowing disaffection among their ranks, and the Sultan's notorious meanness and avarice gave only too much colour to the insinuations of these emissaries; the Turkish troops became less hostile to Tīmūr when they found how liberal he was to his followers. Still Bāyezīd did nothing to allay the growing murmurs of his men, and advanced to meet his adversary with an army estimated vaguely at 120,000. Tīmūr, who is fabled to have commanded six times this number, outmanoeuvred him and secured an open field at Angora, where his superior force could be used to the best advantage.

So far was Bāyezīd from manifesting even common caution in the presence of the enemy, that out of mere bravado he employed his army in a grand hunt in the neighbourhood of Angora. His hunting was ill chosen as to place as well as time, for there was no water, and it is said that no less than five thousand Turks perished from mere thirst, with never a Tartar arrow to speed them. When the infatuated Sultan returned to his camp, he found that Tīmūr had seized it in his absence, and had poisoned the stream that would have refreshed the weary Turks. In this position the Ottoman led his dispirited men against the enemy. On the one side were men thirsty and exhausted, inferior in numbers, and discontented with their leader : on the other, a vast host, strongly posted, splendidly generalled, neglecting no precaution of war, and possessing every advantage of numbers, discipline, and physical condition. The result could not be doubtful. In the battle many of Bāyezīd's troops, among whom were forced contingents from the

III. Et là Sultan se quile dans la Tente magique. A peine de la bonne mere : A vay vng roy. Et commet d'Egipte et par courent ; Comme Egyptien, comme d'y sa hon oyz.
Et ce qui vous et d'agrement se valoit bien Paix et Subm.

A TURKISH MEAL.

recently annexed states of Asia Minor, went over to the enemy, and only the Janissaries who formed the centre, and the Serbian auxiliaries under their king, Stephen Lazarevich, on the left, gave anything like a soldier's account of themselves on that memorable day. The valour of the Janissaries and the Serbs could avail little against Tīmūr's numbers, and the end was utter rout.

Old Knolles tells the story in his quaint and graphic style : " The next day the two armies drew near together and encamped within a league one of the other ; where all the night long you might have heard such noise of horses as that it seemed the heavens were full of voices, the air did so resound ; and every man thought the night long, to come to the trial of his valour and the gaining of his desires. The Scythians talked of nothing but the spoil, the proud Parthians of their honour, and the poor Christians of their deliverance, all to be gained by the next day's victory: every man during the night speaking according to his own humour. All which Tamerlane, walking this night up and down in his camp, heard, and much rejoiced to see the hope that his soldiers had already in general conceived of the victory. Who, after the second watch, returning unto his pavilion, and there casting himself upon a carpet, had thought to have slept awhile : but his cares not suffering him to do so, he then, as his manner was, called for a book wherein was contained the lives of his fathers and ancestors and of other valiant worthies, the which he used ordinarily to read, as he then did ; not as therewith vainly to deceive the time, but to

make use thereof by the imitation of that which was
by them worthily done, and declining of such dangers
as they by their rashness or oversight fell into. . . .

"Now was Tamerlane by an espy advertised that
Bajazet, having before given orders for the disposing
of his army, was on foot in the midst of thirty
thousand Janissaries, his principal men of war and
greatest strength, wherein he meant that day to fight,
and in whom he had reposed his greatest hope. . . .
His army marching all in one front, in form of a half
moon (but not so well knit together as was Tamerlane's
whose squadrons directly followed one another) seemed
almost as great as his ; and so with infinite numbers
of most horrible outcries still advanced forward ;
Tamerlane and his soldiers all the while standing fast
with great silence.

"There was not possible to be seen a more furious
charge than was by the Turks given upon the Prince
of Ciarcan, who had commandment not to fight before
the enemy came up to him : neither could have been
chosen a fairer plain, and where the skilful choice of
the place was of less advantage for the one or the
other ; but that Tamerlane had the river on the left
hand of his army, serving him to some small
advantage. Now this young Prince of Ciarcan with
his forty thousand horse was in this first encounter
almost wholly overthrown, yet having fought right
valiantly and entered into them, even into the midst
of the Janissaries (where the person of Bajazet was),
putting them in disorder, was himself there slain.
About which time Axalla set upon them with the
avantguard, but not with like danger ; for having

overthrown one of the enemy's wings, and cut it all to pieces, and his footmen coming to join with him as they had been commanded, he faced the battalion of the Janissaries, who right valiantly behaved themselves for the safety of their prince.

" This hard fight continued one hour, and yet you could not have seen any scattered, but the one still resolutely fighting against the other. You might there have seen the horsemen like mountains rush together, and infinite numbers of men die, cry, lament, and threaten, all in one instant. Tamerlane had patience all this while, to see the event of this so mortal a fight ; but perceiving his men at length to give ground, he sent ten thousand of his horse to join again with the ten thousand appointed for the rearward, and commanded them to assist him at such time as he should have need of them ; and at the very same time charged himself and made them to give him room, causing the footmen to charge also, who gave a furious onset upon the battalion of the Janissaries. Now Bajazet had in his army a great number of mercenary Tartars [of the Seljūkian States]. . . . These Tartarians and other soldiers, seeing some their friends, and other some their natural and loving princes in the army of Tamerlane, stricken with the terror of disloyalty and abhorring the cruelty of the proud tyrant, in the heat of the battle revolted from Bajazet to their own princes, which their revolt much weakened Bajazet's forces. Who, nevertheless, with his own men of war, and especially the Janissaries, and the help of the Christian soldiers brought to his aid from Serbia and other places of Europe, with great courage maintained the fight: but the multitude and not true valour prevailed ; for as much as might be done by valiant and courageous men was by the Janissaries and the rest performed, both for the preservation of the person of their prince and the gaining of the victory.   But in the end, the horsemen, with whom Tamerlane himself was giving a fresh charge, and the avantguard wholly knit again to him reinforcing the charge, he with much ado obtained the victory." [1]

So on the field of Angora, where the Ottomans had won their spurs in their first combat by the side of the Seljūkian Turks a hundred and fifty years before, now was their empire shattered to the ground. Bāyezīd himself, with one of his sons, was taken prisoner, and the unfortunate Sultan became a part of his victor's pageant, and was condemned in fetters, to follow his captor about in his pomps and campaigns.   The fact that he was carried in a barred litter gave rise to the well-known legend that he was kept in an iron cage.[2]   He died eight months later, and Tīmūr survived his humbled prisoner but two years.   In that time, however, he had overrun the Turkish Empire in Asia, had occupied Nicaea, Brusa, and the other chief cities of the

---

[1] Knolles, i. 152.

[2] Racine, in his tragedy " Bajazet," made the story of this Sultan the means of familiarizing his generation with the history and habits of a people with whom they were little acquainted ; and Bāyezīd appears also in Marlowe's " Tamburlaine the Great."   In the latter he actually beats his brains out against the iron bars of his cage.   The English Rowe and the French Pradon also based tragedies on the same fruitful theme.

coast, had wrested Smyrna from the valiant Knights
of St. John, and had restored the various petty princes
of Asia Minor to their former possessions. The
empire of the Turks, built up with so much skill and
bravery, till it had become the terror of Europe,
crumbled to dust before the Asiatic despot, who well
earned his title of "The Wrath of God." The history
of the Ottomans seemed to have suddenly come to
an end. Seldom has the world seen so complete, so
terrible, a catastrophe as the fall of Bāyezīd from the
summit of power to the shame of a chained captive.

V.

MOHAMMED THE RESTORER.
(1402–1421.)

THE Ottoman power seemed gone for ever. At
one blow Tīmūr, the "Noble Tartarian," had apparently swept it out of Asia, and there were too
many foes waiting their opportunity in Europe to
make the hold of the Turks upon their European
provinces anything but precarious. Hungarians,
Poles, Bulgarians, Albanians, Vlachs, and many
more hovered on the brink of the Turkish provinces,
or were ready to rise in revolt within their borders.
Their enemy was fallen they thought for ever.

The most astonishing characteristic of the rule of
the Turks is its vitality. Again and again its doom
has been pronounced by wise prophets, and still it
survives. Province after province has been cut off
the empire, yet still the Sultan sits supreme over
wide dominions, and is reverenced or feared by subjects of many races. Considering how little of the
great qualities of the ruler the Turk has often
possessed, how little trouble he has taken to conciliate the subjects whom his sword has subdued,
it is amazing how firm has been his authority,

how unshaken his power. At the moment when Tīmūr's armies were ravaging the southern shores of the Bosphorus and the Greek Empire was almost rousing from its long sleep and retaking its lost provinces in Europe, the Turkish power might well be said to be annihilated ; yet within a dozen years the lost provinces were reunited under the strong and able rule of Mohammed I., and the Ottoman Empire, far from being weakened by the apparently crushing blow it had received in 1402, rose stronger and more vigorous after its fall, and, like a giant refreshed, prepared for new and bolder feats of conquest.

Mr. Finlay, the gifted historian of medieval and modern Greece, has been to some pains to investigate the reason of the strange phenomenon presented by the progress of the Ottoman power. The same causes which produced their first success must account for their even more astonishing resurrection. "The establishment of the Ottoman Turks in Europe," he says, "is the last example of the conquest of a numerous Christian population by a small number of Musulman invaders, and of the colonization of civilized countries by a race ruder than the native population. The causes which produced these results were in some degree similar to those which had enabled small tribes of Goths and Germans to occupy and subdue the Western Roman Empire ; but three particular causes demand especial attention. First, the superiority of the Ottoman tribe over all contemporary nations in religious convictions and in moral and military conduct. Second, the number of different races which composed the population of the country between the Adriatic and the Black Sea, the Danube and the Aegean. Third, the depopulation of the Greek Empire, the degraded state of its judicial and civil administration, and the demoralization of the Hellenic race." [1]

As Mr. Finlay goes on to explain, the respect with which Othmān and his successors were regarded by the countless Mohammedan and Christian tribes, subjects who flocked to their standard and gladly submitted to their authority, is a sure proof of real superiority. Other barbarous races have risen to power and conquered rich provinces, only to succumb to the vices of luxury and demoralization. The Ottomans long retained their pristine vigour and morality. The cause of this is to be sought to a great extent in the extraordinary skill with which Orkhan and his brother Alā-ud-dīn organised their new state ; the admirable administration of justice; and the systematic education in the household of the Sultan, both for civil and military purposes, of the Christian tribute-children who formed the nucleus of the Ottoman power, and who, deprived of the natural ties of country and family, became devoted to the Sultan to whom they owed their judicious training and subsequent advancement : " It was by their mental as well as physical power that a vast variety of races both Mohammedan and Christian were held together by as firm a grasp as that by which imperial Rome held her provinces ; and the standard of the Sultan was carried victoriously into the heart of Europe and Asia, and far along the shores of Africa. Never was

[1] " History of Greece," iii. 475.

so durable a power reared up so rapidly from such
scanty means as were possessed by Orkhan and his
Vezīr, when they conceived the bold idea of exter-
minating Christianity by educating Christian children."

The same sound education which was given to the
tribute-children was shared by the Ottoman princes
of the blood, and the result was that the early rulers
of the Turkish Empire were men of sagacity and
progressive views, always ready to improve the administration and the army, and to introduce new
inventions and combinations. Sultans possessed of so
wise a spirit were dangerous opponents of the shifty
and unprincipled Greek emperors, and their ably
organized and educated followers were infinitely the
superiors of the disunited and corrupt subjects of the
Palaeologi. These subjects, moreover, belonged to
various hostile and jealous races ; they were Slavs,
Greeks, Bulgarians, Vlachs, Albanians, and all degrees
of mixture, nor were the several races collected together, but scattered in various quarters of the empire. And that empire itself was so degraded and
corrupt in its government that it possessed no power
of uniting its motley subjects or stemming the tide
of demoralization that was swamping the whole
population. The road was open to the Ottomans,
and they were prepared to take it : they had served
a worthy apprenticeship to the trade they were to
follow.

Such causes led to the success of the Turks
against the empire, and though the temporary overthrow of the Ottoman power by Tīmūr checked their
progress for the moment, the elements of success

were not abolished.   The Ottomans were still the trained, educated, disciplined force, civil and military, they had ever been.   The Greek Empire was not the less decrepit because its antagonist was for an instant laid low.   It needed but a wise and patient sovereign to retrieve the disaster and restore the Ottoman power to its former supremacy and renown.

Such a ruler was Mohammed I., the son of Bāyezīd.   The Greeks described him as " persevering as a camel," and to his prudence and sagacity the Ottoman Empire owed as much as it did to the fighting qualities of his predecessors and successors.   No other dynasty can boast such a succession of brilliant sovereigns as those who conducted the Ottomans to the height of renown in the fourteenth, fifteenth, and sixteenth centuries.   Orkhan, the taker of Nicaea and founder of the Janissaries ; Murād I., the conqueror at Kosovo ; Bāyezīd I., the victor of Nicopolis ; Mohammed I., the restorer of the shattered empire ; Murād II., the antagonist of Hunyady and of Skanderbeg ; Mohammed II., the conqueror of Constantinople ; Selīm I., who annexed Kurdistan, Syria, and Egypt ; and Suleymān the Magnificent, the victor on the field of Mohács and the besieger of Vienna. Never did eight such sovereigns succeed one another (save for the feeble Bāyezīd II.) in unbroken succession in any other country ; never was an empire founded and extended during two such splendid centuries by such a series of great rulers.   In the hour of dismay, as well as in the moment of triumph, the Turkish Sultan was master of the situation.

It was in the hour of dismay that Sultan Moham-

med I. displayed his statesmanlike qualities. He
began without an empire, and the least encouraging
sign of the times was the jealousy which prompted
his brothers, aided by the crowd of jealous Seljūk
nobles and princes, to dispute with one another for
the throne. Mohammed was the youngest son of
Bāyezīd, and his elder brothers naturally asserted
their prior right to the crown. While he set up a little
shadow of a principality at Amasia, Prince Suleymān
raised his standard at Adrianople and claimed the
homage of the Turkish subjects in Europe ; Prince
Isa established himself at Brusa, and seized part of
the Asiatic provinces ; while Prince Mūsa, after bringing his father's body to Brusa to be buried, joined in
the race for power. Suleymān, who had made himself odious to his troops by his savage cruelty and
debauchery, was deserted by his army and killed
(1410). Mūsa, who reaped the advantages of his
brother's death and emulated his brutality, waged a
campaign against the Serbians, in which he ravaged
the country with all the ruthlessness that a Turkish
army can display, and is said to have feasted his
officers upon tables constructed of the corpses of three
Serb garrisons. He then laid siege to Constantinople, and the emperor called Mohammed to his aid.
After several reverses Mohammed, assisted by Stephen, king of Serbia, the old ally of Bāyezīd, routed
the besieging army, and in the flight Mūsa was killed.
Prince Isa had meanwhile disappeared into obscurity,
and Mohammed I. was now (1413) sole Sultan over
the undivided Turkish Empire.

His reign as absolute Sultan lasted only eight

years, but in that brief space he worked wonders.
He did not indeed attempt the warlike achievements
of his father, though he was prompt to resist any
encroachment upon his dominions.   He suffered
more than one defeat from the Christians of his
northern frontier, and his fleet was severely beaten
off Gallipoli by the Venetians under Admiral Loredano. Mohammed had, however, clearly grasped his
position, and had realized that his policy must be
steady consolidation rather than extension; and he
did not allow a few trifling reverses to tempt him
into dangerous campaigns. What he aimed at he
accomplished : to maintain the boundaries of his empire and strengthen the ties between the sovereign
and his subjects, which the disaster at Angora must
have sorely strained.   With this object his chief
desire was for peace, and he made the Greek emperor
his friend, first by supporting him against Mūsa, and
then by surrendering to him certain places on the
Black Sea and some fortresses in Thessaly.   He
received ambassadors from the rulers of Serbia,
Wallachia, and Albania, with assurances of good-will,
and concluded a treaty of amity with Venice.   In
Asia his authority was established with more difficulty, for the prince of Karaman, who had been
reinstated by Tīmūr, asserted his ancient independence and, not being an effete Greek, but a plucky
Turk, seized the moment of anarchy to invade the
chief cities of the Ottoman dominion in Asia.   Mohammed defeated him, but wisely refrained, in the
convalescent state of the empire, from endangering its
complete recovery by any very stringent measures

A VENETIAN GALLEY.

against the petty dynasties of Asia Minor. He received their homage, but left it to his successor to reduce them once again to the position of Turkish provinces to which Bāyezīd had brought them shortly before his fall.

A revolt of the dervishes, and the appearance of a pretender to the throne, further disturbed the Sultan's pacific designs ; but they were suppressed, and he was able to devote himself again to those measures of consolidation and to those cultivated tastes for poetry and literature for which he was distinguished. He was called Chelebi Mohammed, " Mohammed the Gentleman " ; and no name could better express the refinement and humanity of his character. It is recorded to his discredit that he caused his only surviving brother Kāsim to be blinded, and killed the child of Suleymān ; but it must be remembered that Mohammed had experienced too terribly the evils of rival claimants to the throne to be prone to suffer the empire to be again plunged into the intestinal troubles which had marked the beginning of his own reign. It appears to be the rule that a Turkish prince is never satisfied with anything short of the Sultanate ; and it becomes a matter of sheer necessity, and not a question of jealous suspicion, to make it impossible for him to attain his ambition. In the present day this is done by imprisoning him in the seraglio till he becomes almost idiotic. The old, and perhaps the more merciful, way was to kill him outright.

Mohammed I. died in the spring of the year 1421, and was buried near the beautiful mosque which he had built at Brusa, known as the Green Mosque, from the colour of the tiles that adorned its domes. Brusa was no longer the capital of the Turks. Mohammed had taken an ominous step : he had transferred his capital to Europe. Adrianople was the metropolis of the Ottomans.

VI.

MURĀD II. AND HUNYADY.
(1421–1451.)

THE new Sultan, Murād II., who succeeded in 1421, possessed all the clemency and prudence that characterized Mohammed the Gentleman ; but his temper was of that ambitious adventurous order which the state of the empire at that time demanded. Mohammed's conciliatory disposition, his peaceful and consolidating policy, had been of the utmost service to the State. The Turks were now ready to resume the career of conquest which had been interrupted by the thunderstorm of Angora, and Murād was the very leader they wanted. He lost no time in giving abundant proofs of his mettle. The Greek emperor, forgetful of his old ties with Mohammed, and con-temptuous of the stripling of eighteen years who now ascended the Ottoman throne, let loose a supposititious son of Bāyezīd, Mustafa, who had claimed the throne some years before, and had ever since been kept in close custody at Constantinople. Mustafa enjoyed a transitory gleam of triumph, and subdued the Euro-pean provinces for awhile ; but he was soon found wanting, and Murād had him hanged " to convince

the world that he *was* an impostor." Murād then
resolved to punish the duplicity of Manuel, and laid
siege to the imperial city. Already had Yildirim
Bāyezīd sat down before the city of Constantine,
but he had been recalled to Asia by the coming of
Tīmūr. In like manner Murād had made some
progress in the siege ; he had drawn his lines from
the Golden to the Wooden Gate, and an assault had
been attempted and vigorously repulsed by the
defenders, when a revolt in Asia Minor put an
end to the attack, and Murād hastily crossed the
Bosphorus to put down a brother's insurrection. On
his return he did not recommence the siege, but
accepted a heavy tribute from the emperor, and left
him in possession of Thessalonica (until 1430), and
some forts in Thrace and Thessaly. To prevent
any further opportunities for the disaffected in Asia,
Murād finally annexed most of the various petty
states which Tīmūr had resuscitated, and henceforth
we hear little of wars with the dynasties that had
once been the rivals of the Ottomans in the succession to the kingdom of the Seljūks.

Murād's fighting qualities were soon to be put to
such a test as no Asiatic prince could offer him. The
Christian states were again in arms, and they had
found a leader whose name is famous in the front
rank of European generals. So long as Stephen
Lazarevich lived, the treaty which bound Serbia to
alliance with the Turks was faithfully observed ;
but on his death in 1427 a new king arose, George
Brankovich, who knew not Murād, and who began
to collect the forces of Serbia, Bosnia, Hungary,

Poland, Wallachia, and Albania, against the common enemy.

Hunyady was the name the Christians conjured with. When King Sigismund of Hungary was flying from one of his unsuccessful engagements with the Ottoman armies, he met and loved the beautiful Elizabeth Morsiney, at the village of Hunyadé, and John Hunyady was believed to be the fruit of this consolatory affection. " Whatsoever his parents were," says Knolles, " he himself was a politic, valiant, fortunate, and famous captain, his victories so great as the like was never before by any Christian prince obtained against the Turks ; so that his name became unto them so dreadful that they used the same to fear their crying children withal." Hunyady had won his spurs in the wars in Italy, where his silver armour had gained him the sobriquet by which De Commines styles him, " the White Knight of Wallachia." Returning to his own country, he was chosen Ban of Szörény and Voyvode of Transylvania, and soon displayed his prowess. " This worthy captain," again to quote Knolles, " began to keep the Turks short by cutting them off whensoever they presumed to enter into his country, and also by shutting up the passages whereby they were wont to forage the country of Transylvania ; and when he had put his own charge into good safety, he entered into Moldavia, and never rested till he had won it quite out of the Turks' hands. And not contented with this, passed many times over Danubius into the Turks' dominions, making havoc of the Turks, and carrying away with him great booty, with many captives." For twenty years he was the terror of the Ottomans and the saviour of the kingdom of Hungary, of which, during the minority of Vladislaus V., he was chosen governor. The great events in his career were the battles of Hermannstadt and Nissa, the passage of the Balkan, the defeat at Varna, and the storming of Belgrade.[1]

The first of these encounters took place during the siege of Hermannstadt, in Transylvania, which Murād's general, Mezīd, was pressing as some compensation for a repulse which the Ottoman troops had recently received at Belgrade. Hunyady came to the rescue of the beleaguered city with a small force in 1442, and aided by a sally of the garrison totally routed the Turkish army, killed 20,000 of the enemy, and having taken their general prisoner had him publicly hacked to pieces. Hunyady was as cruel and bloodthirsty as even the traditional Bashibozuk. It was his delight to have his banquets accompanied by the sight of the slaughtering of his enemies, just as other princes prefer to eat their dinner to the sound of music; but Hunyady's music was the shriek of a dying prisoner. Soon after his success at Hermannstadt, he heavily defeated the Turks at Vasag, or Vaskapu, and in 1443 commanded a magnificent army, composed of the flower of Hungary, Serbia, and Wallachia, together with a band of crusaders from Italy whom the Pope had excited to the holy war. King Vladislaus of Hungary was present, and Cardinal Julian brought the weight of papal authority. They met the Ottoman troops on the

[1] For some account of the career of the Hungarian hero see " The Story of Hungary," chap. ix.

banks of the Morava, near Nissa, and routed them completely. The Turks fled over the Balkan, and Hunyady pursued them.

To cross the Balkan in winter from north to south against armed opposition is a feat rarely accomplished. Diebitsch and Gourko are the only generals besides Hunyady who have achieved it. The Turks had skilfully barricaded the passes, and poured water down the approaches, which froze into an icy wall during the night. The passage seemed impracticable. Yet nothing daunted, and braving the weapons of the Turks with the same inflexibility as the rigours of the cold, the Hungarians forced the pass of Isladi, and kept Christmas on the southern slope of the famous range. In the plain below they once again inflicted a defeat upon the discomfited Ottomans. It seemed as though the Turkish Empire in Europe was at the feet of the intrepid general, and we read with amazement that instead of advancing upon Adrianople Hunyady abandoned the fruits of his triumphant campaign and returned to Buda, there to display his booty and his captives to his admiring countrymen. Murād seized the opportunity to offer terms of peace, and the Treaty of Szegedin, by which Serbia regained her independence and Wallachia was annexed to Hungary, was solemnly sworn upon the Gospel and the Koran, and peace was concluded for ten years.

Murād, like Charles V., had already tasted enough of the joys and the sorrows of empire, and the death of his eldest son so sorely afflicted him that he longed for the peace and retirement which he could never attain upon the throne. He abdicated

in 1444, soon after the conclusion of the Treaty of
Szegedin, and his son Mohammed II. reigned in his
stead. Murád contentedly retired to Magnesia, where
he intended to enjoy what remained of his life in
cultivated leisure.

No sooner were the Christians aware of the abdication of the famous Sultan, whose generalship,
despite the reverses his Pashas had received at the
hands of Hunyady, was still an article of faith with
his foes, than they resolved to forsake their treaty.
The Pope and the Greek Emperor used their spiritual
influence to induce Hunyady to break his oath, and
Cardinal Julian employed the celebrated and in-
famous argument which Cardinal Ximenes with equal
success urged upon the conscience of Isabella of Castile
—that oaths are not to be kept with infidels. Hunyady was with difficulty persuaded, but the promise of
the kingship of Bulgaria was too much for his honour,
and he agreed to perjure himself. The treaty had
hardly been sworn a month when this perfidy was afoot ;
but the conspirators waited till the Turks had loyally
carried out their part of the bond and had evacuated
the forts of Serbia, before they began to disclose their
plans.

Nothing more derogatory to the chivalry of Europe
and the fame of a great general could be imagined
than the manner in which this treachery was carried
out. As soon as they had obtained the full advantages of the treaty they were about to disown, by the
retirement of the Ottoman garrisons, Hunyady, with
the King of Hungary, and Cardinal Julian, marched
upon the unsuspecting Turks, and with only 20,000

men began to invade the Ottoman dominions. They
took many strong places, and massacred the garrisons or threw them over precipices. Reaching the
Black Sea, they turned south, and had advanced
as far as Varna, which surrendered to their siege,
when they learned that Murād had been roused from
his retreat, had resumed the sceptre, and collected an
army of 40,000 veterans, who were then being conveyed across the Bosphorus for a ducat a man in
Genoese vessels. By forced marches the Sultan
pressed forward, and soon the news was brought that
he was close at hand.

Hunyady, notwithstanding the smallness of his
force, and the awe which the Sultan's name inspired,
was not dismayed. He was confident of victory, and,
refusing to entrench his camp, declared he would
fight in the open field,

"On the eve of the feast of St. Mathurin," says
Sir Edward Creasy, "the 10th of November, 1444,
the two armies stood arrayed for battle. The left
wing of the Christian army consisted chiefly of
Wallachian troops. The best part of the Hungarian
soldiery was in the right wing, where also stood
the Frankish crusaders under Cardinal Julian. The
king was in the centre, with the royal guard and
the young nobility of his realms. The rearguard of
Polish troops was under the Bishop of Peterwaradin.
Hunyady acted as commander-in-chief of the whole
army. On the Turkish side the two first lines were
composed of cavalry and irregular infantry, the Beglerbeg of Rumelia commanding on the right, and the
Beglerbeg of Anatolia on the left. In the centre,

behind their lines, the Sultan took his post, with his
Janissaries and the regular cavalry of his bodyguard.
A copy of the violated treaty was placed on a lance-
head and raised on high among the Turks as a
standard in the battle and a visible appeal to the
God of Truth, who punishes perjury among mankind.

"At the very instant when the armies were about to
encounter, an evil omen troubled the Christians. A
strong and sudden blast of wind swept through their
ranks, and blew all their banners to the ground, save
only that of the king. Yet the commencement of
the battle seemed to promise them a complete and
glorious victory. Hunyady placed himself at the
head of the right wing, and charged the Asiatic
troops with such vigour that he broke them and
chased them from the field. On the other wing, the
Wallachians were equally successful against the
cavalry and Azabs of Rumelia. King Vladislaus
advanced boldly with the Christian centre, and Murād,
seeing the rout of his two first lines and the disorder
that was spreading itself in the ranks round him, des-
paired of the fate of the day, and turned his horse for
flight.

" Fortunately for the house of Othmān, Karaja, the
Beglerbeg of Anatolia, who had fallen back on the
centre with the remnant of his defeated wing, was
near the Sultan at this critical moment. He seized
his master's bridle, and implored him to fight the
battle out. The commandant of the Janissaries,
indignant at such a breach of etiquette, raised his
sword to smite the unceremonious Beglerbeg, when

JANISSARY IN MUFTI.

he was himself cut down by a Hungarian sabre. Murād's presence of mind had failed him only for a moment, and he now encouraged his Janissaries to stand firm against the Christian charge. King Vladislaus, on the other side, fought gallantly in the thickest of the strife ; but his horse was killed under him, and he was then surrounded and overpowered. He wished to yield himself a prisoner, but the Ottomans, indignant at the breach of the treaty, had sworn to give no quarter. An old Janissary cut off the king's head, and placed it, helmeted in silver, on a pike—a fearful companion to the lance on which the violated treaty was still reared on high.

"The Hungarian nobles were appalled at the sight, and their centre fled in utter dismay from the field. Hunyady, on returning with his victorious right wing, vainly charged the Janissaries, and strove at least to rescue from them the ghastly trophy of their victory. At last he fled in despair with the wreck of the troops that he had personally commanded and with the Wallachians who collected round him. The Hungarian rearguard, abandoned by their commanders, was attacked by the Turks the next morning, and massacred almost to a man. Besides the Hungarian king, Cardinal Julian, the author of the breach of the treaty and the cause of this calamitous campaign, perished at Varna beneath the Turkish scimitar, together with Stephen Bahory, and the bishops of Eilau and Grosswardein." [1]

The result of this decisive victory was the complete subjugation of Serbia and Bosnia, which were the more

[1] Creasy, 69–70.

willing to re-enter the Moslem dominion as they had
been threatened with persecution and forcible conver-
sion to the Latin faith in the event of the triumph of
Hunyady. Murād again retired to Magnesia; but
his son was still too young to manage the empire,
and a revolt of the Janissaries recalled the father to
his responsibilities. He did not retire a third time,
but reigned for six years in undiminished glory, and
once more defeated his old enemy Hunyady at a
second long contested battle at Kosovo.

At last he died in 1451. "Thus lieth great Amurath,"
writes Knolles, compelled into a sort of enthusiasm as
he contemplates the death of the mighty Sultan, " erst
not inferior unto the greatest monarchs of that age.
· . . Who had fought greater battles ? who had gained
greater victories, or obtained more glorious triumphs
than had Amurath? who by the spoils of so many
mighty kings and princes, and by the conquest of so
many proud and warlike nations, again restored and
embellished the Turks' kingdom, before by Tamerlane
and the Tartars in a manner clean defaced? He it
was that burst the heart of the proud Grecians,
establishing his empire at Hadrianople, even in the
centre of their bowels: from whence have proceeded
so many miseries and calamities unto the greatest
part of Christendom as no tongue is able to express.
He it was that subdued unto the Turks so many
great countries and provinces in Asia; that in plain
field and set battle overthrew many puissant kings
and princes, and brought them under his subjection;
who, having slain Vladislaus, the King of Polonia and
Hungary, and more than once chased out of the field

Hunyady that famous and redoubted warrior, had in his proud and ambitious heart promised unto himself the conquest of a great part of Christendom. . . . Where is that victorious hand that swayed so many sceptres? where is the majesty of his power and strength that commanded over so many nations and kingdoms? He lieth now dead, a ghastly carcase, a clod of clay unregarded, his hands closed, his eyes shut, his feet stretched out, which erst proudly traced the countries by him subdued and conquered."

But the clod of clay was not quite unregarded: it was buried with great solemnity at Brusa, where "he now lieth in a chapel without any roof, his grave nothing differing from the manner of the common Turks: which they say he commanded to be done in his last will, that the mercy and blessing of God might come unto him with the shining of the sun and moon and falling of the rain and dew upon his grave." [1]

Hunyady survived the Sultan whose armies he had so often met. Five years after Murād had gone to sleep with his fathers at Brusa, his son Mohammed laid siege to Belgrade—the Gate of Hungary. Then came the crowning triumph of Hunyady's career. He stirred up the garrison to a valiant defence, at first by his single efforts; but soon with the aid of a no less heroic spirit. John Capistran came to his aid, followed by a fiery band of 60,000 Crusaders, whom the monk's martial ardour and zeal for the faith had gathered together to fight for Christendom in this hour of its sore distress. At the

[1] Knolles, i. 227.

moment when the Janissaries had forced their way into the devoted city, Hunyady and the gallant old priest fell upon them with the fury of despair; and so fierce was the charge that the Turks fell back.[1] Then the holy man, leading his Crusaders with a glorious recklessness straight to the tent of the Sultan, and followed by Hunyady and the inspirited garrison, routed the Ottomans so utterly, that they even abandoned their camp and artillery to the Christians and fled for dear life. Mohammed himself was wounded, and 25,000 Turks lay stretched upon the field. Twenty days after this, Hunyady, the hero of many fields, died, and two months later was followed to the grave by John Capistran, who had seen his threescore years and ten, and had ended them in a flash of glory. He was canonized at Rome, and all Christians must agree that the noble old monk had well earned the veneration of all the churches of Europe.

[1] See Vámbéry, "The Story of Hungary," for the Hungarian account of the siege.

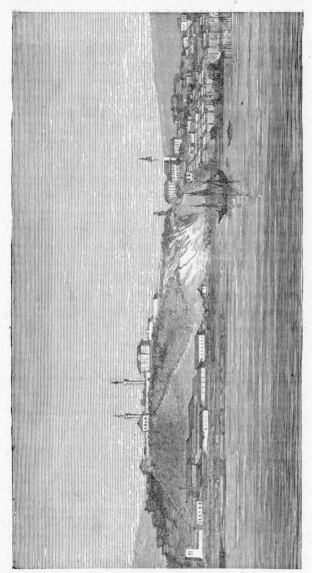

BELGRADE.

7.

VII.

THE FALL OF CONSTANTINOPLE.
(1451–1481.)

Character of Mah. II.

MURAD'S long reign of thirty years was soiled by no breath of dishonour ; his character was as noble as it was commanding. His son and successor Mohammed II., reigned also thirty years, but his rule was marked by violence and treachery, and the new Sultan, though possessed of surpassing ability and intelligence, had none of the high moral qualities that distinguished his father. Again and again he emulated the perfidy of the Hungarians and broke a solemn pledge ; again and again garrisons confided in his honour only to meet with ruthless slaughter. His first act was to murder his baby brother, whose powers of hostility could hardly yet be dangerous ; and it is difficult to imagine the state of mind of a sovereign who, granting the wisdom of removing possible pretenders to the throne, could consistently carry out the principle on the person of an infant at the breast.

Cruel, perfidious, and sensual, the new Sultan was yet, as is not uncommon with Eastern tyrants, a

very cultivated man, devoted to the making of verse
and the society of men of learning. Thirty Ottoman poets received pensions from this Turkish Maece-
nas, and he even sent handsome presents every year to
the Indian Khoja-i-jihān and the Persian Jamī; while
his liberality towards colleges and pious foundations
was so great that he was given the surname " Father
of Good Works" as well as "Sire of Victory."   His
bounty and poetic talent were emulated by his great
officers ; and Mahmūd Pasha, the conqueror of Negropont, was a founder of colleges and a writer of verse.
It was natural that the source of all this poetic culti-
vation should be praised in song ; and we learn from
panegyrists that the countenance of Mohammed II. was
decorated with a pair of red and white cheeks, full and
round, a hooked nose, and a resolute mouth—as we see
in the medal (p. 104); his moustachios were " like leaves
over two rosebuds, and every hair of his beard was as a
thread of gold ! " [1]   Such encomiums sound oddly in
European ears ; but when the poets extolled Mohammed's military genius they were on firmer ground. As a
general he was superior even to his father ; and his
famous reply to one who asked him on a campaign
what were his plans—" If a hair of my beard knew
them I would pluck it out "—gives the key-note of his
success : absolute secrecy and lightning rapidity of
action.

Mohammed II. fought many battles and laid siege
to many cities, but the siege which procured him the
name of " the Conqueror " was that of Constantinople
in 1453. It seemed as if the Greek Empire were

[1] E. J. W. Gibb, " Ott. Poems," 171–2.

MEDAL OF MOHAMMED II.

MEDAL OF MOHAMMED II. (REVERSE).

doomed to precipitate its end by signal acts of folly whenever a new Sultan came to the throne. The Christians had lost their opportunity when the Turks lay prostrate under the heel of Tīmūr, and Europe might have expelled the invaders once and for ever. Europe preferred to wait till the Ottomans had recovered all their pristine vigour, and then, on the accession of Murād II., Manuel the Emperor, committed the folly of setting up Mustafa as a claimant to the throne. But for disturbances in his Asiatic provinces, Murād would probably have taken Constantinople then and there. As it was the Emperor received a lesson that should hardly have needed repetition. Nevertheless, after thirty years, during which the Turks were continually growing in power and military prestige, the new Emperor Constantine Palaeologus, last of his line, impelled by some fatal frenzy, seized the occasion of Murād's death to emulate the insanity of Manuel. He threatened to establish on the throne of Adrianople a grandson of that Prince Suleymān who had once reigned there so gaily among his wine-cups. Constantine was a brave man, as we shall see, but he was not a wise one, and in this instance he had laid too much stress upon the fact that, when Murād had abdicated, the lad Mohammed had shown himself unequal to the task of ruling the wide empire of the Ottomans. Six or seven years, however, had made a great difference in the spirit and resolution of the young Sultan, as Constantine was soon made to understand.

The Turks had longed for the possession of the imperial city ever since Othmān had dreamed that he grasped it in his hand. "Thunderbolt" Bāyezīd had besieged it ; Mūsa had pressed it hard ; Murād II. had patiently planned its conquest. There was little to be won beside the city itself, for all the province round about had long been subdued by the Ottomans ; but the wealth and beauty, the strength and position, of the capital itself were quite enough to make its capture the crowning ambition of the Turks. Mohammed eagerly seized the opportunity offered him by the hostility of the unwary emperor, and immediately began to build a fortress outside the gates of Constantinople, as the manner of the Turks was. Mohammed I. had already erected the fortress known as Anadolu Hisār, "The Castle of Anatolia," on the Asiatic shore, to overawe the Emperor Manuel. Mohammed II. set up the Rumeli Hisār, "Castle of Rumelia," on the opposite side, as a preparation for the conquest of Constantinople, and to the great terror of the emperor. A thousand masons and a thousand labourers were devoted to the work ; altars and pillars of Christian churches were used for the walls, which were thirty feet thick ; and the castle was finished in three months. On the chief tower heavy ordnance was placed in position, which cast stone balls of six hundredweight, and a garrison of four hundred men was established with orders to take toll from all passing vessels. The Castle of Rumelia stands to this day, facing its fellow across the Bosphorus, and keeping guard over the strait.

The Turkish annalist Sa'd-ud-dīn describes the approach of the besieging army in his turgid rhymed prose, the effect of which is preserved in the following translation by Mr. Gibb :—

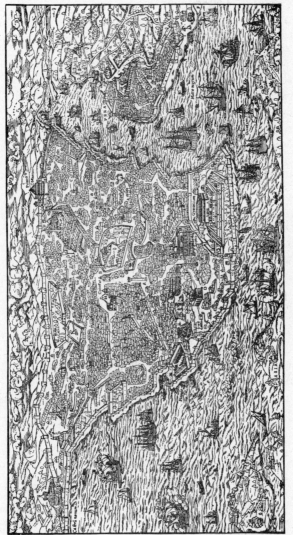

PLAN OF CONSTANTINOPLE.

"One morn, of fortune bright, when the van of the King of the skies [1] had appeared with the hosts of light, from forth the horizon tower, from behind the orient veil, the castle of night to assail, did the victory-shaded avant-guard of the high and lofty Lord [2] likewise attain to the foot of the city-wall. And behind, like a boundless sea, like a hurrying stream, the Imperial host, the victory-tended army, rolled, and did the city on the land-side enfold. With such sternness and such firmness did they that defended burgh, which of burghs is the mightiest, affray, that the footsteps of the courage of the burghers went astray, and the wit and understanding of the wardens passed away."

The greatest of English historians has told the story of the conquest of Constantinople in such a manner, that subsequent research has succeeded in modifying almost nothing of his famous narrative. After careful and detailed preparations, the siege of the Eastern metropolis began on April 6, 1453. We quote from Gibbon.[3]

"Of the triangle which composes the figure of Constantinople, the two sides along the sea were made inaccessible to an enemy ; the Propontis by nature, and the harbour by art. Between the two waters, the basis of the triangle, the land side was protected by a double wall and a deep ditch of the depth of one hundred feet. Against this line of fortification, which Phranza, an eye-witness, prolongs to the measure of six miles, the Ottomans directed their principal attack ; and the emperor, after distributing the service and command of the most perilous

[1] The sun.   [2] The Sultan.   [3] Milman's ed. viii. 159 ff.

stations, undertook the defence of the external wall. In the first days of the siege, the Greek soldiers descended into the ditch or sallied into the field; but they soon discovered that in the proportion of their numbers, one Christian was of more value than twenty Turks; and after these bold preludes, they were prudently content to maintain the rampart with their missile weapons. Nor should this prudence be accused of pusillanimity. The nation was indeed pusillanimous and base; but the last Constantine deserves the name of a hero; his noble band of volunteers was inspired with Roman virtue; and the foreign auxiliaries supported the honour of the Western chivalry. The incessant volleys of lances and arrows were accompanied with the smoke, the sound, and the fire of their musketry and cannon. Their small arms discharged at the same time either five or even ten balls of lead, of the size of a walnut; and, according to the closeness of the ranks and the force of the powder, several breastplates and bodies were transpierced by the same shot. But the Turkish approaches were soon sunk in trenches or covered with ruins. Each day added to the scene of the Christians; but their inadequate stock of gunpowder was wasted in the operation of each day. Their ordnance was not powerful, either in size or number; and if they possessed some heavy cannon, they feared to plant them on the walls, lest the aged structure should be shaken and overthrown by the explosion. The same destructive secret had been revealed to the Moslems, by whom it was employed with the superior energy of zeal, riches, and despotism. The great cannon of Mahomet—an important and visible object in the history of the times—was flanked by two fellows almost of equal magnitude ; the long order of the Turkish artillery was pointed against the walls ; fourteen batteries thundered at once on the most accessible places.

" The first random shots were productive of more sound than effect ; and it was by the advice of a Christian that the engineers were taught to level their aim against the two opposite sides of the salient angles of a bastion. However imperfect, the weight and repetition of the fire made some impression on the walls ; and the Turks, pushing their approaches to the edge of the ditch, attempted to fill the enormous chasm, and to build a road to the assault. Innumerable fascines, and hogsheads, and trunks of trees were heaped on each other ; and such was the impetuosity of the throng, that the foremost and the weakest were pushed headlong down the precipice, or instantly buried under the accumulated mass. To fill the ditch was the toil of the besiegers ; to clear away the rubbish was the safety of the besieged ; and, after a long and bloody conflict, the web that had been woven in the day was still unravelled in the night. The next resource of Mahomet was the practice of mines : but the soil was rocky ; in every attempt he was stopped and undermined by the Christian engineers ; nor had the art been yet invented of replenishing those subterraneous passages with gunpowder, and blowing whole towers and cities into the air. A circumstance that distinguishes the siege of Constantinople is the reunion of the ancient and modern artillery. The cannon were intermingled with the mechanical engines for casting stones and darts; the bullet and the battering-ram were directed against the walls. Nor had the discovery of gunpowder superseded the use of the liquid and unextinguishable fire. A wooden turret of the largest size was advanced on rollers; this portable magazine of ammunition and fascines was protected by a threefold covering of bulls' hides; incessant volleys were securely discharged from the loopholes; in front, three doors were converted for the sally and retreat of the soldiers and workmen. They ascended by a staircase to the upper platform; and, as high as the level of that platform, a scaling-ladder could be raised by pulleys to form a bridge, and grapple with the adverse rampart. By these various arts of annoyance, some as new as they were pernicious to the Greeks, the tower of St. Romanus was at length overturned; after a severe struggle, the Turks were repulsed from the breach, and interrupted by darkness; but they trusted that with the return of light, they should renew the attack with fresh vigour and decisive success. Of this pause of action, this interval of hope, each moment was improved by the activity of the Emperor and Justiniani, who passed the night on the spot, and urged the labours, which involved the safety of the church and city. At the dawn of day, the impatient Sultan perceived with astonishment and grief, that his wooden turret had been reduced to ashes; the ditch was cleared and restored; and the tower of St. Romanus was again strong and entire. He deplored the failure of his design, and uttered a profane exclamation, that the word of the thirty-seven thousand prophets should

VII. La Ville de Constantinople, avec son beau Chasteau ou temple, Medeline en Egialte, et Codelimine avec les Serpent de Cuyure, ou sept et le Sultan ... Item, combien qu'on y puisse recourse à pied. Tout y tyen ... dessus la ville, lequel est pourtraict en ...

SIEGE OF CONSTANTINOPLE.

not have compelled him to believe that such a work in so short a time could have been accomplished by the infidels."

At this point five Genoese ships forced the Turkish blockade, and brought provisions and relief to the garrison.

"The introduction of this supply revived the hopes of the Greeks, and accused the suspicions of their Western allies. Amidst the deserts of Anatolia and the rocks of Palestine, the millions of the Crusades had buried themselves in a voluntary and inevitable grave; but the situation of the imperial city was strong against her enemies and accessible to her friends; and a rational and moderate armament of the maritime states might have saved the relics of the Roman name, and maintained a Christian fortress in the heart of the Ottoman Empire. Yet this was the sole and feeble attempt for the deliverance of Constantinople. The more distant powers were insensible of its danger; and the Ambassador of Hungary, or at least of Huniades, resided in the Turkish camp, to remove the fears, and to direct the operations of the Sultan.

"The reduction of the city appeared to be hopeless, unless a double attack could be made from the harbour as well as from the land; but the harbour was inaccessible; an impenetrable chain was now defended by eight large ships, more than twenty of a smaller size, with several galleys and sloops; and instead of facing this barrier, the Turks might apprehend a naval sally, and a second encounter in the open seas. In this perplexity, the genius of Mahomet

conceived and executed a plan of a bold and marvellous cast, of transporting by land his lighter vessels
and military stores from the Bosphorus into the higher
part of the harbour. The distance is about ten miles ;
the ground is uneven, and was overspread with thickets,
and as the road must be opened behind the suburb of
Galata, this free passage or total destruction must depend on the option of the Genoese. But these selfish
merchants were ambitious of the favour of being the
last devoured ; and the deficiency of art was supplied
by the strength of the obedient myriads. A level way
was covered with a broad platform of strong and solid
planks ; and to render them more slippery and smooth,
they were anointed with the fat of sheep and oxen.
Fourscore eight galleys and brigantines of fifty and
thirty oars were disembarked on the Bosphorus shore,
arranged successively on rollers, and drawn forwards
by the power of men and pulleys. Two guides or pilots
were stationed at the helm and the prow of each vessel ;
the sails were unfurled to the winds ; and the labour
was cheered by song and acclamation. In the course
of a single night, this Turkish fleet painfully climbed
the hill, steered over the plain, and was launched from
the declivity into the shallow waters of the harbour, far
above the molestations of the deeper vessels of the
Greeks. The real importance of this operation was
magnified by the consternation and confidence which
it inspired ; but the notorious, unquestionable fact was
displayed before the eyes, and is recorded by the pens,
of two nations. A similar stratagem has been repeatedly practised by the ancients. The Ottoman
galleys (I must again repeat) should be considered as

large boats, and if we compare the magnitude and the distance, the obstacles, and the means, the boasted miracle has perhaps been equalled by the industry of our own times. As soon as Mahomet had occupied the upper harbour with a fleet and army, he constructed, in the narrowest part, a bridge, or rather mole, of fifty cubits in breadth, and one hundred in length ; it was formed of casks and hogsheads, joined with rafters, linked with iron, and covered with a solid floor. On this floating battery he planted one of his largest cannon, whilst the fourscore galleys, with troops and scaling ladders, approached the most accessible side, which had formerly been stormed by the Latin conquerors. The indolence of the Christians has been accused for not destroying those unfinished works ; but their fire, by a superior fire, was controlled and silenced ; nor were they wanting in an nocturnal attempt to burn the vessels as well as the bridge of the Sultan. His vigilance prevented their approach, their foremost galliots were sunk or taken ; forty youths, the bravest of Italy and Greece, were inhumanly massacred at his command, nor could the emperor's grief be assuaged by the just though cruel retaliation of exposing from the walls the heads of 260 Musulman captives. After a siege of forty days the fate of Constantinople could no longer be averted. The diminutive garrison was exhausted by a double attack : the fortifications, which had stood for ages against hostile violence, were dismantled on all sides by the Ottoman cannon. Many breaches were opened, and near the gate of St. Romanus four towers had been levelled with the ground. For the payment of his feeble and mutinous troops, Constantine was compelled to despoil the churches with the promise of a fourfold restitution ; and his sacrilege offered a new reproach to the enemies of the union. A spirit of discord impaired the remnant of the Christian strength ; the Genoese and Venetian auxiliaries asserted the preëminence of their respective service, and Justiniani and the great duke, whose ambition was not extinguished by the common danger, accused each other of treachery and cowardice." . . .

Such " was the state of the Christians, who, with loud and impotent complaints, deplored the guilt, or the punishment of their sins. The celestial image of the Virgin had been exposed in solemn procession ; but their divine patroness was deaf to their entreaties. They accused the obstinacy of the emperor for refusing a timely surrender ; anticipated the horrors of their fate, and sighed for the repose and security of Turkish servitude. The noblest of the Greeks and the bravest of the allies were summoned to the palace, to prepare them on the evening of the 28th for the duties and dangers of the general assault. The last speech of Palaeologus was the funeral oration of the Roman Empire: he promised, he conjured, and he vainly attempted to infuse the hope which was extinguished in his own mind. In this world all was comfortless and gloomy, and neither the gospel nor the Church have proposed any conspicuous recompense to the heroes who fall in the service of their country. But the example of their prince and the confinement of a siege had armed their warriors with the courage of despair, and the pathetic scene is described by the feelings of the historian Phranza, who was himself present at this mournful assembly. They wept, they embraced each other ; regardless of their families and fortunes they devoted their lives ; and each commander, departing to his station, maintained all night a vigilant and anxious watch on the rampart. The emperor, and some faithful companions, entered the dome of St. Sophia, which in a few hours was to be converted into a mosque, and devoutly received with tears and prayers the sacrament of the holy communion. He reposed some moments in the palace, which resounded with cries and lamentations, solicited the pardon of all whom he might have injured, and mounted on horseback to visit the guards and explore the motions of the enemy. The distress and fall of the last Constantine are more glorious than the long prosperity of the Byzantine Caesars.

" In the confusion of darkness an assailant may sometimes succeed, but in this great and general attack the military judgment and astrological knowledge of Mahomet advised him to expect the morning, the memorable 29th May, in the fourteen hundred and fifty-third year of the Christian era. The preceding night had been strenuously employed ; the troops, the cannon, and the fascines were advanced to the edge of the ditch, which in many parts presented a smooth and level passage to the breach, and his fourscore galleys almost touched with the prows and their scaling-ladders the less defensible walls of their harbour. Under pain of death silence was enjoined, but the physical laws of motion and sound are not obedient to discipline or fear, each individual might suppress his voice and measure his footsteps, but the march and labour of thousands must inevitably produce a strange confusion of dissonant clamours, which reached the ears of the watchmen of the towers.

"At daybreak, without the customary signal of the morning gun, the Turks assaulted the city by sea and land, and the similitude of a twined or twisted thread has been applied to the closeness and continuity of their line of attack. The foremost host consisted of the refuse of the ranks, a voluntary crowd who fought without order or command, of the feebleness of age or childhood, of peasants and vagrants, and of all who had joined the camp in the blind hope of plunder and martyrdom. The common impulse drove them onwards to the walls. The most audacious to climb were instantly precipitated ; and not a dart, not a bullet, of the Christians was idly wasted on the accumulated throngs. But their strength and ammunition were exhausted in this laborious defence. The ditch was filled with the bodies of the slain ; they supported the footsteps of their companions, and of this devoted vanguard the death was more serviceable than the life. Under their respective pashas and sanjak-begs the troops of Anatolia and Rumelia were successively led to the charge : their progress was various and doubtful, but after a conflict of two hours the Greeks still maintained and improved their advantages, and the voice of the emperor was heard encouraging his soldiers to achieve, by a last effort, the deliverance of their country. In that fatal moment the Janissaries arose, fresh, vigorous, and invincible. The Sultan himself on horseback, with an iron mace in his hand, was the spectator or judge of their valour. He was surrounded by 10,000 of his domestic troops, whom he reserved for the decisive occasions, and the tide of battle was directed and impelled by his voice and eye. His numerous ministers of justice were posted behind the line, to urge, to restrain, and to punish ; and if danger was in the front, shame and inevitable death were in the rear of the fugitives. The cries of fear and of pain were drowned in the martial music of drums, trumpets, and attaballs, and experience has proved that the mechanical operation of sounds, by quickening the circulation of the blood and spirits, will act on the human machine more forcibly than the eloquence of reason and honour. From the lines, the galleys, and the bridge, the Ottoman artillery thundered on all sides ; and the camp and city, the Greeks and the Turks, were involved in a cloud of smoke, which could only be dispelled by the final deliverance or destruction of the Roman Empire. The signal combats of the heroes of history or fable amuse our fancy and engage our affections ; the skilful evolutions of war may inform the mind, and improve a necessary though pernicious science ; but in the uniform and odious pictures of a general assault, all is blood, and horror, and confusion ; nor shall I strive, at the distance of three centuries and 1000 miles, to delineate a scene of which there could be no spectators, and of which the actors themselves were incapable of forming any just or adequate idea.

" The immediate loss of Constantinople may be ascribed to the bullet, or arrow, which pierced the gauntlet of John Justiniani. The sight of his blood, and the exquisite pain, appalled the courage of the chief, whose arms and counsels were the firmest ramparts of the city."

Sa'd-ud-dīn glories over the overthrow of this brave captain in his flowery manner :—

"When the Bicorned Lord [1] of the fourth throne, having risen from the glooms of the west, had himself addressed to subdue the castle of the sphere, and had routed the cohorts of the stars with his sabre and his spear, did the chief of the losel Franks, who, charged with the guard of that rampart rent, thought to war and to fight with the holy ranks, mount on the city-wall, meaning the holy legions to repel.   Thereon did a youth nimble and brave, letting his ne'er oppressing glaive hang like the new moon in the sky, climb spider-wise, by the rope of emprize, the city-rampart high.   Then he raised his remorseless brand, and made that awful flame the doom of yon infernal's fearful frame ; thus making the gates of death, before his hapless face, gape wide, even as the rents in the city's side ; and putting to flight with only one blow, the owl, his soul, from its nest of woe ; and cutting short, with his life, the thread of his thought, and making his unseemly visage black as his disastrous lot.   Soon as the Frankish crew saw their chief assume this hue, did the fray tear its skirt from their clutch away ; and each sped along upon flight's highway, and turned his face to face dismay ; and they sought

---

[1] Alexander the Great, so called on account of the two horns on his coins.   Here the Sun is meant, as being the Ruler of the Fourth Sphere, in the old Ptolemaic astronomy.

their ships in woe, running toward the sea, like a river swift of flow."

" The number of the Ottomans," continues Gibbon, " was fifty, perhaps a hundred, times superior to that of the Christians ; the double walls were reduced by the cannon to a heap of ruins; in a circuit of several miles some places must be found more easy of access or more feebly guarded ; and, if the besiegers could penetrate in a single point, the whole city was irrecoverably lost.   The first who deserved the Sultan's reward was Hasan the Janissary, of gigantic stature and strength. With his scimitar in one hand and his buckler in the other, he ascended the outward fortifications ; of the thirty Janissaries who were emulous of his valour eighteen perished in the bold adventure.   Hasan and his twelve companions had reached the summit ; the giant was precipitated from the ramparts ; he rose on one knee, and was again oppressed by a shower of darts and stones.   But his success had proved that the achievement was possible ; the walls and towers were instantly covered with a swarm of Turks ; and the Greeks, now driven from the vantage ground were overwhelmed by increasing multitudes.   Amidst these multitudes the emperor, who accomplished all the duties of a general and a soldier, was long seen, and finally lost.   The nobles who fought round his person sustained till their last breath the honourable names of Palaeologus and Cantacuzene ; his mournful exclamation was heard, ' Cannot there be found a Christian to cut off my head ? ' and his last fear was that of falling alive into the hands of the infidels.   The prudent despair of Constantine cast away the purple ;

amidst the tumult he fell by an unknown hand, and his body was buried under a monument of the slain. After his death resistance and order were no more ; the Greeks fled towards the city, and many were pressed or stifled in the narrow pass of the Gate of St. Romanus. The victorious Turks rushed through the breaches of the inner walls ; and, as they advanced into the streets, they were soon joined by their brethren, who had fought and forced the gate of Phenar on the side of the harbour. In the first heat of the pursuit about 2,000 Christians were put to the sword, but avarice soon prevailed over cruelty ; the victors acknowledged that they should immediately have given quarter if the valour of the emperor and his chosen bands had not prepared them for a similar opposition in every part of the capital. It was thus, after a siege of fifty-three days, that Constantinople, which had defied the power of Chosroes, the Chakan, and the Caliphs, was irretrievably subdued by the arms of Mahomet II. Her empire had been subverted by the Latins ; her religion was trampled in the dust by her Moslem conquerors. . . .

"On the assurance of this public calamity the houses and convents were instantly deserted, and the trembling inhabitants flocked together in the streets like a herd of timid animals, as if accumulated weakness could be productive of strength, or in the vain hope that amid the crowd each individual might be safe and invisible. From every part of the capital they flowed into the church of St. Sophia ; in the space of an hour the sanctuary, the choir, the nave, the upper and lower galleries, were filled with a mul-

SANTA SOPHIA.

titude of fathers and husbands, of women and children, priests, monks, religious virgins ; the doors were barred on the inside, and they sought protection in the sacred dome.

"While they expected the descent of the tardy angel the doors were broken with axes, and, as the Turks encountered no resistance, their bloodless hands were employed in selecting and securing the multitude of their prisoners. Youth, beauty, the appearance of wealth, attracted their choice; and the right of property was decided among them by a prior seizure, by personal strength, and by the authority of command in the space of an hour. Male captives were bound with cords, the females with their veils and girdles ; the senators were linked with their slaves ; the prelates with the porters of the church ; and young men of a plebeian class with noble maids, whose faces had been invisible to the sun and their nearest kindred, and in this common captivity the ranks of society were confounded, the ties of nature were cut asunder, and the inexorable soldier was careless of the father's groans, the tears of the mother, and the lamentations of the children. The loudest in their wailings were the nuns, who were torn from the altar, with naked bosoms, outstretched hands, and dishevelled hair ; and we should piously believe that few could be tempted to prefer the vigils of the harem to those of the monastery. Of these unfortunate Greeks, of these domestic animals, whole strings were rudely driven through the streets ; and, as the conqueror was eager to return for more prey, their trembling pace was quickened with menaces and blows. At the same

hour a similar rapine was exercised in all the churches
and monasteries, in all the palaces and habitations of
the capital ; nor could any place, however sacred or
sequestered, protect the persons or the property of the
Greeks.   Above 60,000 of this devoted people were
transported from the city to the camp or the fleet ;
exchanged or sold, according to the interest or caprice
of their masters, and dispersed in remote servitude
through the provinces of the Ottoman Empire.

" From the first hour of the memorable 29th of May
disorder and rapine prevailed in Constantinople till
the eighth hour of the same day, when the Sultan
himself passed in triumph through the gate of St.
Romanus.   He was attended by his vezīrs, pashas,
and guards, each of whom (says a Byzantine historian)
was robust as Hercules, dexterous as Apollo, and
equal in battle to any ten of the race of ordinary
mortals.   The conqueror gazed with satisfaction and
wonder on the strange though splendid appearance of
the domes and palaces, so dissimilar from the style
of Ottoman architecture.   In the hippodrome, or
At-Meydān, his eyes were attracted by the twisted
column of the three serpents, and, as a trial of his
strength, he shattered with his iron mace or battle-
axe the under jaw of one of those monsters, which
in the eyes of the Turks were the idols or talismans
of the city.   At the principal door of St. Sophia he
alighted from his horse and entered the dome ; and
such was his jealous regard for that monument of his
glory that, on observing a zealous Moslem in the act
of breaking the marble pavement, he admonished him
with his scimitar that if the spoil and captives were

granted to the soldiers, the public and private buildings had been reserved for the prince. By his command
the metropolis of the Eastern church was transformed
into a mosque ; the rich and portable instruments of
superstition had been removed ; the crosses were
thrown down low ; and the walls, which were covered
with images and mosaics, were washed and purified,
and restored to a state of naked simplicity. On the
same day, or on the ensuing Friday, the muezzin, or
crier, ascended the most lofty turret, and proclaimed
the azān or public invitation in the name of God and
His Prophet, the Imām preached, and Mahomet II.
performed the *namāz* thanksgiving on the first altar,
where the Christian mysteries had so lately been celebrated before the last of the Caesars. From St. Sophia
he proceeded to the august but desolate mansion of
one hundred successors of the great Constantine, but
which in a few hours had been stripped of the pomp
of royalty. A melancholy reflection on the vicissi-
tudes of human greatness forced itself upon his
mind, and he repeated an elegant distich of Persian
poetry : "—[1]

" Now the spider draws the curtain in the Caesars' palace hall,
And the owl proclaims the watch beneath Afrasiab's vaulted dome."

The Turkish historian's [2] account of the fall of Constantinople has been faithfully rendered by Mr. Gibb.
A few extracts will suffice :—

" When by the aidance of the One beyond gainsay

---

[1] " The Decline and Fall of the Roman Empire," chap. lxviii.
[2] Sa'd-ud-din, " The Capture of Constantinople," Glasgow, 1879
(revised by the translator).

the strength of the defenders of the burgh was passed
away, and the happy tidings : ' Verily, our hosts, the
conquerors are they ! ' [1] were become the stock of the
support of the victory-crowned array, the gladness-
fraught address, ' Enter ye in peace! ' [2] sounded in
the ear of the army of the Fay.   With leave from the
threshold of the world-conquering King to plunder
and to spoil, did those eager after booty into the city
sweep, where, laying hands on their families and their
wealth, they made the worthless misbelievers weep.
They acted by the order : ' Slaughter their elders and
capture their youth ; ' and those profitful properties,
which in the days of old, the years that are told, had
been unstricken of the hand of profligacy, became the
portion of the champions of the Truth.   And that fair
and fruitful site, through the advent, twin of delight,
of the Sovereign, just of spright, became the home of
flashing light, of the stead of the Faith of Right. . . .

   " And so that spacious land, that city strong and
grand, from being the seat of hostility, became the
seat of the currency ; and from being the nest of the
owl of shame, became the threshold of glory and of
fame.   Through the fair efforts of the Moslem King,
in the place of the ill-toned voice of the graceless
paynim's bell, were heard the Mohammedan screed,
and the five-fold chant of the Ahmedī creed, noble of
rite ; and the harmony fair of the call to prayer on
the ears of all men fell. . . . The temples of the
paynims were made the mosques of the pious ; and
the rays of the radiance of Islam drave the hordes of
gloom forth from that ancient home of the heathen

[1] Koran, xxxvii. 173.   [2] Ibid. xv. 46, and l. 33.

reprobate, and the gleaming of the dawn of the Faith did the darkness of the tyranny of the accursed dissipate ; and the mandate, strong as fate, of the Sultan fortunate, was supreme in the ordinance of that new estate."

The conquest of Constantinople is the great event of Mohammed's reign. Yet it was by no means his sole achievement. He overthrew the Wallachian tyrant, Vlad the Impaler, and completed the final annexation of Serbia and Bosnia. The king of Bosnia and his sons capitulated on promise of their lives being spared ; but Mohammed had this promise annulled by the chief Muftī or Mohammedan judge ; and this spiritual magistrate actually hacked the king down in the Sultan's presence, with the treaty of capitulation in his hand.

It was the violation of the Szegedin Treaty reversed. Mohammed, however, did not greatly advance the Ottoman frontier in the north. He laid siege to Belgrade, but was ignominiously repulsed by Hunyady and St. John Capistran, as has been already related, and after Hunyady's death his son Matthias Corvinus, at the head of his famous " Black Troop,' was strong enough to hold the Turks at bay. In Albania, too, the Sultan met opposition which neither his father nor he was able to overcome. For in Epirus had risen a patriot warrior, no less famous and valiant than Hunyady. This was Skanderbeg, the national hero of the Epirots. His proper name was George of Castriota, and he belonged to a princely family of Epirus. As a boy he had been sent as a hostage to the court of Murād II., where his high bearing and

courage soon won him the Sultan's favour. He was
converted to Islam, and Murād treated him like his
own son and advanced him to high rank in the army,
where he acquired the name of Skanderbeg (properly
Iskender Beg), or " Prince Alexander."

Skanderbeg, however, though petted by the Sultan,
was not satisfied with being sent in chief command of
an army into Asia, or with holding high posts in the
wars with Hungary : he wished to rule his own country,
and he ungratefully seized an opportunity to desert
from the Sultan's forces, and to obtain by stratagem
possession of Croia, the chief city of Epirus. He privily
seized the Sultan's secretary, made him write in his
master's name an order to the governor of Croia to
surrender the place, and then ran the luckless scribe
through the body. The governor suspected nothing
and surrendered the keys, and Skanderbeg, once in
command of the town, massacred the Turks, renounced
Mohammedanism, and called the Epirots to arms.
During the rest of the reign of Murād, and most of
his successor's, Skanderbeg held the mountains of
Epirus against all comers. Murād sent three Turkish
armies against him, and all three were disgracefully
routed. The old Sultan himself had experienced the
like misfortune when his mortal illness seized him at
Adrianople. Mohammed was no more successful than
his father ; but personal admiration and perhaps old
ties of friendship may have made the attacks of both
Sultans somewhat half-hearted. It is certain that they
would willingly have left Skanderbeg alone in consideration of a payment of tribute. The Epirot, however,
declined to pay tribute ; on the contrary, he exacted a

handsome revenue out of the terrified towns of Macedonia and Thessaly.   Eventually Mohammed, after
fruitless endeavours to oust the rebel from the fast-
nesses he knew so well how to defend, was forced to
make a treaty by which he acknowledged Skanderbeg
as prince of Epirus and Albania.   This was in 1461 ;
and six years later the gallant *condottiere* died, worn
out with a quarter of a century of perpetual warfare.
He died game ; for his last act was to defeat an army
which Mohammed had sent out against him with
positive instructions to conquer the land.   After
Skanderbeg's death, the Sultan easily subdued
Albania, though the lawless character of the people
has made it a difficult country to rule to this present
day.

The work of Skanderbeg was important, not so much
in its local influence, as in the bulwark it set up against
Ottoman advance in the direction of Italy.   Just as
Hunyady and St. John Capistran set a northern
limit to the Turks for a while, so Skanderbeg fixed
their boundary on the west.   No sooner was the
barrier removed than we find them contemplating the
invasion of Venice.   The maritime Republic had long
cringed before the Turkish Sultan, and had signed a
humble peace in 1454; but the successes of Skanderbeg
had roused its spirit, and after his death it was
punished for its temerity.   After six years' war the
Ottoman troops in 1477 pushed so far west that they
crossed the Tagliomento and reached the banks of the
Piave.   The smoking ruins that marked their progress
could be seen from the palaces of the Queen of the
Adriatic.   Venice hastily concluded a treaty offensive

and defensive with Mohammed in 1479, but he had already taken from her the island of Euboea or Negropont, the governor of which surrendered the citadel after a long and desperate siege by Mahmūd Pasha in 1470, on condition of safety to the garrison ; whereupon Mohammed, after his treacherous manner, had marched the garrison out and put them to death, sawed the governor in two, and murdered his daughter because she refused dishonour. Greece and the islands of the Aegean were now mainly in the power of the Turks ; on the Black Sea, Sinope and Trebizond had been conquered, and David Comnenus, who reigned in the latter city, had been treacherously executed ; and in 1475 the Crimea was taken from the descendants of Chingiz Khān, by Mohammed's admiral, the Grand Vezīr Gedik Ahmed. Rhodes was besieged in 1480, but the Knights were better prepared than they had been when Tīmūr expelled them from Smyrna. After a tedious siege the Turks made their great assault ; but, either discouraged by the obstinacy of the Knights, or irritated by the proclamation that the spoils of the city were to be reserved for the Sultan himself, the soldiery wavered, and the Knights, driving them furiously back, forced them to raise the siege. Nevertheless, the command of the seas rested to a large extent with the Turks. They had most of the Levantine islands ; their castles commanded the Hellespont and the Bosphorus, so that Loredano vainly sought to force a passage. The Sea of Marmora was closed to European vessels, and the Genoese ports in the Crimea and Sea of Azov were of little value now that their communi-

RHODES.

cations were severed ; and, as Admiral Jurien de la
Gravière observes,[1] it was hardly necessary for Mohammed to send a fleet of three hundred sail to eject
them in 1475. With such advantages, the Turks were
able to contest the seas with the galleys of Venice and
Rhodes.

The day that saw the failure of the storming of
Rhodes was marked by a notable event further west.
Gedik Ahmed, on the 28th of July, 1480, landed on
the southern coast of Italy and stormed the castle of
Otranto, near Brindisi, a fortnight later. Most of the
inhabitants were massacred, and the Ottoman foot was
planted in the Western Empire. Next year Mohammed was preparing an immense expedition, whither
destined no man knew but he, when he suddenly died.
It is hard to say what might have happened had he
lived another year. The capture of Otranto might
have been followed by the sack of Rome. *Sed Dis
aliter visum.* The death of the Conqueror saved
Europe.

[1] " Doria et Barberousse," 32.

VIII.

PRINCE JEM.
(1481–1512.)

THE long reign of Bāyezīd II. (1481–1512) which
surpassed that of his father and grandfather, so that
the three together nearly completed a century, was
marked by a general lethargy and incapacity on the
part of the Turkish Government. Bāyezīd himself
possessed none of the energy and ambition of
Mohammed, and was not only unequal to the task
of carrying on his father's plans, but had enough
to do to keep what he had inherited. His authority
was weakened by the attacks of the Mamlūks of
Egypt, who for five years waged successful war upon
the Turks in Asia; and by insurrections in Karaman
and other parts, where the Shia doctrines of the new
Sūfī dynasty of Persia found adherents in the discontented descendants of the Seljūk princes. Bāyezīd
made no attempt to extend his boundary in the
direction of Hungary; and though Lepanto and
Modon, in Greece, were added (in 1500) to the
Turkish Empire, and two castles were built to command the Gulf of Patras, the bold adventure that had
planted the Turkish flag on Italian soil was rendered

nugatory by the recall of Gedik Ahmed and the loss of
Otranto. The Sultan's later years were disturbed by
the rivalries and insubordination of his three sons, of
whom the most unscrupulous managed to induce his
incompetent old father to abdicate in his favour, and
the victorious Selīm accordingly ascended the throne
in 1512. Family dissensions were indeed the leading
incidents of Bāyezīd's reign, and for many years he
was kept in a state of anxious uncertainty by the
ingenious intrigues of the Christian Powers concerning the custody of his brother, the unfortunate Prince
Jem.

The adventures of Prince Jem (the name is short
for Jemshīd, but in Europe it has been written Zizim)
cast a very unpleasant light upon the honour of the
Christians of his time, and especially upon the
Knights of Rhodes. Of the two sons of Mohammed
II. Jem was undoubtedly the one who was by nature
fitted to be his successor. Instead of the melancholy
dreamy mystic who was incapable of walking in the
proud steps of his father, this other son had all
Mohammed's energy and vigour, his grace and culture, his ambition and imperious pride ; and but
for the accident that Bāyezīd was the first to reach
Constantinople after the death of the Conqueror, and
was thus able to secure the support of the Janissaries
with the customary largesse, it might have been that
in the hands of Jem the Ottoman Empire would have
continued on its triumphant course and pushed its
conquests in Europe in the same spirit that had
animated his ancestors. Jem, however, was not the
first to hear of his father's death, and a year's warfare

against his brother ended in his own defeat. The younger prince then sought refuge with the Knights of Rhodes, who promised to receive him hospitably and to find him a way to Europe, where he intended to renew his opposition to his brother's authority.

D'Aubusson, the Grand Master of Rhodes, however, was too astute a diplomatist to sacrifice the solid gains that he perceived would accrue to his Order for the sake of a few paltry twinges of conscience ; and he had no sooner made sure of Prince Jem's person, and induced him to sign a treaty, by which, in the event of his coming to the throne, the Order was to reap many sterling advantages, than he ingeniously opened negotiations with Sultan Bāyezīd, with a view to ascertain how much gold that sovereign was willing to pay for the safe custody of his refractory brother. It is only fair to say that Bāyezīd, who had no particle of cruelty in his nature, did all he could to come to terms with Jem. He had indeed been stern and uncompromising while his brother was in open hostility, and to the entreaty of their grandaunt that he would be gentle and accommodating to his own flesh and blood, he had replied that "there is no kinship among princes ; " yet had he offered to restore to his brother the profits, though not the power, of the province of Karaman, which Jem had formerly governed, on condition that he should retire and live peaceably at Jerusalem. Jem, however, would have nothing less than independent authority, and this the Sultan could not be expected to allow. " Empire," said he, " is a bride whose favours cannot be shared." All negotiation and compromise having

BATTLE WITH PRINCE JEM.

proved ineffectual, he listened to the proposals of the crafty Grand Master, and finally agreed to pay him 45,000 ducats a year, so long as he kept Jem under his surveillance.

The Knights of St. John possessed many commanderies, and the one they now selected for Jem's entertainment was at Nice, in the south of France. In 1482 he arrived there, wholly unconscious of the plots that were being woven about him. Here, being something of a poet, he wrote his famous ode beginning—

"Quaff, O Jem, thy Jemshīd beaker ; lo, the land of Frankistan !
 This is fate ; and what is written on his brow shall 'tide to man." [1]

He desired to start at once for Hungary, whence he proposed to raise his adherents in Turkey. But he was gently restrained from his purpose. On one pretext or another the knights contrived to keep their prisoner at Nice for several months, and then transferred him to Rousillon, thence to Puy, and next to Sassenage, where the monotonies of captivity were relieved by the delights of love, which he shared with the daughter of the commandant, the beautiful Philipine Hélène, his lawful spouse being fortunately away in Egypt. The last device of the knights, when such friendships made captivity precarious, was to build a lofty tower for their valuable prey, of which the seven

[1] E. J. W. Gibb, "Ottoman Poems," 175 (revised). The reader may be interested to see the original—

 "Jām-l-Jem nūsh eyle, ey Jem, bu Firankistān dir ;
   Her kulun bashina yazilan gelir, devrān dir."

stories were entirely arranged with the object of the prisoner's safe custody.

Meanwhile, Grand Master D'Aubusson was driving a handsome trade in his capacity of jailor. All the potentates of Europe were anxious to obtain possession of the claimant to the Ottoman throne, and were ready to pay large sums in hard cash to enjoy the privilege of using this specially dangerous instrument against the Sultan's peace. D'Aubusson was not averse to taking the money, but he did not wish to give up his captive ; and his knightly honour felt no smirch in taking 20,000 ducats from Jem's desolate wife (who probably had not heard of the fair Hélène) as the price of her husband's release, while he held him all the tighter. Of such chivalrous stuff were made the famous knights of Rhodes : and of such men as D'Aubusson the Church made cardinals !

A new influence now appeared upon the scene of Jem's captivity. Charles VIII. of France considered that the Grand Master had made enough profit out of the unlucky prince, and the king resolved to work the oracle himself. His plan was to restore Jem to a nominal sultanate by the aid of Matthias Corvinus, Ferdinand of Naples, and the Pope. He took Jem out of the hands of the knights and transferred him to the custody of Innocent VIII., who kindly consented to take care of the prince for the sum of 40,000 ducats a year, to be paid by his grateful brother at Constantinople. Bāyezīd was greatly impressed by the Pope's friendly feeling, and received his ambassador with enthusiasm. All the time these

PALACE OF THE GRAND MASTERS, RHODES.

negotiations were proceeding the good Pope, like many worthy knights and holy prelates before, had condoled with Prince Jem on his unhappy fate, and had drawn him bright pictures of the future, when he should stand side by side with Matthias Corvinus, the gallant king of Hungary, in the great campaign that was to be made against the Turks in order to set the injured prince upon his father's throne at Constantinople. Nothing could be more consolatory than the promises and hopes of all the kindly Christian kings and princes who visited Jem in his thirteen long years of captivity ; but none of them reaped, though all sought, so rich a reward as the large-minded and large-pocketed Grand Master of Rhodes and the solicitous and amiable Pope. Unfortunately Innocent did not live long enough to turn Jem to all the account he had anticipated ; but his successor, Alexander Borgia, was not the man to be cheated out of his bargain by such an accident as death. He began negotiations at Constantinople, whither he sent a special ambassador, to extract a capital sum in return for Prince Jem's proposed removal to a world more congenial to his many virtues ; he endeavoured, in short, to get the lump sum of 300,000 ducats for the assassination of his prisoner. Just at this point of the negotiations, Charles, the king of France, invaded Italy, entered Rome, and, among other terms, demanded the cession of Jem, who was accordingly, with a very wry face, given up to him. But poor Jem was not destined much longer to be tossed about from jailor to jailor. The Pope, either in pursuance of an agreement with

Bāyezīd, or more probably because a Borgia could not help it, had the unfortunate Turk poisoned before he left the country. How it was done is not certain—the scratch of a poisoned razor, or a harmless white powder introduced into his sherbet, are two of the theories ; but some there are who say that he died of mere misery and weariness of life—such weariness as he expresses in his melancholy verse :—

" Lo ! there the torrent, dashing 'gainst the rocks, doth wildly roll ;
 See how all nature rueth on my worn and wearied soul !
 Through bitterness of grief and woe the morn hath rent its robe ;
 Behold, in dawning's stead, the sky weeps blood beyond control !
 Tears shedding, o'er the mountain tops the clouds of heaven pass ;
 List, deep the bursting thunder sobs and moans through stress of
   dole ! " [1]

The balance of probability, however, inclines towards poison, and Alexander Borgia has so many crimes on the place where his conscience should have been, that it can do him no harm to bear one murder more. The curious conclusion one draws from the whole melancholy tale is that there was not apparently a single honest prince in Christendom to take compassion upon the captive ; nor one to reprobate the ungenerous and venal intrigues of the Grand Master, the Pope, and Charles VIII. Each contended with the other for the prize of perfidy and shame. Bāyezīd may be excused for his desire to see his brother in safe keeping ; but what can be said for the head of the Christian Church, and the leader of an Order of religious knights, who eagerly betrayed a helpless

[1] E. J. W. Gibb, " Ott. Poems," 20 (revised).

refugee for the sake of the infidel's gold ?   When we come to read of the heroism of the Knights of Rhodes and Malta, it may be well to recall the history of Prince Jem, and to weigh well the chivalry that could fatten upon such treason.

IX.

THE CONQUEST OF EGYPT.
(1512–1520.)

WHEN Selīm I. had deposed his father Bāyezīd,
who did not long survive his humiliation, he resolved that the trouble and anxiety of another
Prince Jem should not disturb his own reign. His
father had had eight sons, of whom two, besides
himself, were still alive, and, including grandsons,
there were no less than eleven dangerous persons to
be made away with. "Selīm the Grim," as the Turks
still call him, did not shrink from the task; he
delighted in blood, whether it were that of animals
slain in the chase, to which he was passionately
addicted, or that of his enemies on the battle-field;
and the bloodless slaughter by the bow-string,
which is the privilege of the progeny of Othmān,
was hardly sufficiently exciting for this sanguinary
tyrant, whose fierce blazing eyes and choleric com-
plexion well accorded with his violent nature. He
watched from an adjoining room the ghastly scene,
when the mutes strangled his five orphan nephews,
and the resolute resistance of the eldest and the
piteous entreaties of the little ones could not move

him from his cruel purpose. The rest, save two, were soon captured and strangled. His brother, Prince Korkud, begged for an hour's grace, and spent it in composing a reproachful poem addressed to Selīm, which the Sultan afterwards perused with tears. It was no doubt the elegance of the verse that moved him, rather than the fate of the poet; for Selīm, like so many of his race, was devoted to letters and poetry. He wrote a volume of Persian odes, liberally rewarded men of learning, and when he went on a campaign liked to take with him historians and bards, who should record the events of the war and cheer its progress by reciting the great deeds of yore. The combination of a high degree of intellectual culture with cruel and savage barbarity is one of the commonplaces of history.

Selīm had no intention of pursuing the inactive policy of his father; but he turned his eyes in a different direction from his remoter predecessors. Murād, Bāyezīd, and Mohammed had pushed the frontier to the north and the west; Selīm would conquer the east and the south. He received courteously the ambassadors who came to offer him congratulations on the part of the Doge of Venice, the King of Hungary, the Czar of Russia, and the Mamlūk Sultan of Egypt. He had no intention for the present of quarrelling with any of them. His care was first directed to the state of affairs on his eastern frontier, where there was imminent danger of a serious invasion. The Sefevi Shah Ismaīl, founder of the Sūfī line, had triumphed over the various local dynasties that had partitioned the pro-

vinces of Persia among themselves, ever since the
break up of the Mongol kingdom.

Hulāgu, the conqueror of Baghdad, and grandson of
Chingiz Khān, had in the thirteenth century exterminated the Abbaside Khalifate in all but name, and
substituted his own sway for that of the numerous
petty dynasties who at that time held rule in Persia
and the country round about. His dynasty, called
the Ilkhāns, lasted about one hundred and fifty years,
and their dominions then became a prey to the feuds
between various Tartar and Kurdish chiefs, of whom
the Jelayirs and the Turkomans of the White and of
the Black Sheep were the most prominent. Tīmūr had
overrun their territory at the beginning of the fifteenth
century ; but the " noble Tartarian's " descendants
proved unable to retain his vast dominion, and the
Kurds and Turkomans and other tribal chiefs soon
re-established their authority in the lands bordering
the Euphrates. Shah Ismaïl, the Sefevi, now appeared
upon the scene, and after a long and obstinate
struggle, succeeded in winning the Persian provinces
from the descendants of Tīmūr and in subduing the
lesser houses of Turkomans and Kurds.

The Persian dominions now marched with those of
the Ottoman, and friction was the more certain and
irritating because the two parties belonged to two
hostile sects of Islam. The Turks were orthodox
Sunnīs, or believers in the conventional doctrine of
the Koran and in the Traditions handed down by the
respectable divines of the orthodox school. The
Persians, on the other hand, were *Shīas*, or believers
in a somewhat mystical variety of Islam, which per-

sented many and important differences from the orthodox teaching, and offered not a few temptations to political as well as religious revolution. Wherever Shiïsm exists, there is always a chance of insurrection against the powers that be. The pernicious doctrine had penetrated the Ottoman dominions in Asia. A carefully organized system of detectives, whom Selīm distributed throughout his Asiatic provinces revealed the fact that the number of the heretical sect reached the alarming total of seventy thousand. Selīm determined to crush the heresy before it came to even more abundant fruit. He secretly massed his troops at spots where the heretics chiefly congregated, and at a given signal, forty thousand of them were massacred, or imprisoned. Christian ambassadors at the Porte, not only expressed no horror at the work, but endorsed the title of " The Just," by which Selīm was now styled in compliment to his severe vindication of orthodoxy.[1] According to them, the massacre of heretics was always a proof of justice.

Having got rid of the enemy within his gates, Selīm now proceeded to attack the head of the Shīas, the great Shah Ismaïl himself. In such slight engagements as had already occurred, Ismaïl had gained a trifling advantage. He had also committed the unpardonable sin of harbouring three of Selīm's nephews, who had been lucky enough to escape from the general slaughter of his kindred by which his accession had been celebrated. The Sultan sent various epistles to the Shah, couched in that bombastic language to

[1] Von Hammer, i. 710.

which Oriental potentates are addicted, and meanwhile collected a great army, with which he prepared to invade the territories of his rival. Ismaïl does not appear to have been adequately impressed either by the correspondence or the preparations for the attack. To Selīm's vainglorious letters, he replied that he had given him no provocation, and desired not war, and that he could only imagine that the epistles were the result of an extra dose of opium taken by one of the Sultan's secretaries, to whom he therefore presented a box of the favourite drug. As Selīm particularly prided himself on his literary skill, and with reason, this reply only increased his rage, and the circumstance that he was himself rather too fond of opium did not make the gift of the box any the more palatable. The sarcasm went home, and Selīm prepared for mortal conflict.

It was no light task that he was undertaking. Ismaïl, when the contest became inevitable, had laid waste the whole country that intervened between his capital, Tebrīz, and the Ottoman headquarters ; and the Turks would be compelled to traverse a desert land. So serious was the campaign felt to be, that when the Sultan informed his council of Vezīrs what his intentions were, they all kept silence, and on his repeating his purpose, again not one made answer, till the very sentry who guarded the door, catching the Sultan's enthusiasm, fell at his feet and cried that he would lay down his life for him against the Persians. That Janissary was made a Bey on the spot. Despite the warnings of his ministers, Selīm set forth with an army estimated at over 140,000 men, 80,000 of which

were cavalry, and after making every possible preparation for transport and commissariat, entered upon the
long and arduous marches which the Persians had
rendered doubly difficult by their previous forays.
The soldiers, afflicted with hunger and thirst, began
to murmur ; but Selīm harangued them, and bade such
as were cowards to step out of the ranks and go home,
for he would only lead brave men against the heretics.
Then he gave the order to march, and not a man
dared leave the ranks. At last, after weary and
painful marching, the Ottomans forced Ismaīl to give
battle at Chāldirān. The Persians had only cavalry,
and no cannon ; but they were fresh, while the Turks
were exhausted with their long tramp across the
desert : the Shah had no fears for the upshot. The
Janissaries, however, had not forgotten how to fight,
and Selīm and his chief commander, Sinān Pasha,
knew how to marshal the battle. The Persians
charged gallantly, but Sinān let his Azabs or light
infantry fall back between his artillery, and when the
Persians rashly followed the retreating squadrons, the
guns opened upon them so deadly a fire that the day
was practically won. It had been fatal to many on both
sides, the Turks lost fourteen Sanjak-Begs, and the
Persians an equal number of Khans of high rank. The
Shah himself was wounded and thrown from his horse,
and was only saved from capture by the devotion of
one of his soldiers, who gallantly personated his
master, and took his fate. The Sultan entered Tebrīz
in triumph, massacred all his prisoners, except the
women and children, and sent back to Constantinople
a trophy in the shape of a thousand of the skilful

workmen for which Tebrīz had long been famous, and who had supplied architects, carvers, and workers in metal and on the loom, to Cairo, Damascus, and Venice, and all places where fine workmanship was prized. The artisans were established at Constantinople, where they continued to ply their trades with success in embellishing the Turkish capital.

The victory of Chāldirān (1514) might have been followed by the conquest of Persia, but the privations which the soldiery had undergone had rendered them unmanageable, and Selīm was forced to content himself with the annexation of the important provinces of Kurdistān and Diyārbekr, which are still part of the Turkish Empire ; and then turned homewards, to prosecute other schemes of conquest. No peace, however, was concluded between him and the Shah, and a frontier war continued to be waged for many years.

During the campaign against Persia, the Turks had been kept in anxiety by the presence on their flanks of the forces of the Mamlūk Sultans of Egypt and Syria, whose frontiers now marched with the territory of the Ottomans, and who were regarding the operations of Selīm in Diyārbekr with no little apprehension. They had indeed waged successful warfare with Bāyezīd II., but they recognized a very different leader in Selīm, and began to tremble for their old supremacy. The Mamlūk Sultans had long borne a very high renown as soldiers and rulers. Mamlūk means " owned," " a slave," and the origin of this celebrated dynasty, or rather the two dynasties into which they were divided, is found in the bodyguard of pur-

chased white slaves with whom the Ayyūbī Sultan
Es-Sālih, grandnephew of Saladin, surrounded his
state in the middle of the thirteenth century. Es-Sālih
found such protection necessary, not only against the
Franks who were threatening his kingdom in one of
their crusading manias, but also against his own kinsmen, who were at once too numerous and too powerful
for his peace of mind. Like most great conquerors,
Saladin had left his empire to be fought for by a
numerous progeny and kindred, and the result was
that individual weakness which seeks to support itself
on mercenary arms, and is eventually compelled to
yield to the very power which it has called in to its
aid.

The Mamlūks of Es-Sālih were a fine body of
Turkish soldiers, recruited by capture or purchase
from various parts of the Mohammedan territories,
and reinforced from the same regions. They were
loyal servants while their master lived ; their brilliant
charge under Beybars put the French to route at
Mansūra, and brought about the surrender of the king,
St. Louis himself. In the troubles that succeeded upon
the death of Es-Sālih, when the intrigues of the beautiful Queen with the picturesque name of Shejer-ed-
durr, or " Tree of Pearls," roused hot blood among
the grandees, the dynasty of Saladin came to an end,
and for two centuries and a half the throne of Egypt
and Syria was occupied by a series of Mamlūk chiefs.
These rulers, who often bore no relationship to each
other, but succeeded to power by force of arms and
factious influence, were among the best that Egypt
ever had. They valiantly repulsed the Mongols

and Tartars in many a sanguinary field : they drove
the Christians from the Holy Land, and they made
Cairo and Damascus, their two capitals, homes of
civilization, art, and literature. These apparently
rude soldiers, " merciless to their enemies, tyrannous
to their subjects, yet delighted in the delicate refine-
ments which art could afford them in their home life,
were lavish in the endowment of pious foundations,
magnificent in their mosques and palaces, and fas-
tidious in the smallest details of dress and furniture :
the noblest promoters of art and literature and of
public works that Egypt has known since the time of
Alexander the Great." [1]

At the time at which we have arrived, the Mamlūks
had lost little, if anything, of their character as patrons
of art and learning. The great Sultan Kāït Bey was
but lately dead, who had covered Cairo with his stately
mosques and other buildings, and whose encourage-
ment of men of letters was not less marked. The
Sultan who surveyed Selīm's progress in Persia was
an old man, Kānsū El-Ghūrī, the same whose two
mosques in the principal street of Cairo are familiar
sights to every traveller in Egypt. He posted an
army of observation on his Syrian frontier, to watch
the course of the Ottoman advance. Selīm took this
as a menace, and consulted his Vezīrs as to what was
to be done. His secretary, Mohammed, urged him to
make war upon the Mamlūks, and the Sultan was so
delighted with this spirited proposal, that he made the
secretary Grand Vezīr on the spot, though it was found
necessary to administer the bastinado to the excellent

[1] S. Lane-Poole, " The Art of the Saracens in Egypt," 12–40.

man before he consented to accept so dangerous a
dignity. Selīm was famous for executing his Vezīrs,
and it was a common form of cursing at the time to
say, "Mayest thou be Selīm's Vezīr," as an equivalent
for "Strike you dead!" Acting upon the advice of
the new Vezīr, Selīm set out in 1516 for Syria, and
meeting the Mamlūk army on the field of Marj Dābik
near Aleppo, administered a terrible defeat, in which
the aged Sultan El-Ghūrī was trampled to death.

He found a brave successor in Tūmān Bey, but in
the interval the Turks had mastered Syria, and were
advancing to Gaza. Here the Mamlūks made another
stand, but the generalship of Sinān Pasha was not to
be resisted any more than the preponderance of his
forces. The final battle was fought at Reydānīya, in
the neighbourhood of Cairo, in January, 1517. The
tremendous charge of the Mamlūks, which had been
their strong point for three centuries, almost secured
the person of Selīm, who was saved only by their mis-
taking Sinān Pasha for the Sultan. The great general
was speared, many pashas and nobles were cut down,
and the Mamlūks rode out of the *mêlée* almost
unhurt; but they had not achieved their object, and
"the efforts of this splendid cavalry were as vain
against the batteries of Selīm's artillery as were in
after times the charges of their successors against the
rolling fire of Napoleon's squares."[1]

Twenty-five thousand Mamlūks lay stark upon the
field, and the enemy occupied Cairo. There a succession of street fights took place; the houses were
defended by the Mamlūks, and only step by step did

[1] Sir E. Creasy, 143.

the Turks reach the citadel. But treason was at work among the followers of Tūmān Bey, and a traitor advised Selīm to offer an amnesty to all who would lay down their arms. Thereupon a truce was made, which Selīm celebrated by beheading the eight hundred Mamlūks who had trusted to his good faith, and by delivering up the unfortunate city to massacre. One of the bravest of the chiefs, whose name was Kurt Bey, or " Sir Wolf," was induced to come before the Sultan with promises of safe conduct, and after a colloquy, in which the Bey made spirited answer alike to the Selīm's promises and threats, his head was cut off before the enraged tyrant's eyes. Tūmān Bey, after some further resistance, was captured and executed, and Egypt became a Turkish province. Twenty-four Mamlūk Beys were constituted a sort of commission for the government of the country, and the traitor Kheyr Bey was appointed Pasha of Egypt.

Sultan Selīm returned to Constantinople in 1518, a much more dignified personage than he had set out. By the conquest of the Mamlūk kingdom he had also succeeded to their authority over the sacred cities of Arabia, Mekka and Medīna, and in recognition of this position, as well as of his undoubted supremacy among Mohammedan monarchs, he received from the last Abbāside Khalif, who kept a shadowy court at Cairo, the inheritance of the great Pontiffs of Baghdad. The *fainéant* Khalif was induced to make over to the real sovereign the spiritual authority which he still affected to exercise, and with it the symbols of his office, the standard and cloak of the Prophet Mohammed. Selīm now became not only the visible chief of the Mohammedan State throughout the wide dominions subdued to his sway, but also the revered head of the religion of Islam, wheresoever it was practised in its orthodox form. The heretical Shīas of Persia might reject his claim, but in India, in all parts of Asia and Africa, where the traditional Khalifate was recognized, the Ottoman Sultan henceforth was the supreme head of the church, the successor to the spiritual prestige of the long line of the Khalifs. How far this new title commands the homage of the orthodox Moslem world is a matter of dispute ; but there can be no doubt that it has always added, and still adds, a real and important authority to the acts and proclamations of the Ottoman Sultan.

The last year of his life was spent by Selīm in immense preparations, both naval and military. His object was concealed, but Rhodes was believed to be his intended victim. He superintended every detail of the arming and building of his navy with unceasing diligence, until his health began to give way, and he felt the approach of the fatal disorder which carried him off on the 22nd of September, 1520. He looked sadly upon his great muniments of war, and said, " For me there is no journey, save that to the Hereafter."

Selīm the Grim was fifty-four years old when he died, and he had reigned less than nine years ; yet in that short space he had nearly doubled the extent of his empire. Egypt, Syria, Arabia, and large tracts in the Euphrates valley were the fruits of his campaigns. On land the Turks had shown themselves invincible. Selīm was

preparing to prove them equally so on sea, when his
career was arrested.　Death, however, did not check
the preparations he had made, nor diminish the stores
of war materials he had collected.　Like another
Philip he had made ready the way for a second
Alexander, and in his son Suleymān the Magnificent
such an imperial conqueror was now found.

Test to here.

X.

SULEYMĀN THE MAGNIFICENT.
(1520–1566.)

THE long reign of Suleymān the Magnificent, who
ascended the throne at the age of twenty-six, in 1520,
and ruled in unequalled glory for nearly half a century,
is fraught with significance to Europe, and teems with
so many events of the first importance that it deserves
a volume to itself.   We can only give a bare outline
of the great wars and sieges that signalized this remarkable epoch : such scenes as the terrible battle of
Mohács, the conquest of Rhodes, the siege of Vienna,
and of Szigeth, and the repulse at Malta, might well
engage each a chapter to itself ; but here they must
be depicted in outline, and the best will have been
attained if the student is incited to read the fuller
records which have been written of them in larger
works.

Suleymān lived at a wonderful epoch.   All Europe,
as well as the East, seemed to have conspired together
to produce its greatest rulers in the sixteenth century,
and to make its most astonishing advances in all fields
of civilization.   The age which boasted of Charles V.,
the equal of Charlemagne in empire ; of Francis I. of

France; of our notable Henry VIII., and Elizabeth, queen of queens; of Pope Leo X.; of Vasili Ivanovich, the founder of the Russian power; of Sigismund of Poland; Shah Ismaïl of Persia; and of the Moghul Emperor Akbar, could yet point to no greater sovereign than Suleymān of Turkey. The century of Columbus, of Cortes, of Drake and Raleigh, of Spenser and Shakespeare, the epoch that saw the revival of learning in Italy by the impulse of the refugees from Constantinople, and which greeted at once the triumph of Christianity over Islam in Spain and the opening of a new world by Spanish enterprise, was hardly more brilliant in the West than in the East, where the unceasing victories of Suleymān, and the successes of Turghud and Barbarossa, formed a worthy counterpart to the achievements of the great soldiers and admirals of the Atlantic. Even the pirates of this age were unique: they founded dynasties.

But the most remarkable feat that the Turks achieved during this glorious century was—that they survived it. With such forces as were arrayed against them, with a Europe roused from its long sleep, and ready to seize arms and avenge its long disgrace upon the infidels, it was to be expected that the fall of the Ottoman power must ensue. Instead, we shall see that this power was not only able to meet the whole array of rejuvenated Europe on equal terms, but emerged from the conflict stronger and more triumphant than ever.

Suleymān ascended the throne surrounded by the glamour which belonged to his youth and charm of manner, and to the affection which his gracious rule

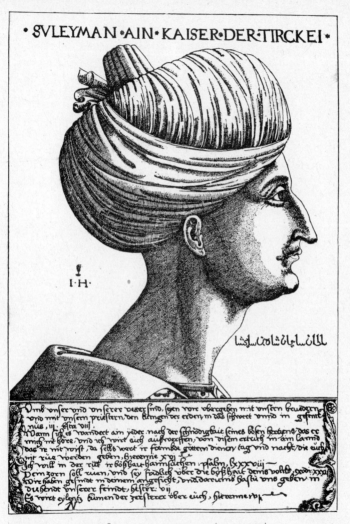

SULEYMĀN THE MAGNIFICENT (IN YOUTH).

in more than one provincial government had inspired ;
but he owed something to the detestation which
Selīm's cruel character had evoked from all classes.
The son differed by the whole heaven from his father.
He was already renowned for his justice and clemency,
and his first acts were calculated to strengthen the
good opinion which had early been formed of his
character. He began by punishing evildoers, and
especially such of the officers and pashas who were
proved to have been guilty of corruption and par-
tiality. His greatest object was the same as that of
the founder of the Ottoman Empire ; he desired to
see even-handed justice administered throughout the
length and breadth of his vast dominions.

"Säulen seines Thron's sind Milde, Biedersinn, und Redlichkeit,
    Und von seinem Wappenschilde strahlet die Gerechtigkeit."

The people rejoiced to see once more a Sultan
they could love as well as fear, and welcomed Suleymān as another Murād.

He had not been long seated on the throne when
the occasion arrived for him to vindicate that title of
" Lord of the Age " which his courtiers bestowed on
him, and which was recorded on his official documents.
The Hungarians had insulted and tortured his envoy,
and vengeance must follow. All the materials for a
campaign were ready ; Selīm had left him a ripe fruit,
and he had only to pluck it.[1] In 1521 he took the
old familiar road of Turkish generals, and marched
upon Hungary. Belgrade, which had repelled Mohammed the Conqueror, yielded to his even greater

[1] Jurien de la Gravière, " Doria et Barberousse," chap. vii. ff.

successor.   The church was turned into a mosque, the fortifications strengthened, and, to the days of Prince Eugene, "der edle Ritter," the key of the Danube formed a jewel in the Ottoman crown.   The effect of the victory was immediate: Venice, in consternation, humbled herself as the Sultan's vassal, and paid him twofold tribute for Zante and Cyprus.   It was only the first rumble of the storm, however.   In the following year, 1522, an even more renowned place fell before Suleymān's assault.   Rhodes, where Mohammed II. had received a second repulse, was now besieged by Suleymān with all the strength of his empire.   A hundred thousand troops by land, and ten thousand by sea, encompassed the devoted island ; and all the efforts of the heroic Grand Master, Villiers de L'Isle Adam, could not avail to prevent the fall of the stronghold of the Knights of St. John.   For close upon five months they met mine with countermine, and repelled four tremendous assaults with heavy loss ; but no garrison, without any prospect of a relieving force, could withstand for ever the skilful engineering of the Turks, who were the masters of Europe in the art of making regular approaches against a fortified position, and possessed the best artillery in the world.   At last, seeing the hopelessness of the contest, the Grand Master and his brave Knights accepted the honourable terms which Suleymān had offered them, but which they had before refused.   The Sultan was no breaker of his word.   They were allowed twelve days to leave the island with their property and arms ; the people of Rhodes were to have full privilege of the exercise of their religion, and to be free from tribute for five

SIEGE OF RHODES.

years. So deeply were the Turks impressed by the valour of the Knights, that even their armorial escutcheons, which stood over their houses, were left undisturbed, and may be seen there to this day.

The first year's campaign had ended in the capture of Belgrade, the second had brought the surrender of Rhodes; the one had opened Hungary, the other had delivered up the Levantine waters to the Ottoman fleets. Now for two years the Sultan busied himself in the internal administration of his empire and in putting down a revolt in Egypt. He soon found out his mistake in intermitting the annual expeditions which had kept his large standing army in good temper. The Janissaries began to mutiny, and though the Sultan at first tried the effect of boldness, and with his own hands slew two of the leaders of the insurrection, he found himself forced at last to pacify them by a large bribe, like Sultans before and since, to the great damage of the imperial authority and impoverishment of the treasury. It became necessary to gratify the soldiers' love of war and booty, and Suleymān resolved on a campaign in Hungary, being the more encouraged to it by the advice of the ambassador sent to the Porte by Francis I. of France, who was anxious to divert his great rival Charles V. from further designs in the west.

The decision was due, however, as much to another voice as to the machinations of the French king. Suleymān, great as he was, shared his greatness with a second mind, to which his reign owed much of its brilliance. The Grand Vezīr Ibrāhīm was the counterpart of the Grand Monarch Suleymān. He was the son of a sailor at Parga, and had been captured by corsairs, by whom he was sold to be the slave of a widow at Magnesia. Here he passed into the hands of the young prince Suleymān, then governor of Magnesia, and soon his extraordinary talents and address brought him promotion. The Turks have a proverb: "When God gives office, he gives also the ability to fill it:" and it was so with the young man who, from being Grand Falconer on the accession of Suleymān, rose to be first minister and almost co-Sultan in 1523. He was the object of the Sultan's tender regard: an emperor knows better than most men how solitary is life without friendship and love, and Suleymān loved this man more than a brother. Ibrāhīm was not only a friend, he was an entertaining and instructive companion. He read Persian, Greek, and Italian; he knew how to open unknown worlds to the Sultan's mind, and Suleymān drank in his Vezīr's wisdom with assiduity. They lived together: their meals were shared in common; even their beds were in the same room. The Sultan gave his sister in marriage to the sailor's son, and Ibrāhīm was at the summit of power. "La douce et féconde union! L'Empire en ressent d'heure en heure le bienfait. Elle dure depuis six ans: puisse-t-elle, pour le salut de la Chrétienté, ne pas être éternelle!" [1] Ibrāhīm deserved his success. He was great in war and in peace. He alone knew how to appease the Janissaries; and he counselled and led the expedition against Vienna.

Accordingly in 1526 the Ottoman army, mustering

[1] Jurien de la Gravière, " Doria et Barberousse," 114.

COUNCIL HALL, RHODES.

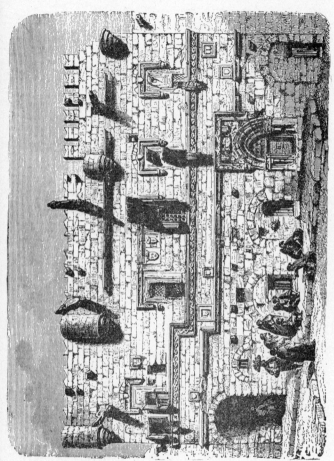

PRIORY OF FRANCE, RHODES.

at least 100,000 men and three hundred guns, marched
north headed by the Sultan in person. Louis II. of
Hungary met him on August 29th on the fatal field of
Mohács with a far inferior force, and the result was
disastrous to the Christians. The king, and many of
his nobles and bishops, and over 20,000 Hungarians
fell on the fatal spot, where the encounter is known as
" The Destruction of Mohács." [1] Buda and Pesth
were occupied, the whole country roundabout ravaged,
and 100,000 captives were driven back to be sold as
slaves. The spoils of the palace of Matthias Corvinus
and its famous library were added to those of the
Palaeologi in the Seraglio at the Golden Horn. For
over a century Hungary had been the rampart of
Europe against the Turks. The campaign of Mohács
made Hungary an Ottoman province for a hundred
and forty years.

The ruling influence which the Sultan exercised over
the appointment of his deputy, the nominal king of
Hungary took him northward again in 1529 to place
his own candidate upon the throne—Zápolya, formerly
Voyvode of Transylvania, who had withheld his
help from Hungary at the battle of Mohács. The
Archduke Ferdinand of Austria, brother of Charles V.,
however, claimed the throne, and Suleymān had to
interfere in the civil war. Ferdinand in vain sent
ambassadors to arrange a truce, and make terms with
the indignant Sultan. The messengers were dismissed,
and Ferdinand was told that the Sultan was coming,
and would expect to meet him at Mohács or at Pesth,
or should he fail to appear, he would breakfast with

[1] See " The Story of Hungary," pp. 286-336.

him at Vienna itself.   And he came with a vengeance, bringing a quarter of a million of men at his heels. In September, 1529, the army retook Ofen (Buda) from Ferdinand's garrison, not without treason from within.   Zápolya was restored, and the Sultan proceeded to execute his threat of advancing upon Vienna. It is worth recording that Suleymān released the commander of Buda on parole that he would not fight against the Turks during the campaign, and this generous act was done in spite of the murmurs of the Janissaries, who were enraged at not being allowed to plunder the Hungarian capital, and even against the urgent representations of the Hungarians of Zápolya's party, who were now ranged with the Sultan ready to attack their countrymen and besiege Vienna.   For a century and a half the capital of Hungary remained a Turkish outpost.

On September 21st Suleymān crossed the Raab at Altenburg, and let loose his terrible troops of irregular cavalry or "Sackmen," as they are called in contemporary German records, upon the stricken land.   Far and wide these fierce riders forayed, under their savage leader Mikhal Oglu, who was a descendant of Scant-Beard Mikhal, a close ally of the first Othmān. They carried devastation and misery among the villages, destroying and burning everything, and bearing off into captivity men, women, and children.   Place after place surrendered, in terror of the Ottoman army and the scourge of the Sackmen.   Pesth fell without a blow.   The Archbishop of Gran surrendered his city, and sought refuge in the Sultan's camp.   Comorn was abandoned : Raab was burned : Altenburg

SULEYMAN ON THE WAR-PATH.

betrayed. Brück, however, made a stout defence, and the Sultan, always pleased with a show of courage, accorded the garrison the lenient condition that they should only do him homage after the fall of Vienna.

Meanwhile Austria was striving to collect some adequate force wherewith to meet the overwhelming hosts of the Turks. Every tenth man was called out for service, and the neighbouring states sent contributions to the army, but it was still miserably unequal to the demand which was to be made upon its valour. Ferdinand implored aid of the empire, and the Diet of Spires, moved by the rumour that Suleymān had sworn not to stop short of the Rhine, voted a puny force of 12,000 foot and 4,000 horse. Even this was not granted without interminable discussion, and the choice of a commander still remained a hotly debated question, when the Turks were already over the Save and had won their way into Pesth. "There were not wanting men hard of belief, pedants of the true German stamp, who maintained that mere apprehension had exaggerated the danger ; and finally it was agreed at Ratisbon, to which city the assembly had transferred itself, to send a deputation of two persons to Hungary to investigate the state of affairs on the spot. They went, and having the good fortune to escape the hands of the Turks, returned with evidence sufficient to satisfy the doubts of their sagacious employers." [1]

It soon became evident that Austria could not muster an army of any service, in time to check the Turkish advance ; and the efforts of the Christians were now devoted to the defence of the capital. " In

[1] Schimmer, "Two Sieges of Vienna by the Turks" (Eng. trans.), 15.

Vienna, the necessary preparations had been made with almost superhuman exertion, but in such haste and with so little material, that they could only be considered as very inadequate to the emergency. The city itself occupied the same ground as at present, the defences were old and in great part ruinous, the walls scarcely six feet thick and the outer palisade so frail and insufficient that the name Stadtzaun, or city hedge, which it bears in the municipal records of the time, was literally as well as figuratively appropriate. The citadel was merely the old building which now exists under the name of Schweitzer Hof. All the houses which lay too near the wall were levelled to the ground; where the wall was specially weak or out of repair a new entrenched line of earthen defence was constructed and well palisaded ; within the city itself, from the Stuben to the Kärnthner or Carinthian gate, an entirely new wall twenty feet high was constructed with a ditch interior to the old. The bank of the Danube was also entrenched and palisaded, and from the drawbridge to the Salz gate protected with a rampart capable of resisting artillery. As a precaution against fire, the shingles with which the houses were generally roofed were throughout the city removed. The pavement of the streets was taken up to deaden the effect of the enemy's shot, and watchposts established to guard against conflagration. Parties were detached to scour the neighbouring country in search of provisions, and to bring in cattle and forage. Finally, to provide against the possibility of a protracted siege, useless consumers, women, children, old men, and ecclesiastics, were as

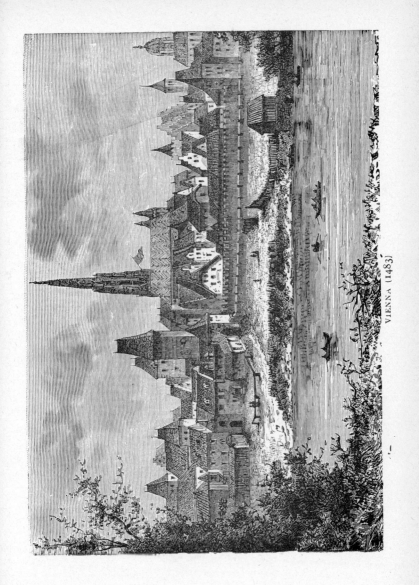

VIENNA (1483)

far as possible forced to withdraw from the city," [1]
too often only to fall into the ruthless hands of the
Sackmen.

Behind these hastily improvised defences, the veteran
Count of Salm, who had seen half a century of
service in the field, posted his garrison of 20,000
foot, 2,000 horse, and 1,000 volunteer burghers, and
manned the seventy guns which formed the artillery
of the city. At the last moment, when the Turks,
having taken Brück and Altenburg, were almost upon
the capital, the order was given to destroy the suburbs,
lest they should afford cover to the besiegers. The
unfortunate inhabitants deprived of their homes thus
late, had no time to escape from the harries of the
Sackmen, who now spread over the whole country
40,000 strong, burning and slaying wherever they
went, murdering unborn children, and brutally destroying helpless girls, whose insulted bodies lay
unheeded upon the roads : " God rest their souls, and
grant vengeance upon the bloodhounds who did this
wrong ! " as a writer of the day indignantly ex-
claims. It was stated at the time that scarcely a
third of the inhabitants of Upper Austria survived
this calamitous invasion.

On the 27th of September, the Sultan and his
Grand Vezīr Ibrāhīm brought the main army before
the city. " The country within sight of the walls
as far as Schwechat and Trautmannsdorf was covered with tents, the number of which was calculated at 30,000, nor could the sharpest vision from
St. Stephen's tower overlook the limit of the

[1] "Two Sieges of Vienna," 16-17.

circle so occupied. The flower of the Turkish force, the Janissaries, took possession of the ruins of the suburbs, which afforded them an excellent cover from the fire of the besieged. They also cut loopholes in the walls still standing from which they directed a fire of small ordnance and musketry on the walls of the city. The tent of Suleymān rose in superior splendour over all others at Simmering. Hangings of the richest tissue separated its numerous compartments from each other. Costly carpets and cushions and divans studded with jewels formed the furniture. Its numerous pinnacles were terminated by knobs of massive gold. Five hundred archers of the royal guard kept watch there night and day. Around it rose in great though inferior splendour the tents of ministers and favourites ; and 12,000 Janissaries, the terror of their enemies, and not unfrequently of their masters, were encamped in a circle round this central sanctuary." [1]

While this immense army of a quarter of a million, of which, however, probably not more than a third was fully armed, invested the city, the circuit was completed by means of the four hundred vessels, which constituted the marine part of the siege, on the Lobau. The work of approaching the walls now began. The Turks had been compelled by heavy rains to leave their siege guns behind them, and they had only field pieces and musketry. Accordingly mines were the chief weapon in which they trusted. For a fortnight they exerted all their noted skill in burrowing under the walls and towers and laying mines in

---

[1] "Two Sieges of Vienna," 26.

the most propitious positions ; but all to no purpose.
The besieged kept a watchful eye upon every approach,
and no sooner was a mine carefully laid, than it was
destroyed by a counter mine, or its powder was ex-
tracted by an exploring party working from the
cellars within the city. The Viennese were in good
spirits and even ventured to indulge in jokes at the
Sultan's expense. Suleymān had vowed to take his
breakfast in Vienna on the 29th of September, and when
the morning arrived, and the city was unsubdued, the
inhabitants sent out prisoners to his tent, to tell him
that his breakfast was getting cold, and they were
afraid they had no better cheer to offer him but the
produce of the guns on the battlements. Such
pleasantries relieved the tedium of mines and counter-
mines, varied by the occasional sallies which the
besieged made from time to time without much result.
On October 9th the Turks effected a broad breach
by the side of the Kärnthner gate, but three successive
storming parties were repulsed, and the breach was
repaired. On the 11th another and greater breach
was made, and for three hours the assailants fought
hand to hand with the defenders, till at midday they
were forced to abandon the assault. All the next
day the walls were the scene of protracted conflicts
between the storming parties and the besieged, who
still manfully resisted every effort of the Turks to
gain a footing inside the defences. The Sultan was
enraged, and his troops afflicted by the severe weather
and bad food, and weary of daily defeat, became
more and more discouraged, so that they had to be
driven to the assault by their officers' swords and

whips. At last, on the 14th, a final attempt was made. Every preparation had been made by both sides, and at nine o'clock the Janissaries and the flower of the Ottoman army came on to the attack. The soldiers however were dispirited, and when the Vezīr and his officers urged them on with stick and sabre, they cried that they would rather die by the hands of their own officers than face the long muskets of the Spaniards and the German spits, as they called the Lanzknechts' long swords. Still when a breach had been made twenty-four fathoms wide the Turks were forced to the assault. The efforts of such unwilling men were of no avail against the resolute defence of the Spaniards and Germans of the garrison. As an instance of the courage of the besieged a story is told of a Portuguese and a German, of whom one had lost his right arm and the other his left in repelling the assault : the two then stood together side close to side, and thus made up a whole man between them. When even the halves of soldiers can fight, such exhausted energies as were left to the Turks might well succumb. The last assault had failed, and Suleymān ordered a retreat. The Janissaries set fire to their camp, and flung into the flames—it is to be hoped without the Sultan's knowledge—the old people and children who were prisoners, and cut to pieces the remainder. After this disgusting and useless revenge, they set out on their retreat, to the music of the salvo of artillery which the delighted garrison now discharged from the ramparts of Vienna, and the ringing of all the bells which during the siege had been silenced. Had they been nearer they would hàve heard the solemn strains of the *Te Deum* which was being celebrated in St. Stephen's, where the defenders were rendering their glad thanks for the victory.

Suleymān pursued his way, harassed by skirmishing bodies of Austrian cavalry, till he reached Pesth, and thence departed for Constantinople, where he made a triumphant entry, and proclaimed that he had pardoned the infidel, and that, as the city of Vienna was so far from his frontiers, he had not deemed it necessary to " clear out the fortress, or purify, improve, and put it into repair." Such was the view sedulously inculcated into the minds of his subjects, when the disastrous siege of Vienna was spoken of. Of the 20,000 or 30,000 men who fell in the siege, Suleymān would probably not be expected to say much.

The 14th of October which saw the abandonment of the siege of Vienna, and the limit set to the rush of Turkish advance, is a famous day in German history : it is the anniversary of the peace of Westphalia and of Vienna, the battles of Hochkirchen, Jena, and Leipzig, and of the capture of Ulm.

Three years later Suleymān returned to the attack, followed by an even larger army ; but the Emperor Charles V. had now taken up the gauntlet, and his forces were too considerable for a rash engagement. Suleymān did not care to risk his long tide of success, already once broken by his failure at Vienna, upon so hazardous a chance as an open battle with Charles ; and after again ravaging the country with the lawless bands of Akinji, made peace at Constantinople in 1533 ; Hungary was divided between the two claimants,

Ferdinand and Zápolya, and the Sultan retained his advantages. The peace was, however, very transitory, for in 1541 the Sultan led his ninth campaign, and after gaining many advantages over the Austrians compelled Charles V. and Ferdinand to sue for peace, so in 1547 a truce was signed for five years. The Archduke Ferdinand was to pay a tribute of 30,000 ducats a year to his master the Sultan, and was proud to be addressed as the brother of his master's Vezīr. Suleymān retained all Hungary and Transylvania, and had certainly come out of the long struggle with the honours of war. Many of the Hungarian cities, however, stoutly resisted his domination, and their defenders performed prodigies of valour. When the five years were over, hostilities were punctually resumed, and continued unceasingly and unproductively until Suleymān's death in 1566.

He died in his tent 6th September, while superintending the siege of Szigetvár, which was heroically defended by Nicholas Zrinyi. The great Sultan expired tranquilly of mere old age, after a reign of forty-six years, filled with a military glory which no similar period could show. As he lay in his tent, while his death was studiously concealed from his troops, Zrinyi made his final sally. He had vowed never to surrender, and had used the Sultan's summons as wadding for his musket. Now seeing that further defence was hopeless, he led the last charge. The Turks were pressing forward along a narrow bridge which led to the castle when the gates were flung open, a mortar filled with broken iron was fired into their midst, and through the smoke and carnage Zrinyi led his men to their death. Like the

SULTAN SULEYMĀN.

famous Light Brigade, the number of these devoted
horsemen was six hundred ; their leader tied the keys
of the castle to his belt, and the banner of the empire
was borne above his head. Zrinyi fell pierced by two
musket shots and an arrow, and the Turks entered the
castle of Szigetvár, only to find that a slow match
had been applied to a mine containing 3,000 lbs. of
gunpowder, which speedily sent as many Turks to
paradise. The castle still remains a ruin : a monument
of the death of a Leonidas and of an Alexander.

Suleymān is perhaps the greatest figure in Turkish
history. His personal qualities were superb : his wisdom, justice, generosity, kindness, and courtesy were
a proverb, and his intellectual gifts were the counterpart of his fine moral nature. His reign had not
passed without its blots ; he had done more than one
cruel deed : he had sacrificed his dear friend and
peerless minister Ibrāhīm in a fit of jealousy in 1536,
and never ceased to find cause to regret his fault ; and
spurred on by a clever and unscrupulous Russian wife,
who rejoiced in the name of Khurrem or Joyous, and
whom all the nations of Europe have adopted
under the name of Roxelana, he had killed the
most hopeful of his sons, his first-born, Mustafa,
who showed such promise of rivalling his father that
Khurrem deemed the chances of her own son Selīm
unsafe while the splendid young prince survived ; and
other executions had stained his career. But these
were the rare exceptions. The rule was justice, prudence, and magnanimity, and Suleymān deserves all
the praises that have been lavished upon him by historians of every nationality. He left his century the

better for his generous example.   He left the Turkish
arms respected by land and sea.   While the horsetails
had waved before Vienna, the Sultan's galleys had
swept the seas to the coasts of Spain.   It was the age
of great admirals, and Charles V.'s splendid Doria
found a rival in Kheyr-ed-dîn Barbarossa, the corsair
of Tunis, and victor over Pope, Emperor, and Doge
at the battle of Prevesa (1538) ;—in Dragut (Torghûd),
who finished his daring career at the fatal siege of
Malta—when, despite the corsair's valour, the Knights
wrought golden deeds of heroism, and dealt as deadly
a blow at Turkish prestige as even the Count of Salm
had struck from the walls of Vienna ;—and in Piali
the conqueror of Oran and worster of Doria himself.
Most of the Turkish naval successes were the work of
semi-independent adventurers, pirates, or buccaneers,
whose venturesome exploits belong rather to the
" Story of the Corsairs " than to the legitimate history
of Turkey.

" Sultan Suleymān left to his successors an empire
to the extent of which few permanent additions were
ever made, except the islands of Cyprus and Candia,
and which under no subsequent Sultan maintained
or recovered the wealth, power, and prosperity which
it enjoyed under the great lawgiver of the house of
Othmān.   The Turkish dominions in his time comprised all the most celebrated cities of biblical and
classical history, except Rome, Syracuse, and Perse-
polis.   The sites of Carthage, Memphis, Tyre,
Nineveh, Babylon, and Palmyra were Ottoman
ground ; and the cities of Alexandria, Jerusalem,
Smyrna, Damascus, Nice, Prusa, Athens, Philippi, and

RVZIÆ SOLDANE.

ANA.

Adrianople, besides many of later but scarce inferior celebrity, such as Algiers, Cairo, Mekka, Medina, Basra, Baghdad, and Belgrade, obeyed the Sultan of Constantinople. The Nile, the Jordan, the Orontes, the Euphrates, the Tigris, the Tanais, the Borysthenes the Danube, the Hebrus, and the Ilyssus, rolled their waters 'within the shadow of the Horsetails.' The eastern recess of the Mediterranean, the Propontis, the Palus Maeotis, the Euxine, and the Red Sea, were Turkish lakes. The Ottoman crescent touched the Atlas and the Caucasus ; it was supreme over Athos, Sinai, Ararat, Mount Carmel, Mount Taurus, Ida, Olympus, Pelion, Haemus, the Carpathian and the Acroceraunian heights. An empire of more than forty thousand square miles, embracing many of the richest and most beautiful regions of the world, had been acquired by the descendants of Ertoghrul, in three centuries from the time when their forefather wandered a homeless adventurer at the head of less than five hundred fighting men." [1]

[1] Sir E. Creasy, 197 (ed. 1877).

NOTE.

The accompanying plan shows in rough outline the growth and the decrease of the Ottoman Empire. Vertically it is measured by years, an inch to a century. Horizontally it is divided into three chief sections, representing Europe, Asia, and Africa, within which the principal provinces are indicated at the time when they became part of the Turkish Empire, and again when they ceased to be Ottoman. The shaded portion represents the dominion of the Turks, whether under their immediate control or under the rule of a vassal king (as Serbia in the earlier period). Thus we see the small beginning of the Ottoman power in Asia; its spread over Bithynia in the first half of the fourteenth century; its progress in Europe during the second half, through Rumelia and Bulgaria to Serbia and Wallachia; its sudden extension in Anatolia at the close of the century, and its equally sudden repression by Tīmūr; and then the steady enlargement indicated by such names as Greece, Constantinople, Albania, Moldavia, Hungary, &c., on the European side, and Karaman, Armenia, Arabia, Syria, Egypt, Algiers, Tripoli, and Tunis on the Asiatic and African side, until, in the last quarter of the sixteenth century, the greatest extent is attained. Then, in the second part of the plan, we see Algiers becoming semi-independent before the seventeenth century was half gone; Tunis following, and Hungary lost by 1700; Russia despoiling the Porte of the Crimea; Mohammed Ali virtually independent in Egypt; various States rising in the Balkan Peninsula,—Greece, Bosnia, Serbia, Rumania; France in Algiers and Tunis, and Russia encroaching in Asia Minor, after the last Russo-Turkish war.

The plan is a modification of a table contributed by Mr. E. J. W. Gibb to my "Catalogue of Oriental Coins in the British Museum," vol. viii.

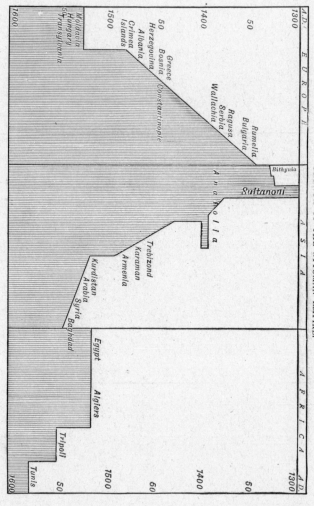

GROWTH OF THE OTTOMAN EMPIRE.

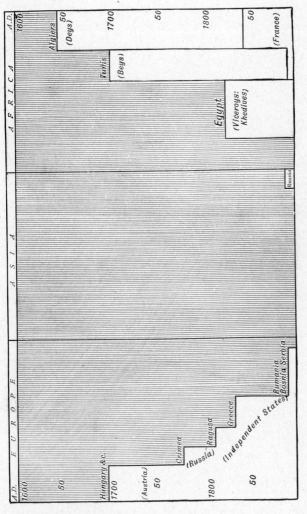

DECLINE OF THE OTTOMAN EMPIRE.

XI.

THE DOWNWARD ROAD.
(1566–1640.)

THE reign of Suleymān the Great forms the climax of Turkish history. In three centuries the little clan of Othmānlis had spread from their narrow district in Asia Minor till they had the command of the Mediterranean, the Euxine, and the Red Sea. Their dominions now extended from Mekka to Buda, from Baghdad to Algiers. Both the northern and southern shores of the Black Sea were theirs ; a large part of modern Austria-Hungary owned their sway ; and North Africa from the Syrian frontier to the boundary of the Empire of Morocco had been subdued by their arms.

The three centuries that remain to be described consist of one long decline, relieved indeed now and then by a temporary revival of the old warlike spirit of the people, but nevertheless a steady and inevitable decline. The causes of this downward course are partly external and partly depend upon the gradual deterioration of the Turks themselves. The growth of Russia and the combination of a group of brilliant leaders in Hungary, Poland, and Austria, are the

most important of the outward causes which led to
the narrowing of the Turkish boundaries : but these
by themselves would hardly have sufficed to reduce
the Ottoman Empire to its present decrepit condition,
had there not been internal cankers which sapped its
ancient vigour.   The very nature of the empire demanded extraordinary energy and wisdom to ensure
its continuance.   A power founded upon military
predominance and exercised upon numerous alien
races and hostile creeds needed peculiar care, both
in maintaining the efficiency of the army and in
conciliating the prejudices and winning the respect, if
not the affection, of the Christian subjects who formed
the majority of the European population.

The Turkish Government, however, cared for none
of these things.   When the energy and genius of a
series of great rulers had brought the empire to the
height of renown, the too common result ensued ; a
line of weak and vicious Sultans succeeded to the
vast dominions which had been won by their ancestors'
swords and retained by their administrative skill, and
these degenerate scions of a heroic stock, thought
only of the enjoyments which their great possessions
permitted, not of the conditions which might ensure
their permanence.   The army, deprived of the valiant
Sultans who once led them to battle, lost all respect
for the idlers who preferred the ignoble luxury of the
harem to the fierce joys of war ; and a disaffected
soldiery, soon learning its power, set up and deposed
Sultans as seemed good to it, and extorted heavy
bribes from each successive puppet of its choice.   The
unbounded exercise of capricious power quickly led to

licence and corruption, and the Janissaries by degrees
lost their martial character and could not be trusted
as of old in the field. A bribe was of more consequence to them than a victory. No efforts, besides,
were made to keep pace with the improvements which
other nations were introducing in the weapons and
tactics of war, and even if their mettle had been as
finely tempered as of old, the Turkish troops were
not equipped as they should have been when they
met the battalions of Prince Eugene, of Sobieski, or
Suvorov. The worst feature of all was their ineffi-
cient officering. Their commanders were appointed
not for merit, but in consideration of bribes, and such
a system naturally entailed the deterioration of every
regiment, and its evil effects are visible to the present
day. With effeminate Sultans, incompetent officers,
and corrupt administrators, with a weak head and
corrupt members, indeed, it was to be expected that
the whole man should also become corrupt and powerless,—the " sick man " for whom Russia prescribed a
euthanasia.

To tell the various stages of decay in detail would
only weary the reader with a catalogue of defeats,
varied by occasional reprisals ; a series of treaties of
peace, each involving loss or humiliation, each sworn
for ever and broken in a few years ; an inventory of
weak, corrupt, or misguided rulers and officers, whose
baseness and incompetence are cast into deeper shadow
by such rare apparitions as the family of the Köprilis,
as Sultans like Murād IV. and Mahmūd II., or
generals like the Dāmād Alī, " the dauntless Vizier,"
the conqueror of the Morea, and the chivalrous Topal

Othmān, the antagonist of Nādir Shāh. It will only
be possible to present a brief outline of the successive
events which marked the gradual shrinking of the
Turkish Empire to its present limits.

The inroads of Russia, not at first the most im-
portant, but growing in force and menace with each
succeeding war, are reserved for another chapter.
The other principal opponents of the Turks were
Austria (aided by Hungary and Poland), Venice, and
Persia.

Venice was the first to dispute the supremacy of
Suleymān's empire. The great Sultan had been
succeeded by his son, who received the too appropriate
sobriquet of Selīm the Sot. But it was not in the
nature of things that the splendid system organized
by Suleymān and his able officers should fall to the
ground in the hands of a single worthless successor.
Many of Suleymān's agents were still alive, and
especially the Grand Vezīr Sokolli Mohammed spared
no pains to carry on the government in the spirit of his
master. Great military exploits were at first contem-
plated. Sinān Pasha reduced Arabia in 1570, and
prayers were said in the Holy City of Mekka for the
" Sultan of Sultans, Khakan of Khakans, lord of the
two seas and two continents, and the two sanc-
tuaries of Islam, Selīm Khan, son of Suleymān
Khan." [1] An expedition was sent to Astrakhān, as
will be related further on,[2] but this was not among
the triumphs of the Porte ; only a fourth of the army
returned alive to Constantinople. The conquest of
Cyprus from the Venetians was the next venture.

[1] Von Hammer, ii. 398.   [2] See page 251.

It was entrusted to a rival of Sokolli, one Lala Mustafa, who conducted it with equal rashness and cruelty. It cost him fifty thousand men, and he revenged himself in the hour of success by flaying alive the gallant commandant Bragadino.

The rule of the sea, thus materially strengthened, was soon destined to receive a check. A great maritime league was formed by the Venetians, Spaniards, Knights of Malta, and others, and a fleet of two hundred galleys and six huge galliasses was collected by the confederates and placed under the command of Don John of Austria, a young man famous for his recent subjugation of the Moors in the Alpuxarras,[1] and reputed the greatest general of the time. Against this formidable array the Turks were able to bring together an even larger fleet. Two hundred and forty galleys, besides sixty smaller vessels, were riding in the Gulf of Patras under the command of Muezzin-zāda, Uluj Alī, and other tried admirals, when, on October 7, 1571, Don John brought his fleet out of the Gulf of Lepanto and gave battle. He formed his centre into a crescent under the command of the celebrated Prince of Parma, and took post himself in the van. The galliasses were ranged like redoubts in front of the line. The Turks were the first to open fire, and pressing forward suffered severely from the broadsides of the tall galliasses which they had to pass before they could come into close action with Don John. The two chief admirals on either sides locked their vessels together, and for two hours a deadly fight went on from the decks. At

[1] See Lane-Poole, " The Story of the Moors in Spain," p. 278.

last the Turkish commander fell, and his flag-ship was boarded : the Ottoman centre was broken, and the right wing gave way. The left, under Uluj Alī, gained some successes over Doria, a nephew of the great admiral of that name, and took some of the enemy's ships, but when he saw the collapse of the centre and right he fought his way out of the melley, and with forty galleys, the remnant of a noble fleet, set sail for the Bosphorus. Ninety-four Turkish ships were sunk or burnt, at least a hundred and thirty were captured ; the Turks lost 30,000 men, and 15,000 Christian galley slaves were set free.[1]

.The result of this tremendous defeat ought to have been the annihilation of the Turkish command of the seas ; but it was nothing of the kind. Its moral effect in showing that the terrible Ottomans were not invincible was lasting, but its immediate influence on the balance of maritime power in the Mediterranean was comparatively slight. The Christian confederates, perfectly satisfied with their triumph, dispersed their fleet, and began to give thanks for their victory and indulge in their favourite jealousies, but the Turks steadily set to work to repair their misfortunes. In a few months, by incredible energy and devotion, in which even the besotted Sultan took a share, a new fleet of two hundred and fifty sail was fitted out; and so little did the victory of Lepanto encourage the Venetians that they threw over their allies and sued for a separate peace. They not only agreed that the Sultan was to remain in possession of Cyprus, but were so good as to repay him thecost of taking it! The

[1] Von Hammer, ii. 423.

SULEYMANIYA MOSQUE, 1556.

memory of Lepanto was wiped out of the Turkish mind.

There was comparative peace with the Venetians for a quarter of a century after this, but it was as much due to harem influence as respect for any treaty. Murād III., who succeeded his father Selīm in 1574, was a feeble creature who let the offices of State be sold by sycophants to the highest bidder, and himself be ruled by his women; but among the latter was fortunately at least one lady of intelligence. Safīa, a captured Venetian of the family of Baffo, governed her imperial husband in the interests of her countrymen, and when he died in 1595, and was succeeded by her son, Mohammed III.—one of Murād's hundred and two children, of whom nineteen were put to death on their brother's accession—she found the power of mother in no way inferior to that of wife. Her chief ally was Cicala, a Genoese of noble birth who had been made prisoner in his youth by the Turks. His father, Count Cicala, had married a captive "Turkess," and the son followed his example by espousing a granddaughter of Suleymān the Great. The combination of personal merit and backstairs influence insured the young man's rise, and in due time he obtained important commands. In 1596 he rendered a signal service to his adopted country. Three days the imperial troops of Austria and Transylvania fought with the Turks on the plain of the Keresztes. The Christians seemed about to triumph, and twice the Sultan thought of flight. Then Cicala swooped down upon them at the head of his horsemen, and in half an hour archduke and prince were riding for dear life, followed by a panting mob of what had once been soldiers, and leaving fifty thousand corpses on the field.

One such success, however, hardly relieved a reign composed of military revolts, petty external wars, provincial tyrants, and general disaffection. It was a sign of the lowered status of the Turkish Empire that a treaty was concluded with Austria, after the usual campaigns, in the reign of the next Sultan, Ahmed I., a boy of fourteen, in which the Porte was treated as an ordinary equal instead of as a dreaded master, and the Austrian tribute was discontinued. Turkey was no longer the terror of Europe. Indeed, had Christendom been less divided and absorbed in the Spanish wars at that time, it is a question whether the Ottoman Empire might not then have come to the end which has so often been predicted. England had an ambassador at the Porte from the time of Elizabeth (1583) who strenuously invited the Sultan to join his mistress against Spain, but England was in no condition to support the Grand Signior against his many and powerful enemies, nor had our traditional policy in the East yet been formulated. The Indian Empire and the preservation of our road thither were in the future. Nothing seemingly but their own divisions kept the Powers from partitioning the Ottoman provinces at the beginning of the seventeenth century. Indeed, Sir Thomas Roe, who wrote an interesting account of his mission to Turkey, looked with confidence to the speedy collapse of the Ottoman State.

But peace reigned for some time on the northern

THE GRAND SIGNIOR IN ROBES OF STATE.

frontiers of Turkey. The emperor of Austria was fully alive to the advantage of keeping on friendly terms in the south when the Thirty Years' War was raging in the north, and the Turks had no motive for aggression, since they had so far retained their conquests. The new Sultan, Murād IV., who ascended the throne in 1623, though fired with something of the old warlike energy of his ancestors, preferred to exert it in another direction, and concluded a fresh peace with the emperor which ensured tranquillity to the Turks on their northern marches during the first half of the seventeenth century.

Murād was the last fighting Sultan of the race of Othmān. The enemy he chose for his attack was Persia. In the time of Murād III. there had been a successful war with the Shāh, which ended in a peace in 1590, whereby the Turks secured Georgia, Tebrīz, and some of the Persian provinces adjoining the southern shores of the Caspian Sea. These acquisitions had again and again been disputed by the Persians, and by a peace in 1619 the Shāh had recovered his losses and the boundary between the two kingdoms had been restored to the limits which had been drawn at the time of Selīm. Murād IV. resolved to regain the conquests of his namesake. He had however to contend with grievous obstacles. He was but a boy of twelve when he came to the throne, and never was an empire more in need of a strong man's hand. Disasters and rebellions were announced from all quarters. The Persians were triumphant, Asia Minor was in revolt, the provincial governors were refractory; the three Barbary states were practically independent;

the treasury was empty, the people were starving, and the army was both turbulent and licentious.

With the help of a capable mother the young Sultan contrived to maintain his authority in some sort in the face of such difficulties, but not without many a painful humiliation. In the ninth year of his reign the Sipāhīs mutinied, and gathering together in the Hippodrome demanded the heads of some of the officers of state, and especially of Hāfiz, the Grand Vezīr. They pressed into the courts of the Seraglio, crying, "Give us the seventeen heads!" The choice lay between submission and abdication. The Sultan vainly used every argument and entreaty. At last he sent for the Grand Vezīr. Hāfiz did not shrink from the sacrifice. "I have seen my fate in a dream to-day," he said, "and I am not afraid to die." He would not however allow the guilt of his blood to rest on his sorrowing master's head, but resolved to seek death in open conflict with the mutineers. "My Padishah," he said, "may a thousand slaves like Hāfiz die for thee:" and after reciting some verses from the Koran, he strode forth into the court, while the Sultan and his retinue sobbed and wept. Hāfiz struck down the first assailant, and then fell pierced by seventeen wounds. The Sultan did not leave the ghastly scene without uttering ominous words to the murderers. "So help me God," he said, "ye men of blood, who fear not God nor are ashamed before God's Prophet, a terrible vengeance shall overtake you."

Gathering together some loyal troops the stern young prince kept his word. The mutineers were slain in every province; the Bosphorus floated thick with the

bodies of Sipāhīs and Janissaries ; while the terrible
Sultan, who had few rivals in sword or bow, patrolled
the streets himself and often carried out his sanguinary
sentences with his own strong hand. The death of
Hāfiz was avenged tenfold, and the authority of his
master was established on the foundation of terror.
His severity indeed outshot the mark ; hundreds of
innocent people were ruthlessly butchered to gratify
the suspicions or even the caprices of the tyrant, in
whom the taste of blood seemed to generate that
fascinating appetite which it creates in beasts of prey.
It is said that a hundred thousand persons paid the
last penalty by his order. An inordinate addiction to
wine still further hardened his fierce temper, but no
habits of indulgence seemed to shake his iron will or
enfeeble his martial frame. He watched over every
department of his administration with vigilant eyes :
law and justice, order and discipline, everywhere prevailed as they had not been known since the days of
the Great Suleymān : tyrant he was, but he allowed no
other man to tyrannize, and the people realized that
the tyranny of one is liberty compared to the aimless
tyranny of the many.

As soon as he could safely leave the capital, Murād
set forth to restore order and peace on his Asiatic
frontiers. In 1635 he reconquered Erivān, and visited
the local governors of Asia Minor with stern punishment for their disaffection. For months his only
pillow was his saddle and his coverlet a horsecloth.
In 1638 he marched to retake Baghdad, which the
Persians had recovered since its first capture by Suleymān. The garrison made a desperate resistance. But

Murād led his men in person, worked in the trenches with his own hands, and, when the Persians sent out a stalwart champion to defy the besiegers to single combat, it was Murād himself who took up the gauntlet and after a hard fight clove the giant's skull from pate to chin. The chain armour in which he fought, a beautiful suit of interwoven steel and gold links, is still to be seen in the Treasury at Constantinople. Baghdad fell and a fearful butchery ensued, in which only three hundred of the thirty thousand men of the garrison escaped, nor did the unarmed inhabitants fare better. Peace was made with Persia on the basis of Suleymān's treaty of 1555 ; Erivān was restored to the Shah, but Baghdad has remained ever since in the hands of the Turks. Murād made his triumphal entry into Constantinople amid the shouts of the people, while the Bosphorus and Golden Horn blazed with salutes.

The following year (1640) he died at the age of 28, the last of the warrior Sultans of Turkey.

XII.

.THE RULE OF THE VEZIRS.
(1640–1757.)

HENCEFORWARD, until we reach the present century and the person of Mahmūd II., the names of the twelve Sultans who succeeded Murād IV. upon the throne of Turkey possess little interest or individuality for us. Secluded in the Seraglio, and abandoned, with few exceptions, to most of the worst vices that can degrade body and soul, they left the care or neglect of their empire to the Vezīrs, and, accordingly as the Prime Minister was a capable or an incapable man, the empire was retarded or accelerated in its downward course. At the beginning of the period upon which we are now entering, the Porte was fortunate in the possession of an Albanian family of remarkable powers, whose influence checked for a while the disastrous tendencies of the empire. Köprili Mohammed, the first of this stock, was chosen Grand Vezīr (1656) at the age of seventy. His inflexible yet just severity restored order in all parts of the empire. For five years his eyes searched out treason and wrongdoing in every corner of the Sultan's dominions, and never was a strong will better obeyed than during this epoch. Thirty-six thousand people were executed by his command, and the chief executioner admitted that in these five years he had with his own hands strangled over four thousand, or nearly three a day. The old Vezīr had previously borne the reputation of a mild and humane man, but he saw that only strong measures could restore tranquillity to the distracted empire, and he did not shrink from the course which his reason dictated. He died in 1661, and was succeeded in his office by his even greater son Ahmed. For fifteen years Köprili-zāda Ahmed was virtual Sultan, and he is admittedly the greatest statesman of Turkey. He had as firm a will and as stern a sense of duty as Mohammed, but he had the advantage of a better education and all the added power and experience due to his father's example. As a civil administrator he was unequalled, but as a general in the field he was doomed to suffer heavy reverses.

The constant intrigues which marked the changes of succession in Hungary and Transylvania once more embroiled the Porte with Austria, and it fell to Köprili-zāda Ahmed to lead the armies of Turkey to the Danube. In the battle of St. Gotthard (1664) he received a terrible defeat at the hands of Raymond, Count of Montecuculi. The Christians were outnumbered in the proportion of four to one, and the contempt of the Turks was increased when they saw the French contingent come riding down with their shaved cheeks and powdered perukes. They ridiculed the charge of the "young girls;" but the "girls" and Montecuculi were too strong for their tried veterans :—ten thousand Turks were left on the field, and the Vezīr was compelled to beat an ignominious retreat.

THE GRAND VEZĪR.

Some compensation for this disaster was found in the success which at length attended the operations of the Ottomans against the island of Candia, or Crete. The Turks were still renowned for their siege works, and though it took them more than twenty years to subdue the determined resistance of the Venetians under their gifted leader Morosini, at last, in 1669, the island was theirs. During the last three years they had made fifty-six desperate assaults, and the garrison had replied with ninety sorties ; more than thirteen hundred mines had been fired on both sides, thirty thousand Turks had fallen, and nearly half as many Venetians. The successful termination of this memorable siege did much to restore the waning confidence of the Porte.

It was, however, but a gleam of sunshine in an Erebus of gloom. A new and formidable enemy appeared in the north. The Cossacks of the Ukraine had been claimed as Polish subjects by the king of Poland against their will, and the Porte proceeded to defend them. The struggle was short ; the king quickly abandoned his pretensions, agreed to pay tribute, and even surrendered Podolia as well as the Ukraine to Turkey. The Polish nobles, headed by John Sobieski, a name which stands in the front rank of European generals, refused to abide by these terms, and, leading their forces against the Turks, administered two crushing defeats, at Choczim in 1673, and at Lemberg in 1675. The Turks, however, were better able to carry on a long war than the Polish nobles, and in spite of their victories, the latter were glad to come to terms, by which the Ottomans retained the advantages which they had previously secured.

A defeat followed by an accession of territory was no very calamitous ending to Köprili's-zāda Ahmed's life, though the Ukraine had soon afterwards to be ceded to Russia. But when the gifted family which had already supplied two eminent men to the highest office in the State suffered a passing eclipse, and a new and temerarious Vezīr was appointed, disasters of a less chequered character poured upon the Turkish arms. The policy of Austria towards Hungary had lately become more and more severe and unconciliatory. The Protestant Magyars especially resented the proselytizing efforts of the Jesuits and the bigotry of the Catholic party towards its unorthodox subjects. Conspiracies were set on foot, and when discovered were punished with unsparing severity; but Hungary remained at least as disaffected to Austrian supremacy as before. Indeed, it was known that the nobles of Hungary preferred the rule of Mohammedans to that of bigoted Catholics. The Porte was fully informed of these matters, and a violent war party sprang up at Constantinople; they eagerly pressed for an advance on Vienna at the moment when Hungary might be counted upon as an ally.

Accordingly in 1682, the new Grand Vezīr, Kara Mustafa, seized this favourable opportunity of putting an end once for all to the detested house of Hapsburg, and marched northwards with a vast host of 400,000 men, officered in part by French captains and engineers, lent for the service by Louis XIV., who was anxious to see the Imperial power humbled in

the dust.   It seemed as if there was nothing to arrest
the advance of the Turks.   The Christians, as usual,
were wholly unprepared.   When once the terrible
horsetails had been seen retreating towards the south,
it was the custom of the princes of Europe to disband
their armies and neglect their fortifications, and to
abandon themselves to all the delights of quarrelling
among themselves.   Charles of Lorraine, indeed, who
had fought beside Montecuculi at the battle of St.
Gotthard, was ready to take his part in the defence ;
but he could only muster 33,000 men, and what
were they against so many, above all, when a large
number of them had to be told off to sundry fortresses
for garrison duty?   Disaffected Hungary sought to
make peace with both sides by sending a miserable
contingent of 3,000 under Esterhazy.   But for one
circumstance the triumph of the Turks might have
been predicted with certainty : this was a treaty of
alliance which had just been signed between the
Emperor Leopold and Sobieski, who was now king of
Poland.   It is a significant fact that when these two
sovereigns bound themselves to make common cause
against the Turk, the memory of many past conventions
of the kind which had been dissolved by the Pope's dispensation, recurred to their minds, and while they swore
an oath, sanctified by the Cardinal Legate, to stand
by one another, they appended a clause which stipu-
lated that this oath was not subject to retractation by
Papal dispensation.   The combination of the Legate's
sacred office, with the guarding clause against its per-
jured misuse, is one of the curiosities of history.

John Sobieski, however, though he had sworn to

help, and was known to be true to his word, was still in Poland, and meanwhile the Grand Vezīr was pushing on to Vienna. Despairing of succour in time, the emperor and his court fled ignominiously to Bavaria. The city was, in truth, very ill prepared to withstand a siege, especially when conducted by such good engineers as the Turks. The fortifications were in a state of decay, and it will hardly be believed that the very tools necessary for their repair were not to be had in Vienna. It was a mere chance that the Grand Vezīr loitered somewhat on his way. Had he used forced marches, he must infallibly have entered the capital of the Holy Roman Empire without so much as striking a blow.

The delay, little as it was, gave the people time to prepare. Count Stahremberg, a true hero, was appointed to conduct the defence, and the whole population laboured incessantly at the work of repairing the fortifications. Students of the University and members of the trades-guilds formed themselves into volunteer corps and drilled with might and main. Out of the population of 60,000 (for half the people had fled) some 20,000 were under arms at the dreaded moment when the flames of burning villages and the news of treacherous butchery told of the near approach of the invaders. At last the orders were given for the burning of the suburbs, that they might not serve as cover to the enemy ; and on the 14th of July the siege began. The island suburb of Leopoldstadt soon fell into the hands of the Turks, and became a smouldering pyre. Assault after assault was made and repulsed ; mine was answered

ST. STEPHEN'S CATHEDRAL, VIENNA.

by countermine ; but Stahremberg, as he looked down upon the operations from the stone seat, which is still to be seen in the lofty spire of St. Stephen's, saw with sadness that inch by inch the Turks were gaining ground.

The assaults so far had indeed been fruitless, for the Turkish scimitar was no match for the German halberd, scythe, and battle-axe : but the mines were creeping towards the walls, and sickness was raging in the city. To sickness followed famine. Cats were so valuable, that a chase after the animal over the roofs became a recognized form of sport. The relieving army was indeed known to be on the move, but would it come in time, or would it succeed in driving away the still immense, though diminishing, hosts of the Turks ?

On the 6th of September, rockets announced that Sobieski was indeed at hand. The people redoubled their efforts when they knew of the presence of the great captain. He had united the Polish, Saxon, Austrian, Bavarian, and other contingents, to the number of some 85,000 men, and had occupied the Kahlenberg, the one strategic position essential for the relief of the city. His men, moreover, were fresh, while the 100,000 troops whom the Vezīr had still in camp were exhausted by a two months' siege, and many privations and labours. On the 10th, the sound of guns was heard in the city. They proceeded from the Kahlenberg. The great contest was beginning. How the thundering of the cannon was listened to in Vienna may be imagined. The people, trembling with anxiety, were held in suspense for many hours. It was a supreme crisis in the history of Europe.

Meanwhile Sobieski had taken his measures for its relief.

" At sunrise of the 12th of September the crest of the Kahlenberg was concealed by one of those autumnal mists which give promise of a genial, perhaps a sultry day, and which, clinging to the wooded flanks of the acclivity, grew denser as it descended, till it rested heavily on the shores and the stream itself of the river below. From that summit the usual fiery signals of distress had been watched through the night by many an eye, as they rose incessantly from the tower of St. Stephen, and now the fretted spire of that edifice, so long the target of the ineffectual fire of the Turkish artilleries, was faintly distinguished rising from the sea of mist. As the hour wore on, and the exhalation dispersed, a scene was disclosed, which must have made those who witnessed it from the Kahlenberg tighten their saddle-girths, or look to their priming. A practised eye glancing over the fortifications of the city could discern from the Burg to the Scottish gate an interruption of their continuity, a shapeless interval of rubbish and of ruin, which seemed as if a battalion might enter it abreast. In face of this desolation a labyrinth of lines extended itself, differing in design from the rectilinear zigzag of a modern approach, and formed of short curves overlapping each other, to use a comparison of some writers of the time, like the scales of a fish. In these, the Turkish lines, the miner yet crawled to his task, and the storming parties were

still arrayed by order of the Vezīr, ready for a
renewal of the assault so often repeated in vain.
The camp behind had been evacuated by the fighting men ; the horsetails had been plucked from
before the tents of the pashas, but their harems still
tenanted the canvas city ; masses of Christian captives awaited there their doom in chains ; camels
and drivers and camp followers still peopled the long
streets of tents in all the confusion of fear and suspense. Nearer to the base of the hilly range of the
Kahlenberg and the Leopoldsberg, the still imposing
numbers of the Turkish army were drawn up in
battle array, ready to dispute the egress of the
Christian columns from the passes, and prevent de-
ployment on the plain. To the westward, on the
reverse flank of the range, Christian troops might be
seen toiling up the ascent. As they drew up on the
crest of the Leopoldsberg, they formed a half-circle
round the chapel of the Margrave, and when the bell
for matins tolled, the clang of arms and the noise of
the march was silenced. On a space kept clear round
the chapel a standard with a white cross on a red
ground was unfurled, as if to bid defiance to the
blood-red flag planted in front of the tent of Kara
Mustafa. One shout of acclamation and defiance
broke out from the modern Crusaders as this emblem
of a holy war was displayed, and all again was
hushed as the gates of the castle were flung open,
and a procession of the princes of the empire and
the other leaders of the Christian host moved forward
to the chapel. It was headed by one whose tonsured
crown and venerable beard betokened the monastic

profession.   The soldiers crossed themselves as he passed, and knelt to receive the blessings which he gave them with outstretched hands.   This was the Capuchin Marco Aviano, friend and confessor to the emperor, whose acknowledged piety and exemplary life had earned for him the general reputation of prophetic inspiration.   He had been the inseparable companion of the Christian army in its hours of difficulty and danger, and was now here to assist at the consummation of his prayers for its success.   Among the stately warriors who composed his train, three principally attracted the gaze of the curious.   The first in rank and station was a man somewhat past the prime of middle life, strong limbed, and of imposing stature, but quick and lively in speech and gesture; his head partly shaved, in the fashion of his semi-Eastern country ; his hair, eyes, and beard, dark, black coloured.   His majestic bearing bespoke the soldier-king, the scourge and dread of the Moslems, the conqueror of Choczim, John Sobieski. . . .

"On his left was his youthful son, Prince James, armed with a breastplate and helmet, and, in addition to an ordinary sword, with a short and broad-bladed sabre, a national weapon of former ages ; on his right was the illustrious and heroic ancestor of the present reigning house of Austria, Charles of Lorraine. Behind these moved many of the principal members of those sovereign houses of Germany.   At the side of Louis of Baden was a youth of slender frame and moderate stature, but with that intelligence in his eye, which pierced in after years the cloud of many a doubtful field, and swayed the fortunes of empires.

This was the young Eugene of Savoy, who drew his maiden sword in the quarrel in which his brother had lately perished. The service of high mass was performed in the Chapel by Aviano, the king assisting at the altar, while the distant thunder of the Turkish batteries formed strange accompaniment to the Christian choir. The prince then received the sacrament, and the religious ceremony was closed by a general benediction of the troops by Aviano. The king then stepped forward, and conferred knighthood on his son, with the usual ceremonies, commending to him as an example of his future course the great commander then present, the Duke of Lorraine. He then addressed his troops in their own language to the following effect : 'Warriors and friends ! Yonder in the plains are our enemies, in numbers greater indeed than at Choczim, where we trod them under foot. We have to fight them on a foreign soil, but we fight for our own country, and under the walls of Vienna we are defending those of Warsaw and Cracow. We have to save to-day, not a single city, but the whole of Christendom, of which that city of Vienna is the bulwark. The war is a holy one. There is a blessing on our arms, and a crown of glory for him who falls. You fight not for your earthly sovereign, but for the King of kings. His power has led you unopposed up the difficult access to these heights, and has thus placed half the victory in your hands. The infidels see you now above their heads, and, with hopes blasted and courage depressed, are creeping among valleys destined to be their graves. I have but one command to give—Follow me !

The time is come for the young to win their spurs.' "[1]

The Grand Vezír's preparations for the fight were very different from those of his Christian opponents. He began, it is said, by slaughtering in cold blood the thirty thousand captives who were confined in his camp. The majority were women who had already been subjected to the degradation of a place in the soldiers' harems. The butchering accomplished, he posted his men. Sobieski, however, had already discovered that Kara Mustafa was no general, and there could be little doubt as to the result of the contest. For many hours the Turks fought bravely, for with all their faults, cowardice in battle is unknown to them ; but the dash of the Polish cuirassiers, the steady persistence of the Saxons and Bavarians, above all, the unerring strategy of Sobieski, won the day. With a final rush, the Christians poured into the Turkish camp, and then all was panic and confusion. The Grand Vezír was carried along in the flying crowd, cursing and weeping by turns, the army melted like a mist before the sun, and the luckless Janissaries who were still in the trenches, forgotten by their flying leaders, were massacred to a man. Over three hundred pieces of artillery fell into the victors' hands, besides nine thousand ammunition waggons, a hundred thousand oxen, twenty-five thousand tents, and a million pounds of gunpowder. The unlucky Vezír paid for his error with his head. Like the Carthaginians, the Turks showed scant mercy to defeated generals.

[1] Schimmer, "Two Sieges of Vienna" (Eng. trans.), 136-138.

Thus was Vienna for a second time delivered out of the hands of the Ottomans; and never again would the horsetails be seen from the steeple of St. Stephen's church; where the preacher triumphantly commented on the text, "There was a man sent from God, whose name was John." It is, perhaps, useless to speculate on the probable consequences of the contrary event. Had Vienna been taken, as it almost was, by the Turks, the course of European history might possibly have been changed; but it may be questioned whether the Turks retained enough of their pristine vigour to hold such a conquest in the face of such powerful and brilliant leaders as the states of Europe could then and afterwards bring against it. Two centuries earlier it might have been otherwise: Mohammed II. might have held Vienna against the world. But Mohammed had slept the last sleep for two hundred years, and no one now sat in his seat at Constantinople who was worthy to wear his armour or wield his sword. At the end of the seventeenth century, the Turks possessed no Sultan or general who could withstand such men as Montecuculi, Charles of Lorraine, Prince Eugene, or Marlborough.

The Sultan, who had been upon the throne for thirty-five eventful years, was no sluggard, indeed; but his energies were wholly absorbed in the chase. "The long reign of Mohammed IV. (1648–87) was the intermediate epoch between the triumphs of the hero, the codes of the legislator, and the pompous nullity of the caged puppets of the seraglio; and while the Ottoman standard was planting on 'Troy's rival Candia,' the now unwarlike, but still spirited, Lord of Constantinople, and successor of the Orkhans, Mohammeds, Selīms, Murāds, and Suleymāns, was chasing the wild deer of Pelion and Olympus, and displaying his sylvan pomp at Larissa and Tirnova. To the remote scene of the Sultan's recreations, Pashas, Generals, Vezīrs, and Embassies, were seen hastening; and the splendour of the seraglio, with its ceremonial, was transferred to mountain wastes and deserts; amid untrodden forests arose halls of Western tapestry, and of Indian texture, rivalling in grandeur, and surpassing in richness, the regal palaces of the Bosphorus. Brusa, the Asiatic Olympus, the field of Troy, the sides of Ida, the banks of the Maeander, the plains of Sardis, were the favourite resorts of this equal lover of the chase and of nature. But the places more particularly honoured by his preference were Jamboli, in the Balkan, about fifty miles to the north of Adrianople, and Tirnova. Whenever he arrived or departed the inhabitants of fifteen districts turned out to assist him in his sport; these festivities were rendered attractive to the people by exhibitions and processions, somewhat in the spirit of ancient Greece, as well as in that of Tartary, where all the esnafs or trades displayed in procession the wonders of their art, or the symbols of their calling, and in which exhibitions of rare objects and grotesque figures were combined with theatric pantomime."

But at home this sporting Sultan was less amiable, or his ministers perhaps took too much upon themselves: for it was in his reign that a French Ambassador was called a Jew by the Grand Vezīr, struck in the face, and beaten with a stool; that a Russian envoy was actually kicked out of the presence chamber; and the Imperial dragoman repeatedly bastinadoed. The Ottoman ministers refused to rise on receiving a foreign representative; yet the ambassadors were regarded as guests at the Porte, and were allowed so much a day for their keep. It was only in the present century that this contemptuous bearing towards Giaours was amended; and as the Grand Vezīr persisted in remaining seated when an Ambassador came for audience, a compromise was arranged, whereby the minister and the envoy entered the chamber simultaneously, by opposite doors, so that neither had the opportunity to seat himself.[1]

Defeated at Vienna, the Turks did not retire from Hungary without striking a blow at the over-confident King of Poland, who in his hot pursuit forgot the ancient valour of his foes and received a severe lesson at Parkany. But this check only made the Imperialists more careful, and the Ottomans found themselves driven step by step from their northern possessions. City after city was retaken by the enemy; a defeat at Mohács, once a name of glory to the Turks, still further discouraged them; Buda was retaken after 145 years of vassalage (1686); the Austrians poured through Hungary and took Belgrade (1688); Louis of Baden entered Bosnia; the Venetians invaded Dalmatia, and their future Doge, the former defender of Candia, Morosini, subdued the Peloponnesus. The great Athenian temple, the Parthenon, after having served the Byzantines as a church and the Turks as a powder magazine, was finally shattered to ruins by the Venetians in

[1] Urquhart, "Spirit of the East," i. 341-345 (ed. 1838).

this campaign.   The Russians and Poles alone had been kept at arm's length on the north-east frontier. The Turkish dominions in Europe were now reduced to half their former extent.

Again the Sultan had recourse to the famous family that had already served his empire so well. Köprili-zāda Mustafa, a brother of the more cele-brated Ahmed,[1] was made Grand Vezīr in 1689.   He saw the first necessity of conciliating the Christian rayas, and this prudent policy prevented any rising of the Greeks and Slavs in Turkey Proper.   He was a wise man, a great reader, and noted for his sincerity, insomuch, that when he could not say a civil thing honestly, he would hold silence for an entire audience. Like his brother, he was more at home in the bureau than the field, yet he led his troops valiantly against the Austrians, marching on foot himself like any common soldier.   He drove back the Christians and retook Belgrade and other places, and pushed forward the Turkish frontier up to the Save.   In the battle of Slankamen (1691), however, he was killed, and his army was put to the rout.   Two other members of his family afterwards succeeded to the chief office, but neither of them attained the fame of Mohammed, Ahmed, or Mustafa.   Yet they served their country well and loyally, and the fifty years of the rule of this family served, like a strong anchor, to hold the drifting ship of State.

A new Sultan, Mustafa II., in 1695 suddenly called to mind the great deeds of his ancestors, and

---

[1] It is Ahmed who is called Fāzil Ahmed=Ahmed the Virtuous (*lit.* Excellent).

inspired by such memories, boldly led forth his armies against the Austrians. At first this unexpected revival of the old traditions of Turkish glory inspired the people with enthusiasm, and his standards were followed by a large and eager force. But zeal was not enough to secure the victory, when Prince Eugene commanded on the other side, and of generalship the Sultan and his advisers had little to spare. The Battle of Zenta in 1697 was a decisive blow: twenty thousand Turks were slain and ten thousand more were drowned in their flight. The unhappy Sultan gave up his dream of military glory.

At this juncture, England, in the person of Lord Paget, her Ambassador at the Porte, offered her mediation, which was accepted. The peace of Carlowitz, a notable landmark in Turkish history, was the result. Here for the first time Russian and Turkish envoys met in a European congress, and Turkey admitted once for all the principle of intervention by disinterested Powers. By this treaty (1699) Austria kept Transylvania and Hungary north of the Marosch and west of the Theiss, with most of Slavonia; Poland recovered Podolia and Kaminiec; Venice retained Dalmatia and the Morea or Peloponnesus; Russia made an armistice which afterwards was changed into a peace. Seventeen years later, after a fresh outbreak of hostilities, Prince Eugene took Belgrade, and by the Peace of Passarowitz (1718), in which England again played the part of mediator, Austria obtained possession of the rest of Hungary, and the Turkish frontier on the north was drawn on very nearly the same line which obtained until the Treaty of Berlin.

Henceforward the Ottoman Empire ceased to hold the position of a dangerous military power : its armies were never again a menace to Christendom. Its prestige was gone ; instead of perpetually threatening its neighbours on the north, it had to exert its utmost strength and diplomatic ingenuity to restrain the aggrandising policy of Austria and Russia. Turkey was now to become important only from a diplomatic point of view. Other Powers would fight over her, and the business of the Porte would be less to fight itself, though she can still do it well, than to secure allies whose interests compelled them to do battle for it. In the hundred and seventy years of Turkish history which remain to be recorded, the chief external interest centres in the aggression of Russia, and the efforts of English diplomacy and English arms to restrain her. The internal changes of the empire, the virtual severance of Egypt, the reforming administration of Sir Stratford Canning, the Russian wars, and the growth of the Christian states, will bring the chronicle up to the present date.

XIII.

THE RISE OF RUSSIA.
(1696–1812.)

WHILE the Ottoman Empire had been growing for centuries, there had been movements to the northward in the region known to the Greeks as Scythia and Sarmatia, which threatened sooner or later to interfere with its progress. Centuries earlier, in fact before Ertoghrul had chivalrously interfered in favour of the Sultan of Iconium, the steppes and seaboards of the north had been under the sway of rulers whose kingdoms had passed through several stages of development, until, at the period which we have reached, they were approaching union and strength.

The early history of this region is involved in the mystery which obscures the first ages of a country. In the Byzantine annals the inhabitants are represented as cruel and filthy, terrible in battle, using the skulls of their enemies as drinking-cups ; yet like the Arabs hospitable to strangers. Other accounts picture them as living in the idyllic innocence and happiness described by the poets of Greece, who imagined that the people beyond the north wind enjoyed peaceful lives that stretched out to a thousand years. They were represented to be of noble presence, bearing instruments of harmony instead of arms, and not even knowing that such a material as iron existed out of which swords might be forged. Travellers seldom gain correct notions of strange lands, and we may suppose that early visitors to the region that was afterwards called Russia took their impressions from the rhapsodies of the bards, in the one case, or, in the other, came into conflict with the strong men who wielded the battle-axe to protect the homes of wives and children. Doubtless these northerners were neither so fierce nor so mild as these conflicting accounts would make them.

Through the steppes and among the mountain ranges commerce had been carried on from a very early period. The river Volga furnished the chief means of communication between the distant east and the Baltic region, in the route of which, on Lake Ilmen, connected with Lake Ladoga and the Gulf of Finland by the rivers Volkhov and Neva, there rose an emporium called Nóvgorod, that became the first capital of the future empire.[1] It is easy to appreciate the importance of a river system in a country like Russia, and especially of such a river as the Volga. It not only drains a vast region, but it falls little more than six hundred feet in a course of twenty-five hundred miles ; but its length and very slight fall are not the only reasons why it was a help to commerce in early times as it is to steam navigation in our own day. A glance at the map shows that there is but a short land passage

[1] The importance of this capital is shown by the early Russian proverb, " Who can resist God and the great Nóvgorod ? "

from its head-waters to those of the Volkhov, as well
as to the Dnieper, through which the trader was able
to convey his merchandise in boats over most of the
long distance from the Caspian to the Black Sea and
the Mediterranean.

About a thousand years ago the inhabitants of this
great territory were harassed on the south by those
terrible Khazars who a century before had crossed the
Caucasus to fall upon the possessions of the Moslems.[1]
At the same time certain Northmen, who are said to
have belonged to the race which afflicted so many
lands in early times, attacked the dwellers about Lake
Ilmen and put them under tribute. These Northmen,
known as Variags or Varangians, were of the family
of Rus, and their leader was Rurik. With him came
his brothers, in the year 862, and brought order to
the misruled and divided people.

For fifty years after the arrival of Rurik, Nóvgorod
was the chief city and the capital, and Russia rejoiced
in a heroic age. It came to pass in time, however,
that Igor son of Rurik was set upon a throne at Kiev,
which for nearly three centuries became the capital.
There Christianity was first planted in the tenth
century, though tradition asserts that St. Andrew the
Apostle first set the Cross up on its heights. On
the death of Igor, Olga his widow reigned during the
minority of her son, and it was in her day that
Christianity began to spread slowly throughout the
middle of the continent. In the year 955 when there
was peace from foreign and domestic enemies, this
queen sailed down the Dnieper and over the Black

[1] See Gilman, "The Story of the Saracens," 345, 346.

Sea to Constantinople, and was there baptized with
much ceremony under the supervision of Constantine
Porphyrogenitus, and received the Christian name of
Helen.

Vladímir the Great, her grandson, received baptism
thirty-three years later, at Kherson, close to the modern
Sevastopol. The legend runs that when he was
besieging the place he said that if he took it he would
be baptized in the holy font excavated in the floor of
the ancient church there, and he kept his word. The
well is still to be seen. He supported the new faith
with zeal, and founded churches and schools. According to Gibbon, all who refused baptism were treated
as enemies of God and their prince, and accordingly
" the rivers were instantly filled with many thousands
of obedient Russians who acquiesced in the truth and
excellence of a doctrine which had been embraced by
the great duke and the boyars." [1]

The descendants of Vladímir did not dwell in peace,
and the kingdom became in time a group of princedoms, which fought innumerable campaigns with each
other and with the barbarians. In the twelfth century
the titular capital was the city of Vladímir, on a river
between the Oka and the Volga ; Kiev and Nóvgorod were among the most wealthy and prosperous
places on the continent ; and the new city of Moskva,
or Moscow, had been founded (1147).

For a century the confederated princedoms were
at war among themselves, and then a new and startling
danger arose in the south-east. The terrible Chingiz
Khān sent a portion of his troops to harass the

---

[1] " The Decline and Fall of the Roman Empire," chapters lii., liv.

Turkish tribes west of the Caspian Sea. They passed through Georgia and over the Caucasus range until they reached the steppes of Russia. There they encountered forces that the Russians had raised to oppose them, and won a complete victory, in 1224, on the banks of a small river that empties itself into the Sea of Azov near the present town of Mariupol. The invaders had crossed the Don, and made considerable progress into the domain of their enemies.

For a dozen years the common people were filled with forebodings of the return of the Tartars, and at the end of that time their fears were realized. Batu, grandson of Chingiz, poured his Mongol hordes upon the inhabitants, slaughtered men, women, and children, and burned their dwellings and cities. Moscow and Vladímir became heaps of smoking ruins; all opposing armies were crushed by the tumultuous Asiatics. Nóvgorod saw the wild horde approaching and expected the fate of its sister cities, but for no reason that could be surmised, Batu turned back, and swept southward to the steppes of the Don. The next year he wasted Southern Russia and retreated to a place of safety. In 1240, he appeared in front of Kiev, which, though already devastated by civil war, beckoned him with its promise of spoils. Soon the bright domes became a prey to the flames, the palaces were rifled; the citizens were butchered or made captive; and smoking walls were all that remained of the splendour that once was Kiev. Batu hurried westward, but was defeated at Liegnitz (1241), in Moravia, and forced to flee to the other side of the Volga, where he laid the foundation of the famous

city of Serāy.[1]   There he pitched his golden camp,
or *ordu*, from which his followers afterwards received
the name "Golden Horde;" while the name of the
city is preserved in the word "seraglio," a palace.

Russia was completely cowed by these invaders,
and for more than two hundred years was in effect a
Tartar province.   The waste places were, however,
cultivated again, and the cities slowly recovered from
their ruined condition; but the hand of the Tartar
was heavy upon the people, and ever and anon the
fearful rumour passed from mouth to mouth that the
invaders were again at hand, and in the imagination
of the terrified folk the scenes of the time of Batu
were repeated in all their frightful horrors.

The yoke was not borne with resignation all this
long time.   Alexander Nevski, the Russian national
hero and canonized Tsar, raised the spirits of his
northern subjects by a mighty victory over the Swedes
on the banks of the Neva in 1240, where St. Petersburg now stands.   In 1378 and 1380, Demetrius IV.,
appointed grand prince by the Mongols, brought
against his masters a well-trained army and twice
routed them.   In one conflict on the Don he killed,
they say, one hundred thousand Tartars; but, in 1381,
the irrepressible horde returned and burned Vladímir
and Moscow, slaying in the latter city alone, it is said,
twenty-four hundred persons.   Peace was purchased at
a heavy sacrifice.

---

[1] This city is mentioned by Chaucer in the Squire's Tale—"the
half-told tale of Cambuscan"—

> "At Sarry, in the land of Tartarye,
>   Ther dwelte a kynge that werreyed Russye."

Nevertheless the importance of Moscow increased as time passed, and in the next century Ivan III., the Great, taking advantage of the weakness which followed the internecine wars which, in the time of Tamerlane,[1] had devastated the Golden Horde, had strengthened himself sufficiently to throw off the yoke. His reign marks a new period in Russian history. He united Nóvgorod, Moscow, and other states, and a kingdom of Russia became for the first time a probability. He married a princess of Constantinople, and expressed his share in the rights of blood-relationship by placing a double-headed eagle upon his escutcheon, instead of St. George and the Dragon, which he had formerly borne.

Under Ivan the Great laws were improved and taxes regulated. The Tartars were now broken up into a number of small khanates—Krim, stretching along the Don ; Kazan, on the Volga ; Astrakhan, on the Lower Volga ; and others further east. In 1502 the golden city of Seräy was taken and destroyed.

The reign of Ivan first brought the Russian Court into peaceful relations with the Porte. Certain Turks had laid burdensome impositions on the Muscovite merchants trading among them, and when, in 1492, the facts came to the knowledge of Ivan the Great, he wrote to Bāyezīd II. and proposed diplomatic intercourse between the two empires.[2] Three years

---

[1] Tīmūr ravaged South-eastern Russia in 1396, and threatened Vladímir and Moscow, but unexpectedly retired.

[2] Diplomacy in the modern acceptation of the term, was then in its infancy. Though it is generally said to have become a science in the

later the Tsar sent his first ambassador to the Golden Horn.

Though this was the first diplomatic connexion between Ottoman and Russian history, it was not the beginning of conflict between Russia and Constantinople. As early as 864, a Russian fleet had appeared at the Golden Horn, and had with some difficulty been repulsed. In 906 the city was panic-stricken by the approach of land and water forces under Oleg, guardian of Igor, the son of Rurik. The inhabitants were plundered, tortured, and put to the sword in great numbers. Again, in 941, Igor himself went down with "thousands" of galleys and ravaged the coasts, destroying towns and crucifying the inhabitants. He was repulsed by the wonderful "winged fire" which had discomfited the Saracens centuries before. In 972, Svätoslav I. made another expedition, but was defeated by the Emperor, John Zimiskes, in the Balkan, after a terrible struggle, and lost his life before he was able to regain his capital. Thus early began the Russians to cast longing eyes upon the beautiful city on the Bosphorus.

Moscow advanced in power. It was blessed with cautious princes, who made a virtue of necessity by bowing to the Tartars when they were too strong to be resisted, but were ever ready to strike in earnest when they had a chance. They contrived at the

reign of Henry IV. of France, under the head of his great minister the Duke of Sully, it had been much cultivated by the Italian republics, and Machiavelli (1467–1527) was ambassador to France as early as 1500.

same time to win the favour of the Greek Church, and they had the support of the *boyars* or nobility. The refractory Lithuanians were gradually subdued, and though not yet Tsars, in the modern meaning, the descendants of Rurik the Norseman were styled "Grand Princes of All Russia." In 1552 the Tartars of Kazan were conquered and made tributary, and a realm comprising some thirty-seven thousand square miles acknowledged the sway of Ivan IV., Grozni, "the Terrible." He in turn, despite his cruel nature, increased his patrimony to more than a hundred and forty thousand square miles, and during the half-century of his reign accomplished more for Russia than any previous sovereign.

The Krim Tartars were fierce foes of this first Tsar [1] of Russia. They were tributary to the Sultan, but he did not take part in their strife with the Tsar. The Turkish Vezīr Sokolli was at that time anxious to revive an enterprize often conceived and even attempted in ancient times. This was the creation of a water-route from Constantinople to the borders of Persia, in the interests alike of commerce and of war. It was to be accomplished by cutting a canal between the Don and the Volga; ships could then sail from the Black Sea, through the Sea of Azov, up the Don and down the Volga, to the Caspian. Astrakhan, at the mouth of the Volga, then held by Russia, was an essential part of the plan. A large force was sent out to take it, but it was routed and obliged to return; and an army of Tartars which went to its assistance, was also defeated by the Russians. The Tsar sent

[1] Or Czar: a contraction of Caesar.

an ambassador to Constantinople to complain of the attack on Astrakhan, and a friendly alliance was arranged. Russia was not yet strong enough to display open resentment. In 1571, a year after this alliance, the Krim Tartars sent an expedition against Moscow. The city was taken by storm and sacked ; thousands of the inhabitants perished in the flames. The Tsar, who had in the previous year been tormenting his subjects in the most fearful manner on suspicion of treason, fled ingloriously from his capital, and found an asylum among his long-suffering people elsewhere.

As the reign of the terrible Ivan wore slowly to its close there was ostensibly peace between the Tsar and the Grand Signior, and after his death came a period of anarchy and rival claims which prevented any attempt at foreign aggrandisement. After the House of Románov, however, had become fairly established on the throne, the natural and constant jealousies between the two peoples increased, and actual conflict became imminent. The Tartars were a perpetual thorn in the side of Russia, and the Cossacks were scarcely less irritating to Turkey. There were frequent petty wars in the latter part of the seventeenth century. In 1696 Peter the Great took Azov and gained a footing on the shores of the Black Sea ; but the Peace of Carlowitz had discouraged the Turks too much for resistance, and in 1700 a treaty of peace was concluded for thirty years. Meanwhile the Tsar went on fortifying Azov, and the Turks met his preparations by building the fortress of Yenikale.   The struggle with Charles XII. of

Sweden diverted Peter from his designs upon Turkey, and when the former took refuge with the
Sultan after the defeat at Pultowa, Ahmed III. had
the courage to refuse to deliver him up to the Tsar.
War broke out between Russia and the Porte in
1710, in spite of the thirty years' treaty, and Peter
the Great found himself surrounded by a superior
force of Ottomans beside the river Pruth. The Grand
Vezīr had the founder of Russian greatness in
his power ; but the quick wit and heavy bribes of
Catherine extricated her consort and saved Russia.
Treaties of peace were common transactions between
the two Powers ; one followed in 1711, and another,
sworn for all eternity, in 1720. The Tsar and the
Sultan joined together in a scheme for the partition
of Persia, and eventually effected an advantageous
peace with the Shah.

It was but few years after this that the belief gained
ground in many parts of Europe that the Ottoman
Empire was tottering to its fall, a belief that has
strengthened with time. In our own century it found
its expression in the historic words of the emperor
Nicholas (in 1844) when, referring to the decline of
the Ottomans, he said to Sir Hamilton Seymour, " We
have on our hands a sick man, a very sick man." It
was at that date generally thought that the Turks
might be speedily driven from Europe and their
possessions divided among the Christian nations.

The humiliation of Peter the Great on the banks
of the Pruth was not forgotten. Resentment for this
disgrace was nursed by the sovereigns and the people
ever after. Peter II. massed materials of war at

convenient places, and was just ready for a campaign when his death occurred in 1727. The enterprise was hindered by circumstances until 1736, when the Tsaritza Anne thought that the moment for revenge had arrived, and in March of that year put her troops in motion. In 1739 the Peace of Belgrade temporarily closed a struggle that had been carried on with frequent attempts at peace ; but it did not afford the expected gratification of revenge. The terms were much too honourable to the Ottomans to satisfy Russia.

It was twenty-nine years, however, before the conflict was renewed. In 1768 indignation arose at Constantinople against Russia on account of the occupation of Poland by her troops, and the fraudulent election of Poniatovski, the favourite of Queen Catherine II., as king, events that resulted in the "dismemberment" of that unhappy state. War was entered upon by the Sultan before he was prepared. It was pursued with very indifferent generalship on both sides, except when Rumiantzov led the Russians, till 1774, and its two most interesting features were the appearance of a Russian fleet, largely officered by Englishmen, upon the coasts of Greece, and the able defence of Silistria in 1773 by the Turks. It was closed by the treaty of Kaynarji, dated July 21st, by design of the Russians, since that was the date also of the disgrace of the Pruth which it was hoped to obliterate. By this treaty Russia gained many advantages. The Crimean khanate and the Danubian principalities were made practically independent, and while resigning her conquests

Russia retained the strong fortresses on the Euxine and Sea of Azov. The treaty of Kaynarji was a definite step towards that dissolution of the Turkish Empire which has long been the dream of the Slavs. One of the empress's grandchildren was named Constantine, and a gate at Moscow was designated " The Way to Constantinople," as expressive of her faith in Russian destiny.

The subsequent progress of the international struggle is marked by the treaties of Jassy, Bucharest, Akkerman, and Adrianople. The Tartars of the Crimea had by the treaty of Kaynarji been declared an independent nation with the internal affairs of which Russia had bound herself not to interfere. In spite of this agreement, however, the empress had laid her plans to take possession of the Crimea, even before signing the treaty in which she so solemnly declared that she would do nothing of the kind. In 1783, the region was accordingly annexed to her dominions, and Constantinople was again agitated. England, however, was then dominated with the idea of a great northern league against France, and would not oppose Russia ; deprived of allies, the Sultan was obliged to acquiesce in the new state of affairs.

In 1787, the empress Catherine visited her new dominions in company with the emperor Joseph of Austria, and set up a pompous inscription on a gate of the city of Kherson, at the mouth of the Dnieper, to the effect that it opened towards Byzantium.[1]

---

[1] For an account of this visit see " Lettres du prince de Ligne á la marquise de Coigny, pendant l'année 1787, publiées avec un préface par M. de Lescure," pp. xxi. 69. Paris, Librairie des Bibliophiles, 1886.

Then the Ottomans could restrain themselves no longer, but, though again unprepared, declared war. In December, 1788, occurred the siege of Ochákov, a strongly garrisoned place which was expected to hold the northerners back from Moldavia and Wallachia. The Russian soldiery, after an exhibition of Turkish butchery in a neighbouring village, were incited to the deepest desire for vengeance, and pressed forward against all odds until the garrison was overcome. Then they gave free reign to their appetite for pillage and murder, and for three days the slaughter was merciless. Only some three hundred persons, chiefly women and children, were left alive out of forty thousand.

The following year, Suvorov, the Russian general to whom the success at Ochákov was due, was directed to advance upon the still stronger fortress of Ismail on the delta of the Danube, some forty miles from the Black Sea. The place was taken by a night assault ; but upon entering it the Russians found that the severest fighting was yet before them, and the struggle was continued in the streets. Throughout all the following day butchery raged without mercy. For three days after they were overcome, the inhabitants were given up to the brutality of their conquerors, and thousands were slain.

War closed with the pacification of Jassy, in January, 1792, a treaty being solemnly signed as usual " In the name of the Almighty." In this document a sincere desire was expressed on the part of the empress and the Sultan to reëstablish peace, friendship, and good understanding, which had been interrupted by "trifling considerations," and to make it enduring.

In the treaty of Kaynarji (1774) the Russians had managed to insert an article intended to make Turkey acknowledge them as exercising in some sort the office of protectors of the Christian subjects of the Porte. In the treaty of Yassy (1791) an article was inserted bearing in the same direction, for Catherine, like Peter the Great, saw the advantages that would accrue to Russia if she could fix her power in that quarter. She did not, of course, honestly feel the sentiments that she expressed through her representatives at Yassy, but went on with preparations for the most formidable campaign that had ever been planned against the Ottoman Empire. Death happily interrupted her schemes in November 1796.

The plans of Russia were, however, simply interrupted, they were to be resumed again at the first opportunity, and accordingly in 1806, we find her armies at Yassy, and marching into Moldavia and Wallachia without a declaration of war. Again there was consternation and indignation at Constantinople. War measures were adopted, but they effected nothing decisive. Meantime a peace was determined at Tilsit in June, 1807, between the Tsar and the Emperor of the French, who theatrically embraced on a raft in the middle of the river Niemen, swore eternal friendship, and agreed that the Ottoman Empire should be at the mercy of Russia.[1] Such was the secret understanding : the public treaty however professed to provide for the evacuation by Russia of the Danubian principalities, and the Tsar made some show of preparing to retreat.

[1] The " eternal " friendship between Alexander and Napoleon lasted five years.

Austria meanwhile was engaged in the disastrous war with Buonaparte which ended in the battle of Wagram and the Peace of Schönbrunn ; and, relieved from any fear of Austrian interference, the Tsar resolved on more active measures against Turkey.

A new and important influence had however arisen at Constantinople. England had been formally at war with the Porte in consequence of our alliance with Russia. When the Tsar embraced Napoleon at Tilsit this purely diplomatic rupture was no longer necessary, and Sir Robert Adair negotiated the Peace of the Dardanelles in 1809. In the following year he left the Embassy, and Stratford Canning, then a young man of 23, became Minister Plenipotentiary. In spite of his youth and inexperience, and notwithstanding a complete want of instructions from England during the entire period of his mission, Canning set himself to defeat the intrigues of the French, and succeeded. Napoleon's object was to weaken Russia, upon whom he was already meditating his attack, by prolonging the war with Turkey, which had been continued in a desultory manner for several years, without any conspicuous advantage to either belligerent. He bribed Austria by a promise of a partition of Turkey, just as he had bribed Russia at Tilsit. He threatened the Turks with his high displeasure, the displeasure of the one overwhelming sovereign of Europe, if they listened to the voice of England—the voice of the one resolute champion of liberty against universal despotism. He promised the Porte his favour and protection if it would prolong the war. Everything seemed in his favour, and it appeared inconceivable that the Porte would throw over so powerful a patron.

In face of these tremendous odds, Canning used his diplomatic genius. It was all he had, for military or naval support was denied him. Yet by mere reasoning, by exposing the treachery of Napoleon, by revealing his successive schemes of partition, by working upon the fears and prejudices of the Turkish ministers with that consummate skill which in after years gained him the title of "the Great Elchi," he prevailed. He induced the Porte to make peace with Russia, even at the sacrifice of territory. A new frontier was drawn at the river Pruth by the Treaty of Bucharest, signed in May, 1812.

This treaty was wholly due to the indefatigable efforts of the British Minister, and Canning had been actuated not alone by the desire to spare the Porte the defeat which must eventually have come upon it, but by other reasons of high European policy. The one chance of overcoming the domineering power of France was to enable Russia to withstand her. Therefore he worked day and night to release the Russian army from its duties in Turkey, and he succeeded just in time. Scarcely was the treaty of Bucharest signed when Napoleon began his fatal march to Moscow, and the action of Chichakov's army of the Danube upon his flank was the *coup de grâce* of the disastrous retreat. English diplomacy finished the work of a Russian winter.

XIV.

STAMBOL.

CONSTANTINOPLE stands on the finest site in Europe. St. Petersburg with its noble river, Stockholm on its many islands, Venice the bride of the sea, cannot rival the ancient city of the Eastern Caesars. To see Rome and die is mere gratuitous suicide when the other Rome, the beautiful city of Constantine, remains to be visited. There is hardly a scene in the world so replete with natural beauty, so rich in storied recollections, as that enclosed betwixt the Bosphorus and

> "the dark blue water
> That swiftly glides and gently swells
> Between the winding Dardanelles."

We have left the Plain of Troy behind, and can almost fancy that we saw the mound of Patroclus; there beyond is "many-fountained Ida," and opposite stands the rocky island of Tenedos, where the Danai moored their fleet during the ten weary years of the siege. We are entering the Hellespont, where the Theban maid fell from the golden ram, and perished in the strait that bears her name. High on the right, ever veiled with clouds, rises Bithynian Olympus, beneath which, we know, cluster the green groves and exquisite mosques of Brusa, the old Turkish capital, invisible from the sea. We are in the enchanted land of Byron when we look upon Abydos, and think of the fatal night,—

> " on Helle's wave,
> When Love, who sent, forgot to save
> The young, the beautiful, the brave ; "

and then suddenly we are carried back to the stormy days of early Christian history, when an inlet in the southern shore of the Propontis indicates the direction of Nicaea, and the ruined site of Chalcedon comes into view. But the islands that fringe the coast take us once more to a new region of association, not ancient history, nor yet romance, but modern politics ; for these are the Prince's Isles, where the British fleet lay during the critical weeks when the death warrant of Turkey was being drawn up at St. Stefano exactly opposite.

As the eye passes St. Stefano an imposing block of grey walls and feudal-looking battlements comes into the vision. This is the Castle of the Seven Towers, where it was the usual custom of the Porte to incarcerate the minister of a foreign power upon declaration of war. These grey walls, in triple ranks, are part of old Byzantium ; there are stones here that were laid in the time of Constantine, and renewed by Theodosius. They enclose the whole city in a circuit of twelve miles, and once they were nearly impregnable. Now they are overgrown with shrubs and creepers; the towers are torn with gaping rents, the breaches of many sieges are discernible in the crumbling ruins, and the scene is one of melancholy decay and desolation.

The old walls run out to a point, and then wind round to the north, bounding the harbour. The Point is crowned by a group of irregular ruinous buildings, and a few better preserved kiosques, which are all that remain of the Seraglio of the Grand Signior. Over them rise the bulbous dome and cupolas of St. Sophia, with its Turkish minarets, and beyond are other domes and minarets innumerable. Rounding Seraglio Point, the vessel glides into the Golden Horn —the wide inlet which forms the splendid harbour of Constantinople, and divides the city into its European and its Turkish quarters. On the left or west side is Istambol, or Stambol, the ancient Byzantium, which is now entirely inhabited by Mohammedans, as might be guessed from the long line of mosques that fringes the Seven Hills, from St. Sophia hard by the Seraglio to the shrine of the conqueror Mohammed II. at the northern extremity, near the picturesque village of Eyyūb; and also from the dilapidated and irregular style of the soft-toned houses that crowd the slopes below and around the mosques. On the right of the Golden Horn is the European quarter, known as Galata near the water's edge, and as Pera on the top of the steep hill where the European colony has its houses and the Embassies their town palaces. Galata is the mercantile and shipping quarter; Pera is the West End of Constantinople in all but the points of the compass. It has not many good looks to boast, how-

F. HERINGTON

SERAGLIO POINT.

ever. Its high street or " Grande Rue " is sloped at the
angle of a roof, and in places is as narrow as an alley ;
the shops are, with few exceptions, poor and dirty, and
very few good houses are to be seen, though there are,
in reality, some comfortable mansions secluded behind
high walls and within dusty gardens.

Further to the east are the country houses of both
Turks and Christians, sheltered in the combes that divide
the swelling downs that bound the Bosphorus on the
north. From the top of the hill of Pera, where the
hideous German Embassy enjoys one of the finest
views in the world, and where one can see the Golden
Horn and the Propontis laid out like a beautiful map, a
couple of miles downhill brings us to the little village
of Ortaköy, with a pretty mosque, and the best
caïques on the Bosphorus. Entering one of these
delicious boats, we round the slight promontory, and
find ourselves at Bebek, a lovely village, nestled in
trees up the bosom of a ravine, and forming a strange
contrast with the frowning Castle of Europe, which,
just beyond, rears its round towers against the sky,
as it did when Mohammed II. built it as a preliminary
to the conquest of Constantinople. Further on are
Therapia and Buyukderé. Therapia is the Richmond
of Pera. When the weather becomes hot, all who can
afford a country-house go to Therapia, where they can
enjoy the cool breeze that blows from the Black Sea.
The British Embassy looks straight down the Bosphorus to the mouth, where Jason found the
Wandering Rocks when he went to seek for the
Golden Fleece. It was in the old residence here that
the Great Elchi passed his summer after he had fought

his famous diplomatic duel with Prince Menshikov. "Living close over the gates of the Bosphorus, he seemed to stand guard against the North, and to answer for the safety of his charge."

The whole tone of the country by night or by day is lovely. As we see it we begin to understand Byron's enthusiasm when he saw

> " the land of the cedar and vine,
> Where the flowers ever blossom, the beams ever shine ;
> Where the light wings of Zephyr, oppressed with perfume,
> Wax faint in the gardens of Gul in her bloom ;
> Where the citron and olive are fairest of fruit,
> And the voice of the nightingale never is mute ;
> Where the tints of the earth and the hues of the sky,
> In colour though varied, in beauty may vie,
> And the purple of ocean is deepest in dye ;
> Where the virgins are soft as the roses they twine,
> And all save the spirit of man is divine."

No scene more perfect can be conceived than the Bosphorus by moonlight, with the red of the sunset dying away into a pale yellow sheen over the minarets of Stambol ; the hills, clothed with dark cypresses, stand out like ramparts on either hand, ever and again cleft with a deep ravine, where a few lights reveal the presence of a little village ; along the shores are ranged the white palaces of the Sultan and his race, many of them deserted and ruinous, shining like pale but stately ghosts in the cold beams of the climbing moon. Beglerbeg and Dolmabaghché are no longer the homes of the Grand Signior. He lives on the top of the hill of Beshiktash, in his new mansion of Yildiz Köshki, or "Star Kiosque," and the old palaces are left to go to ruin, like many another fine old Turkish house which overhangs the water, into which it must speedily fall, a type of the history of the nation.

The Sultan, however, shows judgment in choosing for his residence a height whence a magnificent view is obtained, and where he is far removed from the bad odours and dirt of Stambol. The old Seraglio is incomparably picturesque, but when one approaches it through the filthy streets, and sees the squalor and mud and ruin that make up the Turkish quarter, one ceases to wonder at the removal of the Sultan from Eski Serāy, until one finds oneself inside its enchanted courts, when the dirt is forgotten, and one marvels how any prince could wish for a nobler site wherein to pass his days.

Among the groves of plane and cypress that clothe the apex of the triangle on which the ancient city of Constantinople is built, the domes and minarets of the Seraglio [1] stand forth conspicuously still. Here in the days of their glory dwelt the Othmanli Sultans, surrounded by all the luxury and magnificence that Oriental imagination could devise. This beautiful palace-city, with its marble and gilded kiosques, its gardens, flowers, and fountains, must have recalled the enchanted palaces and fairy cities of the Thousand and One Nights. But admiration must have been touched with horror, for many a gloomy oubliette and grim-looking pile awakened thoughts of

---

[1] Europeans frequently use the word *Seraglio* as a synonym for *harem*, *i.e.*, that portion of a dwelling set apart for the use of the women of the household. It really means the entire imperial residence, being a corruption of the Eastern *serày*, or palace.

the hideous tragedies that were from time to time
enacted within those walls ; and in the end the
ghastly recollections which these monuments called
forth proved its ruin.   Abd-ul-Mejīd, gentlest of
Sultans, unable to endure the sight of a place so
haunted by the crimes of his ancestors, abandoned
the old Seraglio for one of those gay and cheerful
mansions which his father had erected on the shores
of the Bosphorus.   Since that time the old palace of
the Sultans, deserted by its imperial masters, has fallen
to decay ; more than one terrible fire has swept across
the point on which it stands, and now little remains,
save the outer courts, of what was once the favourite
residence of some of the mightiest of monarchs.

In the latter half of the eighteenth century this
palace, which might perhaps be more correctly described as a small town, consisted of a number of
independent buildings erected at different times on
the gardens situated at the point of land where the
Bosphorus enters the Sea of Marmora.   On all sides
but one it was surrounded by the sea, from which it
was protected by a tower-flanked wall some thirty
feet in height, while another similar wall shut it in
from the city, the circuit of the whole being nearly
three miles.   The buildings were, for the most part,
upon the rising ground that runs along towards the
Seraglio Point, while the gardens stretched down to
the sea on either side.   A quay, on which were
mounted several large pieces of artillery, ran along
outside the whole length of the sea-wall, which, as
well as the city-wall, was pierced with a number of
gates, but one only was in general use.   This was

the great gate of the Seraglio, the Bāb-i Humāyūn
or Imperial Gate, that " Sublime Porte," from which
the Ottoman Government derives the name by which
it is best known.   Piled up on one side, just without
this gate, were pyramids of heads, trophies of victory
over Greek or Serbian rebels, as ghastly as the skulls
that once bleached upon London Bridge or over
Temple Bar.

Entering under the lofty arch, where fifty Kapujis
or porters stood on guard, the visitor found himself in
the first of the four courts of the Seraglio.   This
court, which, like the others, lay open to the sky, was
rather mean in appearance for the vestibule of a
palace.   Several buildings stood on each side ; the
public treasury, the orangery, the infirmary, and the
bakery occupying the right, while the timber-yard, the
stables, the armoury, the mint, and several other
offices, were ranged along the left.   The armoury,
which still exists, was an old Byzantine church
dedicated to St. Irene, but turned to its present use
by the Turks on their capture of the city.   In it are
preserved the keys of many cities taken by the Ottomans in the days of their prosperity.   To enter the
second court it was necessary to traverse a passage of
about fifteen feet in length, closed by a gate at either
end.   This passage, which was hung with old arms,
trophies of Ottoman valour on many a hard-fought
field, was one of those places to which terrible
memories clung.   Here Vezīrs and other great men
who had forfeited their master's favour were arrested,
and shown the fatal warrant that contained their
doom ; and here they died by the bowstring.

The outer gate of this passage, which went by the
name of the Orta Kapu, or the Middle Gate, was
guarded by fifty porters. In the second court, which
none but the Sultan might enter on horseback, the
paths alone were paved, the rest of the ground being
laid out in grass plots surrounded by rows of cypresses,
and watered by fountains, while all round the court
ran a low gallery covered with lead, and supported by
marble columns, under which, on days of ceremony,
the Janissaries were drawn up. The whole of the
right side of this court was occupied by the offices
and kitchens, while on the left, among other buildings,
stood the Record Office, the Hall of the Divan, the
Office of the Grand Eunuch, and the Outer Treasury,
where was kept the store of those robes of honour,
which the Sultans used to bestow on such persons as
found favour in their eyes. On certain days in every
week a court of justice, presided over by the Grand
Vezīr, was held in the Hall of the Divan, which was
open to every subject of the Sultan who had cause of
complaint against his neighbour. Here the dis-
putants came and personally pleaded their cause
before the highest tribunal in the empire, with a good
chance of a just settlement of their case ; for the
Vezīrs never knew whether the Sultan himself might
not be watching them from the curtained gallery,
which communicated with the inner courts of the
Seraglio, and had been built in order that the Pādishāh
might be able to come unobserved and see what
manner of justice was administered in his name.
Not far from the Dīvān-Khāna stood the Hall
of the Ambassadors, where the Grand Signior

GATE OF FELICITY IN THE SERAGLIO.

used to receive the representatives of foreign monarchs.[1]

These two courts, the first and second, formed the
outer portion of the Seraglio, and were almost of a
public character.   They were attended during the day
by a vast number of officers, guards, and servants,
collectively known as the Aghayān-i Bīrūn, or Masters of the Outside, not one of whom was permitted to
pass into the third court, where the private establishment of the Sultan began.   This inner division, which
was served by the Aghayān-i Enderūn, or Masters of
the Inside, *i.e.*, the Four Chambers of pages and the
two corps of eunuchs, was entered by a gate called
the Bāb-i Sa'ādet, or Gate of Felicity.   On passing
through this doorway an entirely new scene presented
itself ; instead of the rectangular courts which formed
the outer portion of the palace, there appeared an
extensive garden, studded with many buildings, large
and small, arranged in no apparent order, but all
glittering with gold and marble.   Conspicuous among
the kiosques and fountains, some of which were of
extreme beauty, stood the pavilion of the Sultan, the
Seraglio mosque and library, the immense halls of the
pages—one for each of the Four Chambers—the apartments of the eunuchs, a magnificent suite of baths, and
the imperial Treasury.   In this last were preserved the
priceless art treasures of the Sultans, a dazzling array
of beautiful and costly objects, gifts of princely allies
and vassal kings, or trophies of many a devastated
land and plundered capital ; there, indeed,

[1] The first and second courts of the Seraglio still exist in a nearly
complete condition.

> " Jewels wept from bleeding crowns,
>   Spoils of woful fields and towns."

The treasury was burnt down in 1574, and most of its precious contents were destroyed. Whatever the Turks had preserved of the treasures of old Byzantium and the library of Matthias Corvinus doubtless perished in the flames. But the collection which has since been gathered together in the later building gives one some idea of what the Sultan's treasure house must have contained in the days of Suleymān the Magnificent. Within the badly-lighted and ill-arranged chambers of the modern treasury are such gems and precious stuffs as could not be believed in unless they were actually seen, as the author saw them in 1886. Huge emeralds as large as the palm of one's hand, garments positively plated with great table diamonds, maces and daggers whose hilts held gems as large as hen's eggs, jewelled aigrettes, and robes of state standing up stiff with gold and precious stones. The splendid gems which glow in every inch of the glass cases are almost all uncut, as is the fashion of the East, and their glittering brilliancy is thus concealed within their formless outlines ; and the workmanship of most of the thrones and other objects is rich and elaborate rather than tasteful. Even the arms are not so beautiful as might have been expected, though the coat which Murad IV. wore at the siege of Baghdad is a fine piece of chain armour. Art was never a strong point with the Turks, except when they employed others to work for them, or copied earlier models ; but in magnificence, in solid wealth of gold and precious stones, the Sultan's treasury leaves one in a condition of dazed stupefaction. Nothing to compare with its barbaric splendour exists in any other European capital.

Jealously guarded in another building lay, and indeed still lie, the sacred relics of the Prophet Mohammed. These, which passed into the possession of the Ottoman monarchs when the last of the Abbasides made over to Selīm I. the office and dignity of the Khalifate, consist of a few seemingly trivial objects, the most prominent among which are the mantle and banner of the great reformer—the mantle which he threw over the old Arab poet, Ka'b ibn Zubeyr, in token of his delight with an ode which the latter improvised and which has ever since been famous as the Poem of the Mantle ;—his banner, that Sanjak-i Sherīf, or Holy Oriflamme, under which in olden days Khalifs and Sultans used to lead their hosts to victory. Near the further end of this division of the Seraglio, in a place called the Chimshirlik, or Boxwood Shrubbery, were twelve pavilions, each containing several rooms, and each surrounded by a high wall enclosing a little garden. This was the Kafes, or Cage, the residence of the imperial princes, sons of the Sultan. Each prince, in his separate pavilion, from which he was not allowed to come forth without the special permission of his father, was attended by some ten or twelve fair girls and a number of young pages ; and these were the only companions whom he might see and converse with, except the black eunuchs to whom his education was confided.

Beyond this third division of the Seraglio,—separated from it by a massive wall, pierced by a single

passage which was closed by four gates, two of bronze
and two of iron, whereat black eunuchs stood on guard
night and day—lay the imperial harem, another large
garden, stretching down to the sea-wall, and dotted,
like the former, with numerous detached buildings.
The harem was exclusively tenanted by the women of
the imperial household; no man save the Sultan himself
was allowed to explore that paradise of earthly houris;
even the Grand Eunuch must receive his imperial master's permission before he ventured to pass through
the fourfold gate. In the middle of the harem garden
rose the Sultan's pavilion, blazing with cloth of gold
and hangings embroidered with precious stones. Each
of the Kadins, or wives of the Pādishāh, (there were
usually four,) had a pavilion containing ten or twelve
rooms and a suite of attendants of her own; while
the other women were provided with apartments suited
to their respective positions. There were, of course,
besides these, numerous baths, kiosques, summer-
houses, and similar places, where the ladies of the
Seraglio, who were forbidden to pass beyond the
harem bounds except on certain stated occasions,
might amuse themselves as best they could.

The palace officials consisted of the Aghayān-i
Bīrūn, or Masters of the Outside, and the Aghayān-i
Enderūn, or Masters of the Inside. The former,
whose duties lay exclusively in the two outer courts
and who might never pass beyond the Gate of Felicity,
were divided into eight classes: the Ulemā, or
Doctors; the Rikāb Aghalari, or Masters of the
Stirrup; the Umenā, or Intendants; the Shikār
Aghalari, or Masters of the Hunt; officers subor-

dinated to the Grand Eunuch, officers subordinated
to the Kilar Kyahyasi, or Comptroller of the Buttery,
the Body-guards, and the Palace Guards.

The class of doctors consisted of five officers : the
Khoja, or titular Tutor of the Sultan, the First and
Second Imāms or Chaplains, the Chief Physician,
the Chief Astrologer, the Chief Chirurgeon, and the
Chief Oculist. The duty of the chaplains was to
replace the Sultan in the mosque at the Bayram
feasts, when, as head of the religion, he was supposed
to lead the public worship. The Chief Physician,
who had under his orders about eighteen members
of his craft, used to derive a considerable profit from
the preparation of ma'jūn. This was a sort of sweet-
meat composed of essence of opium, aloes-wood,
ambergris, and other aromatics, which he composed
and sent in china vases at the Nev-rūz, or Festival
of the Vernal Equinox, to the Sultan and the
members of his family, to the Grand Vezīr and other
great men of the state, from all of whom he received
handsome gifts in return. The Chief Astrologer's
business was to consult the stars as to the prospects
of any projected action, and to prepare an annual
almanac in which all the lucky and unlucky days
were indicated. The Chief Oculist was charged
with the preparation of the surma, or collyrium,
which the ladies of the harem rubbed upon their
eyelids.

The Masters of the Stirrup, so called because they
were supposed to attend the Sultan when he rode,
comprised five great officers : the Lord of the Banner,
the Chief Gardener, the First and Second Lords of

the Stable, and the Comptroller of the Porters.
Besides these functionaries there was a corps of
gentlemen, about five hundred strong, called the
Kapuji Bashis, or Chief Porters, who were all
reckoned among the Masters of the Stirrup. None
but the sons of Pashas or Vezīrs were eligible for
admission into this select body, the members of
which acted as chamberlains on state occasions, when
they wore a long robe of cloth of gold trimmed with
sable and a curious-looking gilt head-dress surmounted by an enormous crest of white plumes,
shaped somewhat like an umbrella. When a foreign
ambassador was admitted into the imperial presence,
it was by the Chief Porters that he was introduced.
One of their number stood on guard every night at
the Middle Gate, at the entrance to the Second
Court of the palace. The Lord of the Banner had
charge of the imperial standards and of the seven tughs,
or horsetails, of the Sultan.[1] He also commanded
the corps of Chief Porters, and was superintendent
of the military music of the palace.

One of the most influential officers of the court
was the Bostanji Bashi, or Chief Gardener. This
functionary was governor of the Seraglio and over-
seer of all the Sultan's gardens and summer palaces.
The shores of the Bosphorus and Sea of Marmora,
from the entrance to the Black Sea as far as the
Dardanelles were all under his inspection ; and no

---

[1] The Tugh, or ensign of the Turkish tribes, was originally the tail of
a yak, but when the Ottomans left Central Asia, that of a horse was
substituted. Governors of provinces received one, two, or three tughs,
according to their rank ; the Sultan alone displayed seven.

one might erect, or even repair, any kind of building on the land subject to his jurisdiction without his permission, which had to be paid for. He was ranger of the forests in the neighbourhood of Constantinople, and had charge of the royal hunt and fisheries. Among his duties was the steering of the imperial barge whenever the Sultan went on the waters over which he exercised control, an office which afforded him many opportunities of confidential communication. He had moreover to preside at the execution of great men, when that took place within the Seraglio precincts, and to superintend the prison where suspected officials were put to the torture. D'Ohsson tells us that the mere mention of this dismal place, which was situated close to the Seraglio bakeries and consequently called the Fur, or Oven, was sufficient to inspire terror.

The First Lord of the Stable had under his orders upwards of a thousand equerries, six hundred grooms, a body of six thousand Bulgarians, known as Voynuks, who acted as grooms to the army in time of war, the Koru Aghas, or rangers of the parks, and finally, all the saddlers, camel-drivers, and muleteers attached to the palace service. All the meadows and prairies belonging to the Crown, that lay between Adrianople and Brusa, were under his charge ; and he was entitled to grant private individuals, on payment of a certain sum, the right of turning out their horses to graze on the same. In times of peace the Voynuks were usually employed in looking after the Sultan's horses out at grass on these vast plains.

The Comptroller of the Porters received the written

petitions which were, and still are, presented to the Pādishāh on his appearance in public. On gala days he, in conjunction with the Chawush Bashi, or Chief Herald, an officer belonging to the eighth class of the Masters of the Outside, exercised the functions of marshal of the court. When the Grand Vezīr was summoned to confer with the Sultan, these two officials, dressed in long fur-trimmed robes and wearing the tall white cylindrical head-dress known as mujevveza, met him at the Seraglio gate and marched slowly five or six paces in front of him, striking the ground at regular intervals with the silver staffs which they carried in their hands, till they reached the Gate of Felicity where the minister was received by two of the great officers of the household. The Second Lord of the Stable had charge of the royal mews.

The Intendants also comprised five functionaries: these were the Intendant of the City, the Intendant of the Mint, the Intendant of the Kitchens, the Intendant of the Barley, and the Imperial Steward. All these officials belonged to the body of Khojagān, or Chancellors.

The five Masters of the Hunt were the Av Aghasi, or Master of the Chase, the Chief Falconer, the Chief Merlin-keeper, the Chief Hawker, and the Chief Sparrow-hawker. These officers were latterly purely titular, as the Sultans had long ceased to be sportsmen.

In the fifth class, or officers subordinated to the Grand Eunuch, we have four functionaries. The Chief Tent-pitcher, who had under his orders a body of eight hundred men whose duty it was to pitch the

Sultan's tents wherever he might wish to pass the day, whether in the Seraglio gardens or in one of his numerous pleasaunces in the environs of Constantinople. The meanest individuals of the corps of tent-pitchers acted as executioners, and four or five of these always stood at the Middle Gate in order to be at hand should their services be required. (2) The Chief Treasurer, who had charge of the old archives of the finance department, and of the store of robes of honour which were bestowed on favoured individuals, and of the satin covers in which the imperial despatches were usually wrapped up—twenty storekeepers obeyed his orders. (3) The Chief Merchant, who had to procure the cloth, muslin, &c., required for the imperial household. And lastly, the Chief Presentkeeper, who had charge of all the presents offered by his subjects or by foreign ministers to the Grand Signior.

The sixth class, the officers subordinated to the Comptroller of the Buttery, the head of the Third Chamber of Pages, consisted of six members. The Chief Assayer, or Taster, under whom were about fifty assayers whose only duty was to wait upon the Grand Vezīr and other ministers when they dined in the Hall of the Divan, which they usually did after holding a court of justice. The title arose in old times when kings and other great men used to have an officer who first tasted their food to see if it was not poisoned. The Chief Musician, who commanded (under the Lord of the Banner) the military band of the palace, which was composed of sixteen hautboys, sixteen drums, eleven trumpets, eight kettle-drums, seven pairs of cymbals, and four great tymbals. The

Chief Baker, who had about five hundred bakers under him. The Master of the Buttery, who was over one hundred servants. The Chief Cook, under whom worked likewise a hundred of his craft. And finally, the Chief Confectioner, who superintended some five hundred comfit-makers. This great array of cooks, confectioners, and so on, all wore the same uniform, a green cloth robe and a pointed cap of white felt, which in shape bore some resemblance to a large champagne bottle.

The seventh class, the Body-guards, formed two corps: the Solaks or Sinistrals, and the Peyks or Couriers. The Solaks consisted of four companies of Janissaries, of one hundred men each, under the command of a captain called the Solak Bashi or Chief Sinistral, and two lieutenants. These soldiers were richly dressed, their gilt headpieces being surmounted by a lofty plume; their officers wore robes of green velvet trimmed with lynx fur. The Peyks or Couriers formed a body of one hundred and fifty men under the orders of an officer who bore the title of Peyk Bashi or Chief Courier. Their uniform was not less splendid than that of the Sinistrals; they wore helmets of gilt bronze adorned with a black crest, and were armed with gilded halberds. Their costume is said to have been borrowed from that of the body-guards of the old Byzantine emperors, whose gorgeous court doubtless furnished the model for many of the institutions which appeared in the Seraglio of their successors. When the Sultan rode in state through the streets, the Sinistrals and Couriers used to march on foot round his horse.

The Palace Guards, who formed the last class of the Masters of the Outside, consisted of the following six corps: the Bostanjis or Gardeners, the Khāssekīs or Royals, the Baltajis or Halberdiers, the Zulfli Baltajis or Tressed Halberdiers, the Chawushes or Heralds, and the Kapujis or Porters. The Bostanjis or Gardeners, who numbered about two thousand five hundred men, nominally formed part of the Ojak or army-corps of the Janissaries. They were the real guards of the Seraglio; and to members of their body was entrusted the protection of the various imperial parks and pleasure grounds. They also acted as gardeners, whence their name. One of their duties was to row the imperial barge when the Sultan was on board. The Gardeners could be recognized by their high cylindrical caps of red felt with a long flap hanging down behind. The Bostanji Bashi or Chief Gardener, whom we have already seen among the Masters of the Stirrup, was the commander-in-chief of this large and important corps; he had under him a number of officers whose special titles it is unnecessary to enumerate here. The Khāssekīs or Royals formed a body of three hundred men usually chosen from among the Gardeners. They wore a red uniform and were armed with a two-edged sword. The Baltajis or Halberdiers, who numbered four hundred, were nominally the guards of the Queens and the imperial princes and princesses; but the only occasions on which they really attended those august personages were when the Sultan took some of the members of his harem to bear him company during a journey or on a campaign. Then the Baltajis marched beside the ladies' carriages and at night camped round their tents. On these occasions they were armed with halberds, whence they received their name. It was they who carried the bier at the funeral of a Sultan or a member of the imperial family. The Zulfli Baltajis or Tressed Halberdiers, who were so called because they wore two artificial tresses of hair which were attached to their caps and hung down, one along each cheek, numbered a hundred and twenty men, and were appointed to serve the pages of the First or Royal Chamber. The Chawushes or Heralds formed a corps of six hundred and thirty men, divided into fifteen companies ; they marched first in all the imperial processions. Whenever the Sultan made his appearance in state the Heralds shouted the Alkish or Acclaim, the Turkish equivalent to *Vive le Roi ;* it was : " God give long life to our lord the Pādishāh !" The Kapujis or Porters, who formed the last division of the Palace Guards, were eight hundred strong ; one of the oldest of the corps always followed the Sultan when he appeared in public, carrying a stool decorated with silver, on which His Majesty placed his foot when mounting or dismounting his horse.

Except those actually on guard, very few of this army of Masters of the Outside passed the night in the Seraglio ; during the day they attended, when necessary, in the two outer courts, or played their part in the gorgeous ceremonies and state processions which were constantly occurring ; but most of them were married and had houses in the city to which they retired when the duties of the day were over. In this they differed widely from the Masters of the Inside, none of whom could leave the inner division of the palace without permission, or marry, or wear a beard. All the officers and servants of the Imperial household, even the Sultan's sons and brothers, had to shave their faces all but the moustaches; the Pādishāh alone might wear a beard. Except in the case of the Bostanjis and the Body-guards, this rule did not hold with the Masters of the Outside, who were permitted to let the beard grow, as was till a few years ago the universal practice with all Turks, other than servants and private soldiers and sailors.

The Aghas or Masters of the Inside, who formed the private household of the Sultan, consisted of two classes, pages and eunuchs. The pages were divided into four companies called Odas or Chambers. The first of these was the Khāss Oda or Royal Chamber which comprised forty members, the Sultan himself being reckoned the fortieth. All the members of this company were officers of high standing and great influence. Their chief who commanded all the Four Chambers and acted as major-domo of the palace, bore the title of Silahdar Agha or Master Sword-bearer, because he always followed the Sultan, carrying the imperial scimitar in its scabbard over his shoulder, grasping it near the point, so that the hilt was behind his head. He wore a magnificent robe of scarlet and gold brocade, and a very strange head-dress adorned, like the cap of the Tressed Halberdiers, with two locks of artificial hair. No one, except perhaps the Grand Eunuch, was more intimate with the Sultan than the Sword-bearer, who often possessed immense influence, and was not unfrequently raised to the

Grand Vezîrship, Grand Admiralship, or some other
important office in the state.   Sixteen of the other
officers of this chamber had titles indicative of the
services they performed about the Sultan's person ;
thus there were the Master Vesturer, one of whose
duties was to follow the Sultan in processions and cast
handfuls of silver coins among the people ; the Master
Stirrup-holder, who held the Sultan's stirrup when he
mounted his horse ; the Master of the Turban, who
had charge of the imperial turbans, one of which he
carried in the processions, inclining it slightly to right
and left as a salutation to the people ; the Master of
the Napkin ; the Master Ewer-keeper, who poured the
water on the Sultan's hands when he made the
ablutions ; the Private Secretary ; the Chief Turban-
winder ; the Chief Coffee-server ; the Chief Barber, and
so on.

The second company of pages was called the Khazîna
Odasi or Treasury Chamber, and was intended to
guard the jewels and art treasures of the Crown.
Among their officers were the Comptroller of the
Treasury, who had among other duties to keep the
accounts of the imperial household : the Aigrette-
keeper, who looked after the aigrettes or ornaments of
jewels and feathers with which the royal turbans were
decorated ; the Robe-keeper, who had charge of the
state robes which were never presented to the Sultan
without having first been perfumed with aloes-wood ;
the Elder of the Plate, to whose care were entrusted
the services of porcelain ; the Chief Nightingale-keeper
and the Chief Parrot-keeper, who had charge of the
Sultan's birds.

The Third Chamber was that of the Buttery, its chief being called the Comptroller of the Buttery. The duty of this division of pages was to look after the bread, fruit, confections, sherbets, and other foods and drinks required for the Sultan and his harem. The Chief Assayer was one of their officers ; another was the Chief Minstrel, who had charge of the music of the interior of the palace, where stringed instruments— lutes, mandolines, and rebecs, enjoyed the greatest favour. The Sefer Odasi or Journey Chamber was the fourth and last. In old times its members used to accompany the Sultan when he went on a campaign ; but latterly it became a sort of school for singing, dancing, playing, &c.

Not one of the members of these Four Chambers was a Turk. They were all sons of Christians, who had been taken prisoner, kidnapped by brigands, or sent as tribute by vassal princes. When the Turks re-captured a rebel Greek town, when the Tartars made a foray into Hungary or Poland, when the Algerines took a Frankish vessel or surprised a French or Italian village,—and such things were of very frequent occur-rence a century or so ago—they invariably seized as many little children of both sexes as they could lay hands on, and sent the best to Constantinople, sure of obtaining a high price or reward if they were deemed of sufficient beauty and promise to be received into the Seraglio. If such was their lot, the boys were educated as Musulmans, either in a school set apart for that purpose in the palace itself or in a special establishment which existed at Galata. The reason for preferring such persons to native Turks was the idea that they would prove more faithful to their master; ignorant of country and parents, brought up with all the pride of Musulman and Turkish nobles, and knowing no master or benefactor save the Sultan who always made a point of treating them with kindness and liberality, and frequently appointed members of their body who displayed the necessary ability to the highest offices in the state, it was thought that they would naturally be more single minded in their loyalty and devotion to his interests and person than any natives, however well affected, who must have had many ties and connections beyond the palace walls. All the eunuchs were foreigners, and all the women of the harem were foreigners, acquired as prisoners of war or purchased from Georgian or Circassian parents; indeed there was not one Turk among all the crowd who dwelt in the inner Seraglio save the Sultan and the members of his family, and even these were always the children of foreign mothers.

The Eunuchs formed two corps, the Black and the White. The black eunuchs, who were all Africans, numbered about two hundred, and were the special guard of the imperial harem. Their chief, whose title was the Kizlar Aghasi or Master of the Girls, was one of the greatest men in the empire. He had the rank of a pasha of three tails, and administered the Holy Cities and the imperial mosques, from which he derived an enormous income. He wore a white robe trimmed with sable and a cylindrical head-dress of white muslin twenty-five inches high. The white eunuchs, eighty strong, who looked after the young pages, obeyed a chief whose style was Kapu Aghasi

GREEK TRADERS.

or Master of the Gate. Besides these, there were in
the inner division of the Seraglio a number of mutes
and dwarfs; the former guarded the door of the room
or pavilion when the Sultan conferred with some great
man, an idle form, as every one in the palace under-
stood and often made use of their peculiar language
of signs; the dwarfs served as buffoons to divert the
Pādishāh and his household.

Penetrating now to the innermost sanctuary of the
Seraglio, the imperial harem itself, we find that an
organization not less systematic than that which prevailed among the male inhabitants of the palace reigned
likewise among the ladies and their attendants. The
women of the Sultan's household were divided into
five classes: the Kadins or Ladies, the Gediklis or
Handmaids, the Ustas or Mistresses, the Shāgirds or
Novices, and the Jārīyas or Damsels. Of these the
Kadins, whose number was usually four, were, so to
speak, the consorts of the Sultan, what Europeans
would call his Sultanas (a term unknown to the
Turks), and each had her own suite of apartments
and attendants. When a Kadin became the mother
of a son she received the title of Khāssekī Sultan or
Royal Princess, when of a daughter, that of Khāssekī
Kadin or Royal Lady. On the birth of a child the
harem was illuminated, and a number of brilliant
ceremonies took place. The Gediklis were a company
of girls on whom devolved the personal service of the
Sultan when he chose to visit or reside in the harem.
Twelve of the fairest of these, the *élite* of the harem,
held offices and titles corresponding to those of the
highest officers of the First Chamber of pages. It was

from among their ranks that the Pādishāh chose his Ikbāls or favourites. The Mistresses were girls attached to the service of the Sultan's mother, a very important personage in the harem, and to that of the Kadins and their children. The Novices were children who were educated to recruit the ranks of the Gediklis and Mistresses. The Damsels were the servants of all the others, and performed the manual work and menial duties of the establishment.

The imperial harem contained as a rule about five or six hundred women, Europeans, Asiatics, and Africans, hardly one of whom knew whence she came. They were under the orders of a Grand Mistress whose title was Kyahya Kadin or Lady Comptroller, and who was usually chosen by the Sultan from among the oldest of the Gediklis. This lady was assisted by another called the Khazīnadār Usta or Mistress Treasurer, one of whose duties was to look after the expenses of the harem.

Such, then, was the Seraglio in the old days of its prosperity before the reforming hand of Sultan Mahmūd had swept away its medieval splendour. The household of the Ottoman monarch of to-day, if more in keeping with the spirit of the times, is very commonplace beside that of last century. Nine-tenths of the old offices and institutions have disappeared ; stiff European uniforms have driven away the flowing Eastern robes of silk and velvet, while all those marvellous caps and turbans, by which more than by anything else the rank of each man might have been known, have vanished to be replaced by the charac- terless and unvarying fez. Nevertheless the modern

Seraglio is hardly an anchorite's cell. The late Sultan Abd-ul-Azīz employed at least six thousand servants and officials, and his privy purse cost two million pounds a year. There were 300 cooks, 400 grooms, 400 boatmen, 400 musicians, and so forth ; while the harem contained 1200 odaliks. Special officers attended to the Sultan's pipe, his coffee, his wardrobe, and his perfumed washing-basin. Somebody must see to the imperial backgammon board, and another to the august chin. £16,000 a year was spent on sugar. There were 600 horses in the stables, and 150 coachmen and footmen. Abd-ul-Azīz was fond of pictures and jewellery, and spent a quarter of a million on them annually. Every year saw him at least three-quarters of a million deeper in debt for his private expenditure.[1]

But, spend how he would, Abd-ul-Azīz could not attain the splendour of the olden times. The Seraglio system indeed, by its very nature, could not last ; all the races of the earth were not created simply in order to furnish slaves or toys to gratify the whims of a Grand Signior; and even if no Sultan Mahmūd had abolished them, the Four Chambers must have passed away or been altogether changed from sheer lack of a legitimate supply of white men. The Sultans would have to recruit their ranks with members of their own race, and the moment this was done their old boasted isolation was at an end.

We may gain some idea of a state ceremony in the old days of the Seraglio from the following description of a reception of imperial ambassadors by Selīm the

---

[1] " The People of Turkey," by a Consul's Daughter. i. 247-9.

Second.   The old-fashioned language of Knolles be-
fits the subject :

" So accompanied in this honourable wise, the
Embassadors enter the first gate of the Great Turk's
Palace.   This gate is built of marble in most
sumptuous manner, and of a stately height, with
certain words of their language in the front thereof,
engraven and guilt in marble.   So passing through the
base court, which hath on the right side very fair
gardens, and on the left divers buildings, serving for
other offices, with a little Moschy, they come to the
second gate, where all such as come in riding must
of necessity alight ; here, so soon as they were entered
in at this second gate, they came into a very large
square court with buildings and galleries round about
it, the kitchens standing on the right hand, with other
lodgings for such as belonged to the Court, and on
the left hand likewise rooms deputed to like services.
There are, moreover, many halls and other rooms for
resort where they sit in Council, handling and executing the public affairs either of the Court or of the Empire, with other matters where the Bassaes (Pashas)
and other officers assemble together.   Entering in at
this second gate, in one part of the court, which seemed
rather some large street, they saw the whole company
of the Solaches (Solaks) set in a goodly rank, which
are the archers, keeping always near to the prison of
the Great Turk, and serving as his footmen when he
rideth ; they use high plumes of feathers, which are
set bolt upright over their foreheads.   In another place
there stood the Capitzi (Kapuji) in array, with black
staves of Indian canes in their hands; they are the

porters and warders of the gates of the palace, not
much differing in their attire from the Janissaries,
who stood in rank likewise in another quarter. And
besides all these, with many more that were out of
order, as well of the Court as of the common people,
those knights of the Court which accompanied the
embassadors thither with other great ones likewise
of same degree, were marshalled all in their several
companies ; and among the rest the Mutarachaes
(Matrakjis), men of all nations and of all religions
(for their valour the only free men which live at their
own liberty in the Turkish Empire), stood there
apparelled in damask velvet and cloth of gold, and
garments of silk of sundry kinds of colours ; their
pomp was greater, for the turbants that they wore
upon their heads being as white as whiteness itself,
made a most brave and goodly show well worth the
beholding. In brief, whether they were to be considered all at once, or in particular, as well for the
order that they kept as for their sumptuous presence,
altogether without noise or rumour ; they made the
Embassadors and the rest of their followers there
present, eye-witnesses both of their obedience and of
the great state and royalty of the *Othoman* Court.
Passing through them the Embassadors were led into
the hall where the Bassaes and other great men of
the Court were all ready to give them entertainment,
they of their train being at the same time brought
into a room that stood apart under one of the aforesaid lodgings all hung with Turkey carpets. Soon
after (as their use and manner is) they brought in
their dinner, covering the ground with table-cloths of

a great length spread upon carpets, and afterwards
scattering a marvellous number of wooden spoons,
with so great store of bread, as if they had been to
feed three hundred persons ; then they set on meat in
order, which was served in forty two great platters
of earth full of rice pottage of three or four kinds,
differing one from another, some of them seasoned
with honey and of the colour of honey ; some with
sour milk, and white of colour ; and some with sugar;
they had fritters also, which were made of like
batter ; and mutton besides, or rather a dainty and
toothsome morsel of an old sodden ewe. The table
(if there had any such been) thus furnished, the guests
without any ceremony of washing sat down on the
ground (for stools there were none) and fell to their
victual, and drank out of great earthen dishes water
prepared with sugar, which kind of drink they call
zerbet (sherbet). But so having made a sort of repast,
they were no sooner risen up but certain young men
whom they call *Grainoglans* (Ajem-Oghlans), with
others that stood round about them, snatched it up
hastily as their fees, and like greedy Harpies ravened
it down in a moment. The embassadors in the
meantime dined in the hall with the Bassaes. And
after dinner certain of the Capitzies were sent for,
and twelve of the Embassadors' followers were appointed to do the great Sultan reverence ; by whom
(their presents being already conveyed away) they
were removed out of the place where they dined
and brought on into an under room, from whence
there was an ascent into the hall where the Bassaes
were staying for the embassadors, who soon after came

forth, and for their ease sat them down upon the benches, whilst the Bassaes went in to *Selymus*, who before this time had made an end of dinner, and was removed in all his royalty into one of his chambers, expecting the coming of the Embassadors. All things now in readiness, and the Embassadors sent for, they set forward with their train, and came to the third gate which leadeth into the Privy-Palace of the Turkish Emperor, where none but himself, his eunichs, and the young pages his minions, being in the eunich's custody, have continual abiding, into which inward part of the palace none entereth but the Capitzi Bassa (Kapuji Bashi) (who hath the keeping of this third gate) and the Asigniers (that serve in the Turk's meat) with the Bassaes and some few other great men, and that only when they have occasion so to do by reason of some great business, or sent for by the Sultan. Being entered in at this gate, which is of a stately and royal building, the Capitzi, by whom they were conducted, suddenly caused them to stay, and set them one from another about five paces in a little room which, nevertheless, was passing delicate, all curiously painted over with divers colours, and stood between the gate and the more inner lodgings, on both sides of which room, when all things were whist and in a deep silence, certain little birds were only heard to warble out their sweet notes, and to flicker up and down the green trees of the gardens (which all along cast a pleasant shadow from them) as if they alone had obtained licence to make a noise. *Selymus* himself was in great majesty sat in an under-chamber, parted only with a wall from a room wherein

the Embassadors' followers attended, whereinto he
might look through a little window, the portal of his
said chamber, standing in counterpart with the third
gate above mentioned. The Embassadors entering
in, were led single, and one after another, to make
their reverence to the Great Turk, and in the meantime certain of the Capitzi, with the presents in their
hands, fetching a compass about before the window,
mustered them in his sight. All this while not the
least sound in the world being raised, but a sacred
silence kept in every comer, as if men had been going
to visit the holiest place in Jerusalem. Yet for all
that the Embassadors' followers, placed one after
another (as aforesaid) were not aware that the
great Sultan was so near, looking still when they
should have been led on forwards all together ; how-
beit they were set in one after another, neither did
they that were so set out return again into the room,
but having severally done their reverence, were all
(except the Embassadors that still staid in the chamber) by one and one sent out another way into the
court ; neither could he that came after see his fellow
that went before him after he was once taken in to do
his reverence, but suddenly as the former was let out
the next was advanced forward to the door where
Isman the Capitzi - Bassa and the Odda - Bassa,
taking him by both arms and by the neck, the one at
the right hand and the other at the left, and so leading
him apace by the way softly left his wrists with their
hands, lest peradventure he might have some soft
weapon in his sleeve. Yet were they all not thus
groped as Marc Antonio Pagasetta (the reporter of

this negotiation) saith of himself and some others also. However, this hath been, and yet is the manner of giving of access unto the person of the Great Turk ever since that Amurath the First was, after the battle of Cassova, murdered by one of *Lazarus* the Despot's men, who admitted in his presence in revenge of the wrong done unto his master, with a short poniard that he had closely hidden about him, so stabbed him in the belly that he presently died. And thus like men rather carried to prison by sergeants than to the presence of so mighty a monarch, they were presented unto his majesty ; he, sitting upon a pallet which the Turks call mastal, used by them in their chambers to sleep and to feed on, covered with carpets of silk, as were the whole floor of the chamber also. The chambers itself, being not very great, was but dark altogether without windows, excepting that one whereof we have before spoken, and having the walls painted and set out in most fresh and lively colours by great cunning, and with a most delicate grace ; yet use they neither pictures nor the image of anything in their paintings. The Visier's Bassaes, before mentioned, were standing at the left hand as they entered in at the chamber door, one by another in one side of the chamber, and the Embassadors on the right hand on the other side standing likewise and uncovered. The Dragomans were in another part of the chamber near the place where the Sultan sat, gorgeously attired in a robe of cloth of gold all embroidered with jewels, when, as the Embassador's followers by one and one brought before him (as is aforesaid) and kneeling on the ground, a Turk stand-

ing on his right hand, with all reverence taking up
the hem of his garment, gave it them in their hands
to kiss. Selymus himself all this while sitting like
an image without moving, and with a great state and
majesty keeping his countenance, deigned not to give
them one of his looks. This done they were led back
again, never turning their backs towards him, but
going still backwards until they were out of his
presence. So after they had all thus made their reverence, and were departed out of the chamber, the Embassadors delivered unto Selymus all the Emperor's
letters, and briefly declared unto him their message ;
whom he, answering in four words as, 'that they
were to confer with his Bassaes ;' presently they were
dismissed. And so coming out of the two inner gates
they mounted on horseback and took the way, leading towards their lodging, being at their return accompanied by the whole order of the Janissaries, with
their aga and other captains, among whom were
certain of their religious men called *Haagi* (which
used to follow the Janissaries) who continually turning
about, and in their going, singing or rather howling
out certain psalms and prayers for the welfare of their
great Sultan, gave the Embassadors and their followers
occasion to wonder, that they either left not for weariness or fell not down like Noddies for giddiness. All
these were sent, the more honourably to accompany
the Embassadors to their lodging ; and beside these,
many more on horseback than attended them at
their coming forth ; in regard whereof the Embas-

[1] Knolles, i. 563-4.

sadors, when they were come to their lodging, to requite their greedie courtesy, frankly distributed amongst them above four thousand dollars, and yet well contented them not." [1]

XV.

OTTOMAN LITERATURE.

THE literature of the Ottomans was, like their civilization, borrowed from the Persians through the Seljūks ; and it is natural that we should find a close resemblance between their writings and those of their Persian masters. We are not then surprized when we see the same tone and sentiment, the same figures of speech, and the same structure of verse, in the literatures of the two peoples. In both the poetry is superior to the prose. Persian and Ottoman poems are, when at their best, marked by extreme grace and finish, by great elegance of diction, and not unfrequently by a beautiful harmony· But they are, on the other hand, highly artificial ; the sentiment is often exaggerated, the ideas either conventional or far-fetched, and the language disfigured by a variety of verbal conceits, too often of a very childish description. If we except the long narrative poems, the range of subjects sung by the muses of Persia and Turkey is very limited. Love, with its woes and its joys, naturally and by right assumes the first place ; then we have the charms of the springtide, the sweet song of the nightingale, the beauty of the flowers, and other delightful things of Nature, generally with an undertone of religious mysticism audible throughout. And that is well-nigh all. It is remarkable that the Turks, though essentially a military people, had no war-poetry worthy of the name; the Persians had none (apart from their epics), and so it never occurred to the Ottomans to write any.

The long narrative poems already mentioned are written in rhyming couplets; but the most marked feature in the rhyme-system of these Eastern literatures is what is known as the monorhyme. A single rhyme-sound, that of the first couplet, is carried throughout the entire poem; this rhyme is repeated in the second line of each that follows, while their first lines do not rhyme at all. Examples of this system, which is very simple, will be seen in most of the translated poems that occur in this chapter. The favourite composition of the Ottoman poets is called the *ghazel;* this is a short monorhythmic poem, usually consisting of less than a dozen couplets, in the last of which the writer generally inserts his name, as though putting his signature to his little work.

The prose in its higher flights is generally bombastic, often involved, and, like the poetry, bristles with equivoques and other verbal tricks, which, though frequently ingenious, are more or less trivial, and always give a forced and unnatural appearance to the style. A peculiarity of ambitious prose is the *sej,* an embellishment which consists in making the last words of the several clauses of a sentence rhyme together, the result being a jingle rather irritating than otherwise to Western ears. The extracts which are here translated from the old chronicler Sa'd-ud-dīn, will give the reader some idea of the effect of the *sej*. The simpler prose is more natural, and consequently more pleasing ; but it is apt to err in the opposite direction, and become bald and uninteresting.

Ottoman literature is very extensive, writers of every kind, but especially poets, having been at all times both numerous and prolific. We shall have to content ourselves here with making the acquaintance of a few of the most eminent of those authors who have won for themselves a high position in the literary history of their country.

One of the earliest of Ottoman poets is Ghāzī Fāzil, a Turkish noble who crossed the Hellespont on the raft with Prince Suleymān that night when the Ottomans gained their first foothold in Europe (p. 34). The following lines, evidently written after some successful fight with the Byzantines, may possibly refer to this expedition in which the warrior-poet helped to win a new empire for his race :—[1]

" We smote the paynim once again, our God did send us grace ;
   The arrows of our holy-war were thorns in the foeman's face.
   All spirits that are in the skies came down to lend us might,
   And from the earth arose to succour us our martyr race.
        We look to God for aidance, they of holy-war we be,
        And in the cause of God our lives and bodies offer we."

Some time after this, Sheykhī of Kermiyan wrote a long narrative poem on the adventures of Shīrīn,

---

[1] In this fragment, as in all the other renderings of verse in this chapter, besides translating almost literally and line for line, I have retained the rhyme-movement and, as far as possible, the metre of the original, hoping in this way to give the reader as accurate an idea as I can of the general effect of Turkish poetry.

the favourite heroine of Persian romance ; and later
still Yaziji-oghlu composed a versified history of the
Prophet, which he named the Mohammedīya. The
most interesting prose work of this early period is
a collection of old popular tales, known as the
" History of the Forty Vezīrs," compiled by an
author of the first half of the fifteenth century, who
calls himself Sheykh-zāda or the Sheykh's son, and
whose personal name was probably Ahmed. The
following story, which is that told by the twentieth
Vezīr, shows at once the character of the tales and
the simple unaffected style in which the book is
written :

" Of old time there was a great king. One day,
when returning from the chase, he saw a dervish
sitting by the way, crying, ' I have a piece of advice ;
to him who will give me a thousand sequins, I will
tell it.' When the king heard these words of the
dervish he drew in his horse's head and halted, and
he said to the dervish, ' What is thy counsel ? ' The
dervish replied, ' Bring the sequins and give me
them that I may tell my counsel.' The king ordered
that they counted a thousand sequins into the dervish's
lap. The dervish said, ' O king, my advice to thee
is this : whenever thou art about to do a deed, consider the end of that deed, and then act.' The
nobles who were present laughed together at these
words and said, ' Any one knows that.' But the
king rewarded that poor man. He was greatly
pleased with the words of the dervish, and commanded that they wrote them on the palace-gate
and other places. Now that king had an enemy, a

great king ; and this hostile king was ever watching his opportunity ; but he could find no way save this, he said in himself, ' Let me go and promise the king's barber some worldly good and give him a poisoned lancet ; some day when the king is sick he can bleed him with that lancet.' So he disguised himself, and went and gave the barber a poisoned lancet and ten thousand sequins. And the barber was covetous and undertook to bleed the king with that lancet what time it should be needful. One day the king was sick, and he sent word to the barber to come and bleed him. Thereupon the barber took that poisoned lancet with him and went. The attendants prepared the basin, and the barber saw written on the rim of the basin, ' Whenever thou art about to perform a deed, think on the end thereof.' When the barber saw this he said in himself, ' I am now about to bleed the king with this lancet and doubtless he will perish, then will they not leave me alive, but will inevitably kill me ; after I am dead what use will these sequins be to me ? ' And he took up that lancet and put it in its place, and drew out another lancet that he might bleed the king. When he took his arm a second time, the king said, ' Why didst thou not bleed me with the first lancet ? ' The barber answered, ' O king, there was some dust on its point.' Then the king said, ' I saw it, it is not the treasury lancet ; there is some secret here, quick, tell it, else I will slay thee.' When the barber saw this importunity, he related the story from beginning to end, and how he had seen the writing on the basin and changed his intention. The king put a

ST. SOPHIA.

robe of honour on the barber and let him keep the
sequins which his enemy had given him. And the
king said, ' The dervish's counsel is worth not one
thousand sequins, but a hundred thousand sequins.'" [1]

But there is little work of real merit before the
capture of Constantinople in 1453. Not very long
after that event certain ghazels of Mīr Alī Shīr
Nevāyī, a contemporary Tartar prince and poet,
found their way to the newly-won capital of the
Ottomans. There they were copied by Ahmed Pasha,
one of the Vezīrs of Mohammed II. Although they
possess no originality, many of them being little
else than translations from Nevāyī, the poems
of this minister are among the landmarks in
Ottoman literary history. It was only after their
appearance that poetry began to be regularly cultivated, and they rendered important service in the
work of settling and refining the language. Sinān
Pasha, another of the Conqueror's Vezīrs, was the
first who excelled in high-flown prose ; he is author
of a religious work entitled Tazarru'āt " Supplica-
tions," the style of which, notwithstanding a lavish
use of the embellishments supplied by Persian
rhetoric, is remarkable for its lucidity and directness.
Here are one or two sentences from it :

" Thou art a Creator, such that nonentity is the
store for Thy creations ; Thou art an Originator, such
that nothingness is the material for Thy formations !
Far-sighted understanding cannot see the horizon of
the summit of Thy righteousness ; swift-winged en-

[1] "The History of the Forty Vezīrs," translated by E. J. W. Gibb, pp. 220–222. (Redway, 1886.)

deavour cannot reach the verge of the pavilion of Thy
mightiness.   The soaring eagle, the human mind, to
which the existences, celestial and terrestrial, are ever
the prey of claw and beak, cannot open the wing and
fly for one moment in the air of Thy sublimity ; and
the peacock, mortal thought and understanding, which
strutteth day and night in the plain of domain and the
mead of might, cannot move one step on the road to
Thy divinity."

The lyric poets Nejātī and Zātī, who follow Ahmed
Pasha, show a marked advance ; while the poetesses
Zeyneb and Mihrī deserve mention among the more
notable writers of the time of Mohammed II.   As
we have seen in a previous chapter, that sovereign,
like most of his house, warmly patronized literature
and men of letters, was himself a poet, and some tole-
rable verses by him are preserved in the old antho-
logies.   His grandson, Selīm I., surnamed Yawuz,
"the Grim," was perhaps the greatest of the Ottoman
Sultans ; high as were his military and administrative
talents, they were hardly more remarkable than his
poetic genius.   Of the four and thirty monarchs who
have occupied the throne of Osmān, twenty-one have
left verses, and of these twenty-one Selīm the First is
unquestionably the truest poet.   His work is, however,
for the most part in the Persian language, a circumstance much to be regretted, as, had he chosen to
write in Turkish, his high talents could hardly have
failed to render valuable service to the language and
literature of his nation.   The following is a translation
of one of the few Turkish ghazels which this great
monarch wrote :

"Down in oceans from mine eyen   rail the tears for grame and teen,
Acheth still my head for all the dolour that my feres have seen.
That the army of my visions o'er the flood, my tears, may pass,
Form mine eyebrows twain a bridge, one-piered, with arches two
   beseen.[1]
Clad in gold-bespangled raiment, all of deepest heavenly hue,
Comes the ancient Sphere each night-tide, fain to play my wanton
   quean.[2]
Lonely had I strayed a beggar through the realms of strangerhood,
Had not pain and woe and anguish aye my close companions been.
O thou Sphere, until the Khān Selīm had nine full beakers drained,
Ne'er did he, on all earth's surface, find a faithful friend, I ween."[3]

Kemāl-Pasha-zāda Ahmed, often called Ibn-Kemāl
a high legal functionary, distinguished himself during
this reign both in verse and prose ; among his works
are a poem on the romantic history of Joseph and
Zuleykhā (as the Easterns name Potiphar's wife), and
a treatise called the Nigāristān, similar in style to the
well-known Gulistān or "Rose-garden" of the Persian
Sa'dī. Mesīhī, another contemporary of Selīm I., is
chiefly known through one poem of great beauty,
which has gained for its author a European celebrity.
This is an ode on spring, consisting of eleven four-
line strophes, four of which I quote :

[1] Indulging in one of those quaint conceits, of which the old poets,
Western as well as Eastern, were so fond, the Sultan here conceives his
nose and eyebrows as forming a bridge for the fancies that throng in his
brain, while his tears represent the torrent that flows beneath.

[2] In Ottoman poetry the Sphere represents our "fickle Fortune."
Here this personified Sphere is purposely confounded with the starry
sky.

[3] The "nine full beakers" refer to the nine spheres of the Ptolemaic
astronomy. The couplet probably means that until the Sultan had
fathomed the mystery of the universe, he had not found the one true
Friend, *i.e.*, God ; but it is rather obscure, as a good deal of old
Ottoman poetry is too apt to be.

"Hark, the bulbul's[1] blithsome carol : 'Now are come the days of
   spring !'
Merry bands and shows are spread in every mead, a maze o' spring ;
There the almond-tree bescatters silvern showers, sprays o' spring.
   Drink, be gay ; for soon will vanish, biding not, the days o' spring !

*   *   *   *   *   *

Rose and tulip bloom as beauties bright o' blee and sweet o' show,
Who for jewels hang the dew-drops in their ears to gleam and glow.
Deem not thou, thyself beguiling, things will aye continue so.
   Drink, be gay ; for soon will vanish, biding not, the days o' spring !

*   *   *   *   *   *

While each dawn the clouds are shedding jewels o'er the rosy land,
And the breath of morning's zephyr, fraught with Tartar musk, is bland,
While the world's delight is present, do not thou unheeding stand ;
   Drink, be gay ; for soon will vanish, biding not, the days o' spring !

With the fragrance of the garden, so imbued the musky air,
Every dew-drop, ere it reacheth earth, is turned to attar rare ;
O'er the garth, the heavens spread the incense-cloud's pavilion fair.
   Drink, be gay ; for soon will vanish, biding not, the days o' spring !"

*   *   *   *   *   *

Up to this time all Ottoman writings had been
more or less rugged and unpolished, but in the reign
of Selīm's son, Suleymān I. (1520–1566), a new era
began. Two great poets, Fuzūlī and Bākī, make their
appearance about the same time ; the one in the east,
the other in the west, of the now far-extending
empire. Fuzūlī of Baghdad, one of the four great
poets of the old Turkish school, is the first writer of
real eminence who arose in the Ottoman dominions.
None of his predecessors in any way approaches him ;
and although his work is in the Persian style and
taste, he is no servile copier ; on the contrary, he
struck out for himself a new path, one hitherto un-

---

[1] The bulbul is the nightingale.

trodden by either Turk or Persian. His chief characteristic is an intense and passionate earnestness,
which sometimes betrays him into extravagances; and
although few Turkish poets are in one way more
artificial than he, few seem to speak more directly
from the heart. His best known works consist of
his Dīvān or collection of ghazels, and a poem on the
loves of Leylī and Mejnūn ; he has besides some
prose writings, which are hardly inferior to his verse.
His works are in a provincial dialect, which differs
considerably from the Turkish of Constantinople ;
and this is perhaps the reason why no school of poets
followed in his footsteps. The two following ghazels
will give an idea of Fuzūlī's usual style:

" O my loved one, though the world because of thee my foe should be,
'Twere no sorrow, for thyself alone were friend enow for me.
Scorning every comrade's rede, I cast me wildly midst of love ;
Ne'er shall foe do me the anguish I have made myself to dree.
Dule and pain shall never fail me, long as life and frame aby ;
Life may vanish, frame turn ashes : what is life or frame to me !
Ah, I knew not union's value, parting's pang I ne'er had borne ;
Now the gloom of absence lets me many a dim thing clearly see.
Yonder Moon [1] hath bared her glance's glaive ; be not unheeding, heart;
For decreed this day are bitter wail to me, and death to thee.
O Fuzūlī, though that life should pass, from Love's way pass not I ;
By the path where lovers wander make my grave, I pray do ye.

Whensoe'er I call to mind the feast of union 'twixt us twain,
Like the flute, I wail so long as my waste frame doth breath retain.
'Tis the parting day ; rejoice thee, O thou bird, my soul, for now
I at length shall surely free thee from this cage of pine and pain. [2]
Lest that any, fondly hoping, cast his love on yonder Moon,
Seeking justice 'gainst her rigour, unto all I meet I plain.

---

[1] " Yonder Moon " is, of course, the beautiful object of his love.
[2] He is about to be parted from his beloved, consequently he will die,
and thus set free his soul from the cage of the body.

Grieve not I whate'er injustice rivals may to me display ;
Needs must I my heart accustom Love's injustice to sustain.
Well I know I ne'er shall win to union with thee, still do I
Cheer at times my cheerless spirit with the hope as fond as vain.
I have washed the name of Mejnūn [1] off the page of earth with tears ;
O Fuzūlī, I shall likewise fame on earth through dolour gain."

Bākī of Constantinople, though much inferior to his contemporary Fuzūlī, was like him far in advance of any of his predecessors. His most celebrated work, an elegy on Sultan Suleymān the First, is unsurpassed in its style. It consists of a number of monorhythmic stanzas, each closed by a rhyming couplet ; I quote the first two, by way of specimen. The reader is addressed in the opening lines :

"O thou, foot-tangled in the mesh of fame and glory's snare !
How long shall last the lust of earthly honour falsely fair ?
Aye hold in mind that day when life's sweet spring shall pass away ;
Alas ! the tulip-tinted cheek to autumn leaf must wear !
And thy last resting-place must be, e'en like the dregs', the dust ; [2]
And mid the bowl of cheer must fall the stone Time's hand doth bear.[3]
He is a man in sooth whose heart is as the mirror clear ;
Man art thou ?—why then doth thy breast the tiger's fierceness share ?
In understanding's eye how long shall heedless slumber bide ?
Will not war's Lion-monarch's lot suffice to make thee ware ?
He, Prince of Fortune's cavaliers, he, to whose gallant Rakhsh,[4]

[1] Mejnūn is the Orlando Furioso of the Moslem East ; driven mad by his hopeless passion for the lovely Leylī, he flies into the desert, where he wanders about until he dies.

[2] It was customary to throw the dregs on the ground after drinking.

[3] A pebble thrown into a beaker was a signal for a party to break up ; and death, as coming after life, is sometimes likened to the end of a banquet when the guests are gone and the lights put out.

[4] Rakhsh, *i.e.*, Lightning, is the name of the charger of Rustem, the hero of the Shāh-Nāma, and the Hercules of all those lands where Persian culture prevails. When the poet here styles the Sultan's steed a Rakhsh, he, of course, intends the reader to infer that the rider was a Rustem.

What time he caracoled and pranced, cramped was earth's tourney-
 square—
He, to the lustre of whose sword the Hunnish paynim bowed —
He, whose dread sabre's flash hath wrought the wildered Frank's
 despair !
 Like tender rose-leaf, gently laid he in the dust his face ;
 And earth, the guardian, placed him like a jewel in his case.

In truth he was the radiance of rank high and glory great,
A king, Iskender-diademed, of Dārā's armied state.¹
Before the ground beneath his feet the Sphere bent low its head;
Earth's shrine of adoration was the dust before his gate.
The smallest of his gifts the meanest beggar made a prince ;
Exceeding boon, exceeding bounteous a Potentate !
The court of glory of his kingly majesty most high
Was aye the centre where would hope of sage and poet wait.
Although he yielded to eternal Destiny's command,
A king was he in might as Doom, and masterful as Fate !
Weary and worn by yon vile, fickle Sphere deem not thou him ;
Near God to be, did he his earthly glory abdicate.
What wonder if our eyes no more life and the world behold,
His beauty sheen as sun and moon did earth irradiate !
 If folk upon the sun do gaze, their eyes are filled with tears;
 For while they look yon moon-bright face before their mind
 appears ! "

*   *   *   *   *   *

During the reign of Ahmed I. (1603–1607) arose
the second great light of old Turkish poetry. This
was Nef'ī of Erzerūm, who is as much esteemed for
the brilliancy of his *kasīdas,* or eulogies, as Fuzūlī
is for the tenderness of his ghazels. Like him, he
elaborated a style for himself, which found many
imitators, the most successful of whom was Sabrī.
Unfortunately for himself, Nef'ī was an able satirist ;
his scathing pen drew down upon him the enmity of
certain great men, who prevailed upon Sultan Murād

¹ Iskender is Alexander the Great ; Dārā, Darius.

IV. to sanction his execution (1635). The following is the opening of one of Nef'ī's most celebrated kasīdas. It is in praise of Sultan Murād IV., at whose command the poet is said to have improvised it as he stood in the royal presence, a story which seems a little doubtful when we consider that the poem is one of the most elaborate and artful in the language. It is a good specimen of Turkish bacchanalian verse, and touches in a characteristic fashion on the charms of the spring season, a theme in which the Ottoman poets greatly delight :

"The early springtide breezes blow, the roses bloom at dawn of day ;
Oh! let our hearts rejoice ; cup-bearer, fetch the bowl of Jem, I pray.[1]
The gladsome time of May is here, the sweetly scented air is clear,
The earth doth Eden-like appear, each nook doth Irem's bower display.[2]
'Tis e'en the rose's stound o' glee, the season of hilarity,
The feast of lovers fair and free, this joyous epoch bright and gay.
So let the goblet circle fair, be all the taverns emptied bare,
To dance let ne'er a toper spare, what while the minstrels chant the lay.
A season this when day and night the tavern eyes the garth wi' spite ;
Though drunk, he loved a winsome wight, excused were Mekka's guardian gray.
Oh! what shall now the hapless do, the lovelorn, the bewildered crew ?
Let beauties fetch the bowl anew, to spare the which were shame to-day.
Be bowl and lovesome charmer near, and so the hour will shine with cheer ;
And he indeed will wise appear who maketh most of mirth and play.
That toper's joy in truth were whole who, drunken and elate of soul,
With one hand grasped the tulip bowl,[3] with one the curling locks did fray.

[1] Jem, or Jemshīd, is an ancient Persian king, celebrated for his love of splendour and festivity.

[2] Irem, the terrestial Paradise.

[3] The wine makes the crystal bowl red like a tulip.

Cup-bearer, lay those airs aside, give wine, the season will not bide,
Fill up the jar and hanap wide, nor let the beakers empty stay.

Each tender branchlet fresh and fine hath hent in hand its cup of wine.[1]

Come forth, O cypress-shape,[2] and shine; O rosebud-lips, make glad the way.

Of this say not 'tis joy or pain; grieve not, but pass the bowl again;
Submit to Fate's eternal reign; and hand the wine without delay.

For wine of lovers is the test, of hearts the bane, of souls the rest,
The Magian elder's treasure blest,[3] th' adorn o' th' idol's festal tray.[4]

'Tis wine that guides the wise in mind, that leadeth lovers joy to find;

It blows and casts to every wind, nor lets grief's dust the heart dismay.

A molten fire, the wine doth flow; in crystal cup, a tulip glow:
Elsewise a fragrant rosebud blow, new-oped and sprent with dewy spray.

So give us wine, cup-bearer, now, the bowl of Jem and Kay-Khusrau;[5]
Fill up a brimming measure thou, let all distress from hearts away.

Yea, we are lovers fair and free, for all that thralls of wine we be,
Lovelorn and stricken sore are we, be kind to us nor say us nay.

For Allah's sake a goblet spare, for yonder moon's that shineth fair,
That I with reed and page prepare the Monarch's praises to assay.

That Sun of empire and command, that Champion-horseman of the land,
As blithe as Jem, as Hātim bland,[6] whom all the folk extol alway,

That Dread of Rūm[7] and Zanzibar, who rides Time's dappled steed in war,
Who hunts the foeman's hordes afar, Behrām, Ferīdūn-fair in fray,[8]

---

[1] *I.e.*, the buds.

[2] The cypress is the regular emblem for a graceful figure.

[3] It is said that wine used to be sold by the Magians in medieval Persia.

[4] The "idol" is the beautiful cup-bearer whom all the revellers adore.

[5] Kay-Khusrau is Cyrus; it is pronounced Key to rhyme with *they*.

[6] Hātim, an old Arabian chief, famed for his hospitality.

[7] Rūm is a general name for the lands that formed the Eastern Roman, or Byzantine, Empire. Rūm and Zanzibar stand for the countries inhabited by the white and black races of mankind, *i.e.*, the whole world.

[8] Behrām and Ferīdūn are kings of old Persia.

That Monarch of the Osmān race, whose noble heart and soul embrace
Arabian Omar's saintly grace and Persian Pervīz' glorious sway.[1]
Sultān Murād, of fortune bright, who crowns doth give and kingdoms
    smite;
Both emperor and hero hight, the Age's Lord with Jem's display."

*　　*　　*　　*　　*　　*　　*

The next notable poet is Nābī, in the time of Sultans
Ibrāhīm (1640–1648) and Mohammed IV. (1648–1687).
About this time the Persian Sāib was introducing in
his own country a new style of ghazel-writing, marked
by a philosophizing, or rather a moralizing, tendency.
Nābī copied him, and consequently brought this new
style into Turkish literature. The greater portion of
his numerous writings are in a didactic strain ; and
some are so closely moulded on his Persian model
that it is difficult to tell that they are intended for
Turkish. He had many followers, among whom
Rāghib Pasha and Sāmī are perhaps the most deser-
ving of mention.

During the reign of Ahmed III. (1703–1730)
flourished Nedīm, the greatest of all the poets of the
old Ottoman school. Nedīm has a style that is
entirely his own; it is altogether unlike that of any
of his predecessors, whether Persian or Turkish, and
no one has ever attempted to copy it. Through his
ghazels, which are written with the most finished
elegance in words of the truest harmony, sings a
tone of sprightly gaiety and joyous lightheartedness,
such as is not to be found in any other poet of his
nation. His numerous kasīdas, while they are more

---

[1] Omar is the second Khalif ; Khusrau Pervīz, a renowned sovereign
of the Sassanian dynasty of Persia.

graceful, are hardly less brilliant than those of Nef'ī, and are at the same time in truer taste and less burdened with obscure and far-fetched conceits. Little is known regarding his life save that he resided at Constantinople, where the Grand Vezīr, Ibrāhīm Pasha, appointed him custodian of the library which he had founded, and that he was still alive in 1727. These two ghazels are by Nedīm:

" Love distraught, my heart and soul are gone for nought to younglings fair,
All my patience and endurance spent on torn and shredded spare.[1]
Once I bared her lovely bosom, whereupon did calm and peace
Forth my breast take flight, but how I wist not, nay, nor why nor where.
Paynim mole, and paynim tresses, paynim eyes, I cry ye grace ;
All her cruel beauty's kingdom forms a Heathenesse, I swear.
Kisses on her neck and kisses on her bosom promised she ;
Woe is me, for now the Paynim rues the troth she pledged while-ere.[2]
Such the winsome grace wherewith she showed her locks from 'neath her fez,
Whatsoever wight beheld her gazed bewildered then and there.
' Sorrowing for whom,' thou askest, ' weeps Nedīm so passing sore ? '
Ruthless, 'tis for thee that all men weep and wail in drear despair.

O my wayward fair, who thus hath reared thee sans all fear to be ?
Who hath tendered thee that thus thou humblest e'en the cypress-tree ?
Sweeter than all perfumes, brighter than all dyes, thy dainty frame ;
One would deem some fragrant rose had in her bosom nurtured thee.
Thou hast donned a rose-enwroughten rich brocade, but sore I fear
Lest the shadow of the broidered rose's thorn make thee to dree.[3]

---

[1] I use the old-fashioned word " spare " to replace the Eastern girībān, which means the opening in a garment from the neck, which enables it to be put off and on. In this line Nedīm means to say that the only result of all his long-suffering is that he has been driven to tear his robe through despair at the conduct of his beloved.

[2] He calls his beloved a Paynim because she has as little mercy as the infidel foe.

[3] So delicate is her skin.

Holding in one hand a rose, in one a cup, thou camest, sweet ;
Ah, I knew not which of these, rose, cup, or thee, to take to me.
Lo, there springs a jetting fountain from the Stream of Life, methought,
When thou madest me that lovely lissom shape o' thine to see."

What may be called the classical period of old
Ottoman literature closes with Nedīm ; its most
brilliant epoch is from the rise of Nef'ī to the death
of Nedīm, or, roughly, from the accession of Ahmed I.
(1603) to the deposition of Ahmed III. (1730).

Turning now to the prose literature, which we have
not looked at since the days of the Conqueror, we
find the Humāyūn-Nāma, an elegant translation of
the Persian Anvār-i-Suheylī, made by Alī Chelebi for
Suleymān I. A little later Sa'd-ud-dīn wrote for his
pupil Murād III. (1574–1595), the Tāj-ut-Tevārīkh, or
" Crown of Chronicles," a history of the reigns of the
first nine Ottoman Sultans. This work, which forms
the first link in an unbroken chain of national annals,
is admired alike for its historical accuracy and for the
elaborate grace of its style. As several extracts from
it have been given in the chapter of this book which
tells the story of the capture of Constantinople, it is
unnecessary to offer any here. The work is written
from beginning to end in *sej* or rhymed prose, and is
embellished with numerous pieces of poetry, sometimes productions of the author himself, and sometimes quotations from the Turkish and Persian poets.
Of the imperial historiographers, Sa'd-ud-dīn's successors, Na'īmā calls for special mention ; his history,
which covers the period between 1591 and 1659, is in
marked contrast, so far as style goes, to the " Crown
of Chronicles," being remarkably simple and direct,

and at the same time very vivid and picturesque. Evliyā Efendi, the Sir John Mandeville of the Ottomans, travelled far and wide through the three continents of the old world, and then came home to Constantinople, where he wrote the story of his wanderings. The celebrated Hājī Khalīfa, sometimes called Kātib Chelebi, who died in 1685, was the author of a large number of valuable works on history, chronology, geography, and other subjects. In 1728 appeared the first book printed in Turkey, a translation of an Arabic dictionary. The press had been founded by Nedīm's patron, the Grand Vezīr Ibrāhīm Pasha, and was under the direction of an Hungarian convert to Islam, who had assumed the name of Ibrāhīm.

The last of the four great poets of the old Turkish school was Sheykh Ghālib, who lived and worked in the time of Sultan Selīm III. (1789–1807). His Husn-u-Ashk, "Beauty and Love," an allegorical romantic poem, is one of the finest productions of Ottoman genius. Like Fuzūlī, Nef'ī, and Nedīm, Sheykh Ghālib successfully originated a style for himself, which is distinct from that of any previous writer.

The reign of Mahmūd II. (1808–1839) was a transition period in Turkish history ; old laws, old customs, old institutions, were all more or less modified. Literature did not remain unaffected by the spirit of the time ; it was then that appeared the first indications of the modern or European school, destined eventually to reign supreme. These indications, however, were visible in prose earlier than in poetry.

Among the more remarkable poets of this transition time are Wāsif who attempted to write verses in the spoken language of Constantinople, Izzet Molla, and the poetesses Fitnet and Leylā.

Some thirty years ago a wonderful change began to come over Turkish literature, and this change has ever since been growing yearly more and more marked, altering the whole tone and spirit, as well as the external form of Ottoman literary work. It is not too much to say that a poem or an essay by a great author of to-day would have been barely comprehensible, certainly not appreciated, by a writer of the first quarter of the present century. This change is a result of the study of the French language and literature, which has become general only within the last twenty years. Marvellous, indeed, have been its effects; the ambition of the modern Turkish aspirant after literary fame is, while writing gracefully, to write naturally; the old *sej* and the traditional conceits and tricks have vanished, to be replaced by direct and simple words, chosen for no other reason than that they best convey the author's meaning. The drama, a form of literature previously unknown in Turkey, has been introduced, and has met with the highest favour from contemporary writers. In poetry likewise, Western forms have well-nigh superseded the monorhythmic ghazels and kasīdas of the olden time. A corresponding change has taken place in the language; many old words have been abandoned as useless, while many others have had their meaning more or less modified to meet the requirements of newly introduced conceptions and ideas, for which no expressions exist in the language as it formerly stood. Of course all these changes have not been effected without opposition ; many Turks of the old school, admirers of the Persian style, and haters of all things Western, opposed them bitterly, and some oppose them still ; but the battle has virtually been fought, the victory won, and for good or for ill Europe has conquered Asia, Paris has replaced Shīrāz.

Although its first distinct notes may be heard in the writings of Akif and Reshīd Pashas, it is to Shināsī Efendi, who died in 1871, more than to any other that the merit of accomplishing this great reform is due. Shināsī was ably supported by the talented and accomplished Kemāl Bey, one of the most gifted men of letters who have ever appeared in Turkey; and the poet Ekrem Bey, who holds at present the position of Professor of Literature at the École Civile of Constantinople, and Hāmid Bey, the most illustrious of Turkish dramatists, deserve to be mentioned in the same sentence with Kemāl.

The tone of the imaginative literature of modern Turkey is very tender and very sad. The Ottoman poets of to-day love chiefly to dwell upon such themes as a fading flower, or a girl dying of decline ; and though admiration of a recent French school may have something to do with this, the fancy forces itself upon us, when we read those sweet and plaintive verses, that a brave but gentle-hearted people, looking forward to its future without fear, but without hope, may be seeking, perhaps unconsciously, to derive what sad comfort it may from the thought that all beautiful life must end in dismal death.

XVI.

THE OTTOMAN ADMINISTRATION.

SUPREME head alike of Church and State, the
Ottoman Sultan has always been an absolute and
irresponsible sovereign, free to act as he pleases so
ong as he observes the commandments of the Koran.
To aid him in the government of the Empire, he
delegates his authority to two great officers : the
Grand Vezīr, who is his lieutenant in all that per-
tains to the temporal administration, and the Muftī,
who is his representative in those matters connected
with the religion and the law. There is little of
interest in the Turkish Government of the present
day, which is conducted by a cabinet of ministers
chosen by the Sultan, and subject to his constant
control and interference, and we shall describe
only the old national system which existed down
to the time of the later Europeanizing reforms.

At first the Ottoman monarchs used to lead their
armies to battle, and personally superintend all affairs
of State ; but this activity gradually subsided, and,
shutting themselves up in their Seraglio, they left
everything in the hands of their ministers and
favourites. Such at least was generally the case, but

MOSAIC IN ST. SOPHIA.

a great deal depended, and still depends, upon the personal character of the ruler ; Murād IV., Selīm III., and Mahmūd II. were anything but nonentities in the Government, and the present Sultan takes an active part in the State.

The Ottoman order of succession to the throne differs from that which holds in Western Europe. The Sultan's heir is his oldest male relative, not necessarily his eldest son ; indeed it is more frequently a brother or nephew who inherits the sovereignty. In old times it was customary for a Sultan on succeeding to the throne to have all his brothers put to death ; they are now usually kept in close seclusion in the palace.

The functionaries of the State were divided into three great classes : those of the Pen, those of the Sword, and those of the Law. The first two of these were under the Grand Vezīr, the third was under the Muftī.

The Ashāb-ul-Kalem, or Companions of the Pen, as they were called, consisted of three classes, the first of which was styled the Rijāl or Grandees, and formed, so to speak, the Ministry of the Empire. Three great officers, the Kyahya Bey, the Reīs Efendi, and the Chawush Bashi, along with six under-secretaries, made up the body of Rijāl. Of these, the Kyahya Bey combined the functions of Minister of War and Minister of the Interior; the Reīs Efendi, whose title was more correctly Reīs-ul-Kuttāb, or Head of the Scribes, was at once Chief Secretary of State and Minister of Foreign Affairs ; while the Chawush Bashi was the Marshal of the Empire and the Minister of Police. The six under-secretaries were the Biyuk Tezkereji and the Kuchuk Tezkereji, who drew up the orders of the Grand Vezīr ; the Mektūbji, or First Secretary of the Grand Vezīr ; the Teshrīfātji, or Grand Master of Ceremonies ; the Beylikji, or Grand Referendary ; and the Kyahya Kātibi, or Secretary of the Kyahya Bey. Among the innumerable subordinate officials who belonged to this class of the Companions of the Pen were two who deserve special mention : the Vak'a-nuwīs, or Historiographer ; and the Terjumān-i Dīvān-i Humāyūn, or Interpreter of the Imperial Divan. To the historiographers we owe that long series of annals which forms so marked and interesting a feature in Ottoman literature, and presents us with so complete and vivid an account of the fortunes of the Empire. The interpreters of the Divan were at first Europeans who had embraced Islām ; but latterly the office became a sort of apanage of certain noble Greek families of Constantinople ; for no Turk till within the last sixty years ever thought of learning a European language.

The second division of the Companions of the Pen was that of the Khojas, or Clerks. These officials were subdivided into four departments. All matters connected with the finances were entrusted to them. Among the functionaries who formed the first department were the Defterdār, or Minister of Finance, and the Nishānji Bashi, whose duty was to trace the Tughra or cypher of the Sultan at the head of all the documents presented to him for that purpose. This Tughra, with the appearance of which most of us are familiar from seeing it on Turkish coins and postage

stamps or on pieces of embroidery or inlaid mother-
of-pearl work, contains, ornamentally written as a
sort of monogram, the names of the reigning Sultan
and his father, together with the title *Khan* and the
epithet *el-muzaffar-dāimā*, or "victor ever." The
Tughra is said to have originated in this way : Sultan
Murād I. entered into a treaty with the Ragusans, but
when the document was brought for his signature, he,

TUGHRA OF ABD-UL-AZIZ.

being unable to write, wetted his open hand with ink
and pressed it on the paper. The first, second, and
third fingers were together, but the thumb and fourth
finger were apart. Within the mark thus formed the
scribes wrote the names of Murād and his father, the
title Khān, and the "victor ever." The Tughra, as
we now have it, is the result of this ; the three long
upright lines represent Murād's three middle fingers,
the rounded lines at the left side are his bent thumb,

and the straight ones at the right his little fing-*r*. The third department of the Khojas consisted of the Intendants who formed the fourth class of the Aghayān-i Bīrūn of the Seraglio.

The third division of the Companions of the Pen was that of the Aghas, which comprised, besides the six Masters of the Stirrup and the Bostanji Bashi, or Chief Gardener, all of whom were attached to the service of the Seraglio, and whose duties will be found mentioned in the chapter describing the Imperial Palace, the following officers among others : the Topji Bashi, or Chief Gunner, who was the Grand Master of Artillery; the Top Arabaji Bashi, who had charge of the material of the artillery ; the Jebeji Bashi, who was in command of the arsenal and armoury ; the Laghimji Bashi, who was chief of the corps of sappers and miners ; the Khumbaraji Bashi, or Chief Bombardier ; and the Mi'mār Bashi, or Chief Builder, who was the Sultan's architect.

The second great class of State functionaries, that of the Companions of the Sword, comprised the governors of the provinces and their subordinates. The Ottoman Empire was divided into provinces styled eyālets, the number of which was constantly varying, owing to administrative changes and the fortunes of war ; these again were subdivided into districts termed sanjak or livā, both words meaning a flag.[1] The eyālets were governed by Pashas who

[1] The Turkish Empire of to-day is divided into a number of provinces termed vilāyets, each of which is under a governor-general, who has the title of Wālī ; these vilāyets are subdivided into districts called sanjaks, which in their turn are parcelled out into kazās or parishes. The administrator of a sanjak is styled a Mutasarrif ; that of a kazā, a Kāimmakām.

held the rank of Vezīrs, and had three Tughs, or horsetails, as their standard.

These rulers lived in almost regal splendour in their provincial capitals, and often shamefully oppressed the people who were entrusted to their charge. The expenses attendant on their position were very great ; they had to make handsome presents to the principal officers of the Court and Government at Constantinople, not only at the time of their appointment, but every now and again in order to secure the support of powerful friends against the intrigues which their enemies were constantly setting on foot, and the complaints of their misgovernment which might from time to time reach the capital. This, added to their private extravagance, caused them to be constantly in want of money, and of course their subjects had to pay, or else to suffer for their obstinacy. If matters became so bad that the people rose in revolt, an officer called a Mufettish, or Inquisitor, was despatched from Constantinople ; but he rarely did any good, for although the Pasha might be deposed or bowstrung, and his property confiscated, no one ever thought of returning the plundered wealth to its proper owners, and another Pasha was sent out as governor-general, who in all probability walked in the steps of his predecessor.

The livās were under governers who bore the style of Mīr-i Livā, or Sanjak Beyi, two titles, both of which mean Flag Lord. This name arose in early times, before the institution of eyālets, when the Ottoman possessions were portioned out into a number of small governments, the ruler of each of which received on his appointment a Tugh or horsetail stan dard as the symbol of his authority. The provincial governors had each a council with which he was bound to consult on all matters connected with his administration. A certain number of the members of this council were prominent natives of the district elected by the notables of the place. The object of this arrangement was of course to give the natives some say in the government of their own district, and to place some check on the Pasha should he incline to act unjustly ; but these native councillors were usually as corrupt as the governor himself, and quite as ready as he was to get all they could for themselves out of their fellow-citizens.

Besides these governors, and independent of them, save in military matters, there was in the provinces an ancient hereditary feudal aristocracy. These were old families, the ancestor of which, as a recompense for services against the enemy, had received a portion of the land which he had helped to conquer. This territory, in which he was practically supreme, and exercised all signiorial rights, was to remain in the possession of his representative for ever. In return he or his heir was required to attend with a certain number of armed and mounted followers whenever summoned by the Sultan to take part in any military expedition. For several centuries these feudal soldiers formed a large proportion of the Ottoman armies, and during medieval times they were at least a match for any similar troops that the Christians could bring against them ; but when the nations of Europe began to maintain regular standing armies, the Turkish feudal militia, without modern arms or systematic training, was no longer able to meet them upon equal terms. In conformity with one of the conditions on which they held them, these Sipāhīs, as the Turkish feudal nobles were called,[1] resided on their estates, where they occupied themselves with hunting and military sports ; they never left their old castles save when called upon by the Pādishāh to muster outside the capital for a march on Vienna, or Tebrīz. They took no share in the government of the province where their domains lay, but in these domains they lorded it at their pleasure, and neither Pasha nor Sanjak Beyi had any jurisdiction there. As we have seen, these feudal troops gradually became useless ; the Sipāhīs obstinately opposed all attempts at reform, so that their abolition became necessary. This was accomplished by Mahmūd II., who, as they no longer rendered any effective service in the field, confiscated their properties and abolished their rights. Thus the present century has witnessed the close of two ancient feudal systems, which had come down intact and unchanged through many centuries : that of Turkey and that of Japan.

At the head of the third great class of State functionaries, that of the Ulemā, or Doctors of the Law, stood the Sheykh-ul-Islām or Elder of Islām, the most important of whose duties was to interpret

---

[1] European writers generally call them Timariotes, a name derived from the Turkish word Timar, which means a fief. Larger fiefs, assessed at a higher value, were termed Ziyāmets. The number of soldiers which a Sipāhī, or Turkish knight, was bound to bring with him to a campaign depended on the value at which his fief was assessed. The name Sipāhī was also applied to an old corps of regular cavalry, which has frequently been mentioned in this volume in connexion with the Janissaries ; those Sipāhīs were quite distinct from the feudal knights.

the sacred Law by declaring whether any proposed
action was in accordance with the precepts of the
Koran. No war could be begun, no peace could be
concluded, no public matter of any kind could be
gone on with until the Sheykh-ul-Islām had been
consulted and had pronounced the projected undertaking lawful. Immediately under the Sheykh-ul-
Islām, were two great legal officers called the Kāzī-
ul-'Askers of Rumelia and Anatolia. The title Kāzī-
ul-'Asker, which means Judge of the Army, was originally conferred on a magistrate whom the Sultan used,
in early times, to take along with him when he went
on a campaign, in order to settle any disputes which
might arise among the soldiers. As time went on,
two of these magistrates were appointed, and for the
sake of distinction the territorial titles were added ;
but the Rumelian or European judge (who represented
the original military magistrate) always took prece-
dence of his Anatolian or Asiatic colleague. Next
came the Istambol Kadisi or Judge of Constantinople ;
then the Mollas or Magistrates of the two sacred cities
Mekka and Medīna ; then the Mollas of the " Four
Burghs," *i.e.*, of Adrianople, Brusa, Cairo, and Damascus ; and then the Makhrej Mollalari or Mollas Aspirant, including the Magistrates of Galata, Scutari,
Eyyūb (all suburbs of Constantinople), Jerusalem,
Smyrna, Aleppo, Yeni Shehr, and Salonica. This
division embraced, besides these, some of the 'Ulemā
attached to the service of the Seraglio, and an officer
called the Nakīb-ul-Eshrāf or Representative of the
Nobles, *i.e.*, of the Sherīfs or recognized descendants
of the Prophet Muhammed, in the Turkish Empire.

All these functionaries belonged to the first rank of legal dignitaries ; the second consisted of the Mollas or Magistrates of certain other of the more important cities ; the third of a number of officials termed Mufettishes or Inquisitors, whose duty was to see that the legacies bequeathed to mosques and other religious or charitable institutions were properly administered. The fourth rank was that of the Kādīs or ordinary judges of the less important towns ; and the fifth and lowest that of the Nāibs or Judge-substitutes.

The Divan, as the Council of the Empire was called, consisted at first of only three Vezīrs, but was gradually increased to nine. These ministers, who were styled the Kubba Vezīrleri or Cupola Vezīrs, because the room in which they carried on their deliberations was roofed by a cupola, were superseded during the reign of Sultan Ahmed III., on account of the rivalry which had sprung up between them ; and a new Divan was instituted. This was composed of eight members ; the Grand Vezīr, who was President of the Council ; the Kapudan Pasha or Grand Admiral ; the two Kāzī-ul-'Askers ; the three Defterdārs or chiefs of the financial department ; and the Nishānji or Tracer of the Sultan's cypher. By the end of last century this Divan, which was held in the hall specially set apart for the purpose in the second court of the Seraglio, had become a mere tribunal for the redress of private grievances, and met only once in six weeks or so, while the real business of the State was transacted in councils called Mushāvaras, which were held at the residence of the Grand Vezīr, and at which all the heads of departments assisted.

The fleet was under the command of the **Kapudan Pasha** or Grand Admiral, one of the greatest officers of the Empire. The islands of the Grecian Archipelago were under his jurisdiction, and every summer he used to go with the fleet into the Mediterranean on a tour of inspection, and to receive his rents from the officers to whom he had farmed his government.

There was no similar officer in command of the army ; the Grand Vezīr being, under the Sultan, the generalissimo of the forces. He usually took command of an army when marching against an enemy, but he was always assisted and sometimes replaced by other Pashas of the highest rank. Each division of the army had its own general ; thus the Janissaries had their Agha, but he did not interfere with the cavalry or artillery or with any branch of the infantry except his own.

Formerly, when the Ottoman Government declared war against a foreign state, it used to seize the ambassador of that state at Constantinople and shut him up in the State prison of the Seven Towers. Its object in so doing was not only to emphasize its hostility against the enemy, but to prevent the latter from learning any of those particulars concerning the condition of the Turkish Empire which the minister would most probably be able to afford, as well as to hold a hostage for the good treatment of any Ottoman subjects who might chance to be in the territories of that State against which the war was to be waged.

All the great functionaries of the Empire were distinguished by the magnificence and variety of their

IN THE HAREM.

State costumes. The Grand Vezīr wore a long robe
of white satin trimmed with sable, and a curious head-
dress, some five and twenty inches in height, called a
kilavi, which was made of white muslin and shaped
like a sugar-loaf with the top cut off ; a band of gold
lace four inches wide fell across this from right to left.
The dress of the Grand Admiral was the same, save
that his robe was of green instead of white satin.
This was the costume of all the Pashas of the
first rank, those of three Tughs, the Grand Vezīr
alone wearing white satin. Similarly the Sheykh-ul-
Islām had a robe of white cloth, while all the other
chiefs of the Ulemā wore green cloth. Their turban,
which was termed 'urf, was egg-shaped, and was white,
excepting in the case of the Nakīb-ul-Eshrāf, when it
was green. Unless when travelling or on a campaign,
none of these high officials carried a sword ; but they
all (except the legal dignitaries who were unarmed)
had a jewel-hilted dagger stuck in the girdle which
they wore under the fur-trimmed outer robe.

Of all this gorgeous apparel little or nothing is now
visible at Stambol. His Majesty, Abd-ul-Hamīd Khan,
may be seen driving to mosque in a plain landau, and
habited in a black frock-coat and trousers, with a red
fez on his head. Save for the fez, he and his ministers
might be mistaken for Frenchmen of a sedate order.
Old Turkey, with its pomp, its power, its gorgeous
ceremony, is gone for ever ; and the time has not yet
come for New Turkey to feel comfortable in its tight
European clothes.

XVII.

"THE SICK MAN."
(1812–1880.)

THE present century has witnessed many stirring events in and around the Ottoman Empire, but they have nearly all been marked by a novel characteristic. In former ages Turkey fought for herself, to win lands or to repel invaders. In the present day other nations fight for Turkey, not for her sake, but for their own. The City on the Bosphorus has become a bone of contention to the Powers of Europe : one of them is determined to possess it, and the others, afraid to claim it for themselves, have resolved that no one shall touch it. All fears of the ancient military prestige of the Ottomans have passed away, and what anxiety there is depends, not upon their strength, but their weakness. Turkey is a weight in the European equilibrium, and the danger is that she may slip off the scale and overturn the balance. How far this estimate of the feebleness of the Sultan's resources is true may perhaps be questioned. The Turks have never been honestly beaten in the present century. In the Russian war of 1809–12 they were but slightly worsted ; in the Greek war of 1822–8 they were at a disadvantage on account of a military revolution, but would never have given in without the pressure of three Great Powers ; in the war of 1828–9, Russia won by a *coup de théâtre*, and Mahmūd was surprised into surrender on false information ; in the Crimean war the Turks drove the Russians from before Silistria and over the Danube before the Allies came up, and afterwards were never given a chance ; in the latest war it has been boldly asserted that the Russians won by roubles, more than by powder and shot, and that the Turks would have been fully their match had their officers been superior to bribes. Be this as it may, it is well to be cautious in prejudging the issue as between Russia and Turkey. With good officers and subsidies for arms, the splendid material of which the Ottoman rank and file is composed might possibly be backed against the multitudinous hordes of Russia. Asia Minor is the recruiting-ground of the Turk, and is still almost untouched by the invader. What Turkey might be able to accomplish in the event of another Russian war, with voluntary aid from abroad, and fair play, must remain a problem ; but so long as Russia remains what she is, the odds are not perhaps so very heavy on the Tsar.

Nevertheless it has become almost an axiom in politics to regard Turkey as a more or less defenceless State, and most of the wars and negotiations which have centred in the Bosphorus have been conducted on the assumption that she is a necessary evil, necessary to be kept where she is, but perfectly hopeless in herself, and incapable of development or reform. Certainly she is not what is called a progressive

nation, though the changes which have taken place
in her social, intellectual, and administrative ideas
within the last sixty years are, for a Mohammedan country, almost revolutionary. Christians and
foreigners who now visit Constantinople can hardly
believe the condition of society when the Russian
ambassador was thrown into the castle of the Seven
Towers; when no Turkish minister would deign
to rise to a foreign representative ; and when the
Sultan would as soon think of visiting a kennel as
touching the hand or entering the house of a Giaour.
Now a Turk of rank or position is very much like
any one else, often cultivated, generally well-bred,
and, whatever he may feel as a Moslem, scrupulously
tolerant and polite to " infidels " of every description.
This change, however, applies to the minority : the
mass of the people remain much what they were. Experience and frequent intercourse has perhaps made
them more tolerant or indifferent, but they are still
Moslems, and, as such, practically stationary. The administration remains corrupt, and will remain so until
Turkey is permitted to enjoy a long period of immunity
from external dangers, and to devote the energies of
her best sons, not to playing off several jealous Powers
against one another, but to developing her own resources and thoroughly revising her executive system.
That period, however, is a very uncertain speculation.
No one, perhaps, not even Lord Stratford de Redcliffe,
has ever believed that Turkey could be saved entirely
from within ; and the Powers have always acted on
the principle that somebody must serve as a dyke between Russia and the Bosphorus, and that Turkey,

being there, had better be maintained in her position. The "Sick Man" of the morbid mind of Nicholas must be galvanized into sufficient vitality to sit up and pretend to be well. The policy of the European Powers towards the Porte has been uniformly selfish ; and the policy has reacted upon themselves : for the Turks are keen-witted, and will do nothing for those who will do nothing for them. We can hardly expect Turkey to don every European habit we cut for her, when we never couch a lance beside her except for our own benefit.

The nineteenth century has seen a process of gradual dismemberment which bids fair to deprive the Sultan of his last foothold in Europe. When Mahmūd II. ascended the throne in 1808, a mere child, he was at first the puppet of the mutinous Janissaries, who had slaughtered his predecessors, and only spared him because for awhile he was actually the last survivor of the august race of Othmān. He began his reign in a war with Russia, and the open hostilities of the Tsar were overshadowed by even more menacing intrigues and plots of partition put forward by Napoleon. The Treaty of Bucharest (1812) terminated the first, and helped to put an end to the second danger. External enemies now gave place to the foes of his own household. Great pashas consolidated their power in distant provinces, and ruled as kings in defiance of the Sultan's authority ; local squires or Derébeys held a sort of feudal state in their districts, and set the Sultan's officers at naught. Two men especially threatened the empire with division : one was Mohammed Alī (Mehemet Ali), who made Egypt virtually independent in the second decade of the century, and so firmly established his power that he was able to transmit it to his descendants, one of whom still reigns in name in the capital of the Mamlūks; the other was Alī Pasha of Janina, who held his own in Albania, with barbaric splendour and barbarous cruelty, until he was slain by the Sultan's troops in 1820. To make head against such opponents required a strong and disciplined army, and the support of the people. But the people liked their local lords, and hated the corrupt government of the Sultan's officers; and the army was at once untrustworthy in the field and mutinous in quarters. Mahmūd, who was possessed of an iron will, considerable political sagacity, and invincible patience, quietly set to work to remedy these evils. It took him twenty years to mature his plans, but in 1826 he dealt the blow. People living in Pera, looking across the Golden Horn, one June morning perceived two columns of smoke ascending to the skies over the minarets of Stambol. The Janissaries had mutinied, but the Sultan was ready for them; and the smoke announced that their barracks had been blown up. The famous corps, which had long survived only to tarnish its ancient renown by deeds of cowardice, venality, and turbulency, was exterminated. The sword, the bowstring, and the exile's galley finished the work, and Mahmūd was free to form a new army, disciplined after the manner of European troops, and fit to be trusted with the honour of the old Ottoman name. The Sultan himself studied French books of tactics, drilled his men in person, mounted like any dragoon, with long English stirrups and a trooper's saddle. He worked hard, but fate was against him. He deprived himself of his old army, and had not yet collected a new one, just at the moment when any sort of army would have been serviceable.

The danger that menaced him sprang from Homer. But for the associations with great deeds and noble words which the very name of Hellas awakens, no sane man assuredly would have meddled in the Greek " War of Independence." The impulse which stirred up the insurrection was not so much the sublime passion of freedom as the suggestion of Russian agents and that delight in noisy excitement which is the heritage of the Greek. Whatever the cause, philanthropists, scholars, and enthusiasts, in England and France, fancied that in the revolutionary movement, which was partly the effect of the ground-swell raised in France a quarter of a century before, they could trace the echoes of Thermopylae and Marathon ; the songs of the klephts were sung in the same tongue—somewhat degraded—that Sophocles and Aeschylus had spoken ; and a general, natural, and very creditable feeling spread over Western Europe in favour of the oppressed Greeks. Poets like Byron flung themselves into the fray in a spirit of patriotic antiquarianism; soldiers like Church, who loved adventure, and habitually espoused the cause of the weak against the strong, cast away the scabbard ; and a crowd of knights-errant of various ranks, nations, and motives, joined in the " War of Independence." Wise heads as well as brave hearts took up the cause of the Greeks. France would have been pleased to see a prince of her royal race on the throne of Athens ; and England, as represented by George Canning the Foreign Secretary, had adopted the policy of giving struggling nationalities fair play. The Continental doctrine, rigorously upheld by Prince Metternich, consisted in a jealous police to be exercised by the Great Powers in the maintenance of the established order of things as formulated in the Treaty of 1815, and in the stern repression of all "Jacobinical" movements. Mr. Canning detested the policy of the Holy Alliance, and saw in the Greek rebellion no Jacobinical tendency, but simply the desire of an oppressed Christian people to cast off the Turkish yoke. He strove to effect a reasonable compromise between the belligerents, and succeeded in inducing Russia, and afterwards France, to join England in forcing terms upon the Sultan (Treaty of London, 1827). Mahmūd remained obdurate, however ; he naturally saw no reason why, when on the whole he was winning, he should voluntarily deprive himself of his Greek provinces. An accidental encounter between the Turkish fleet and the Allies in the harbour of Navarino (Oct. 1827) ended in the destruction of the former ; and the peaceful, if somewhat domineering, mediation of the Three Powers was exchanged for a naval blockade, the landing of a French force in the Morea, whence they speedily expelled Mahmūd's Egyptian contingent, and, finally, a Russo-Turkish war (1828–9). This was what Russia had been wanting all along. The rupture had been staved off at a heavy sacrifice by the Treaty of Akkerman in 1826, because the Sultan's army was then in no state for a great war. The alliance of the Three Powers in 1827

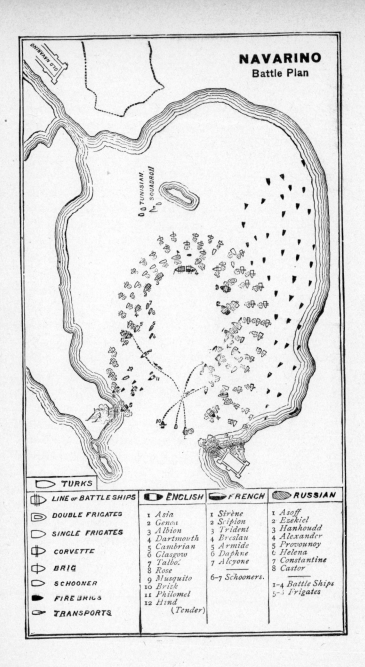

NAVARINO
Battle Plan

OLD NAVARINO

TUNISIAN SQUADRON

TURKS			
LINE OF BATTLE SHIPS	ENGLISH	FRENCH	RUSSIAN
DOUBLE FRIGATES	1 Asia	1 Sirène	1 Asoff
SINGLE FRIGATES	2 Genoa	2 Scipion	2 Ezekiel
CORVETTE	3 Albion	3 Trident	3 Hanhoudd
BRIG	4 Dartmouth	4 Breslau	4 Alexander
SCHOONER	5 Cambrian	5 Armide	5 Provounoy
FIRE BRIGS	6 Glasgow	6 Daphne	6 Helena
TRANSPORTS	7 Talbot	7 Alcyone	7 Constantine
	8 Rose		8 Castor
	9 Musquito	6-7 Schooners.	
	10 Brisk		1-4 Battle Ships
	11 Philomel		5-8 Frigates
	12 Hind		
	(Tender)		

seemed to forbid separate action. But Mr. Canning
was now dead, and Lord Aberdeen's presence at
the Foreign Office gave Russia free scope for action.
The result was Diebitsch's daring march over the
Balkan, and the humiliation of Mahmūd in the Treaty
of Adrianople (1829), in presence of a Russian army
which could hardly have exceeded 15,000 men. At
the point of the sword the Sultan was forced to con-
cede what all the arguments of ambassadors, and even
the fatal catastrophe at Navarino, had failed to extort.
Greece was made free, and in 1832 her boundaries
were extended to very nearly their present limits.
Prince Leopold refused the crown, and the Bavarian
Otho, as King of the Hellenes, taught the people that
a constitutional government by Christian foreigners
may be almost as corrupt and exasperating as even
the rule of a Turkish pasha.

The severance of Greece was a sore blow to
Mahmūd's hopes ; yet, even now, had he been allowed
ten years of tranquillity he might have been able
to carry out the reforming policy upon which his
heart was set. Such however was not to be his
fortune. Shorn of his fleet by the Allies, weakened
in arms and prestige by the Russian war, he became
the natural prey of his powerful vassal the Viceroy
of Egypt. Mohammed Alī pushed his forces across
Syria and even threatened the Bosphorus ; the timely
interposition of Russia (duly recompensed in the
Treaty of Hunkiar Iskelesi, 1833) saved Constantinople. This treaty was a rude surprise to the
Western Powers, for it gave Russia the exclusive
right of way through the Dardanelles : but they too¹

time before they ventured to assert themselves. France was on the side of Mohammed Alī; and England, under the Whig administrations of Grey and Melbourne, was too much harassed at home to retain a free hand for foreign affairs. Palmerston admitted that he had delayed too long before supporting the Sultan, but at length the English fleet sailed for the Levant, Acre was taken, and Mohammed Alī, by the Treaty of 1841, was confined to his Egyptian possessions, under the suzerainty of the Sultan, the integrity and independence of whose empire were now placed formally under the guarantee of the Great Powers. The Treaty of 1841 was a new and vital departure: Turkey was for the first time placed in a state of tutelage, but how far the protection of the Great Powers has benefited her must be considered in the light of more recent events.

Meanwhile Mahmūd had died in 1839, when his empire seemed doomed to fall into the hands of his dangerous vassal. Had he lived, the fourteen years of peace which followed might have been turned to immense account; his masterful will might have reformed the whole system of administration. But his son and successor, Abd-ul-Mejīd, while possessed of many amiable and loveable qualities, was timorous and infirm of purpose. Whatever good was done in the interval of tranquillity which filled the fifth decade of the century was principally the work of the great statesman who then held the post of British Ambassador at the Porte.

Sir Stratford Canning began his diplomatic career in 1807, when he was secretary to a mission sent to

Copenhagen to effect a reconciliation with the Danes after the impounding of their fleet. At the age of twenty-three he was Minister Plenipotentiary at Constantinople, and in 1812, without aid or advice from his Government, but wholly of his own motion and by his own diplomatic skill, he brought about the Treaty of Bucharest, which, as we have seen, released the Russian army of the Danube just in time to attack Napoleon on his disastrous retreat from Moscow. He subsequently served in Switzerland, was present at the Congress of Vienna, held the post of Minister to the United States, and returning to Turkey in 1826 took a principal part in effecting the freedom of Greece, and especially in securing her an adequate and defensible boundary. At the beginning of 1842 he resumed his former post at Constantinople, and began that series of reforms which nothing could have carried but the supreme influence which gained him the name of *the Great Elchi*, or Ambassador *par excellence*. Long experience of the Turks, personal friendship with the Sultan, and the support of the young Turkish party, who had learnt something of Western civilization, were among the causes of his success ; but the mainspring lay in his personal character. Truthful and straightforward in all his ways, he never condescended to the tricks of diplomacy, and the Turks soon began to perceive that what Canning spoke was the truth. Gifted moreover with a sedate gravity which gave dignity and importance to the smallest negotiations,—and which was the more valuable because men knew that beneath the calm and polished surface lay a

impetuous passionate spirit, impatient of restraint,—
the manner of the Great Elchi was full of charm and
persuasion. His refined and intellectual countenance
was the index to his courteous and chivalrous
nature. When circumstances so required, none
could be more urbane ; but when he scented de-
ception or trickery, the man's fiery nature blazed up,
and in his anger he was terrible — few dared to
withstand him. The Turkish ministers and the
Sultan himself bowed themselves down before his
righteous indignation. By force of character, by a
certain admirable violence, necessary in dealing with
dilatory and prevaricating people, by a kingly grace
and courtesy which stamped him a gentleman of the
true sort, but above all by a manly unswerving
honesty and straightforwardness, Stratford Canning
acquired that extraordinary influence which no
Christian has exercised before or since over the
princes and statesmen of the Ottoman Empire.

In 1842 he began his long struggle with Turkish
corruption. Reshid Pasha, the most enlightened of
the statesmen of the Porte, had in 1839 induced the
Sultan to promulgate a sort of Turkish Magna
Charta, called the *Hatti-Sherīf of Gulhané*, (or the
Tanzimat,) whereby many of the anomalies, cor-
ruptions, and disabilities of the administrative and
judicial system, especially in regard to the Christian
rayas, were abolished—on paper. The reform was
premature and was followed by the fall of Reshid
and a strong reaction in favour of the old Turkish
system. It was Canning's design to overturn the
reactionaries and restore Reshid, and in this, after

three or four years, he succeeded. Step by step he obtained the dismissal of fanatical and ignorant officials, and replaced them by men of Reshid's way of thinking. With the aid of the liberal party in the Divan, he carried reform after reform—none very sweeping, for the time had not yet come, and there was no Mahmūd to enforce a complete change, —but each essential to the well-being of the Sultan's Christian subjects. His object was to reform Turkey from within, by removing those glaring injustices which marked so many branches of the executive Government. He did not work for the Christians merely because they were Christians, but because they had the least measure of justice, and so required more support to bring them up to the level of their Moslem neighbours. Equal citizenship for all was his policy. With this view he wrung from the Sultan, after a herculean struggle, in 1844, the promise that thenceforward no one who apostatized from Islam and became a Christian should, as heretofore, be executed; and that the Christian religion should suffer no molestation in the Ottoman dominions. The concession was the more noteworthy since it repealed what was believed to be a part of the sacred law of the Koran. This was followed up by a formal abolition of torture, by the repeal of obnoxious taxes, notably the poll-tax on non-Musulmans which belonged to the ancient constitution of Islam, by the admission of Christian evidence in Moslem law courts, and by various other improvements, which were all eventually summarized and completed in the famous edict—the Hatti-

Humayūn of 1856, which forms part of the Treaty of
Paris. An immense deal remained to be done, but
it was impossible to drive the Turks at a fast pace,
and Canning had to be content with what he could
get. So long as he was at his post reforms accumulated, and his vigilant eye watched every quarter
of the Ottoman Empire to see where offences were
and from whence they came, and to bring condign
punishment on the offender. No pasha was safe,
even so far off as Baghdad, if a complaint against him
reached the ear of the Great Elchi. His power was
unique, and he used it for no selfish or ambitious
end: his arm was stretched forth in the cause of
right and justice alone.[1]

Then, in the midst of this stage of gradual reformation, came two shocks from without. The first passed
off without more than a temporary interruption of
progress. It happened in 1849 that sundry refugees
from Hungary and Poland, where the mid-century
revolutions were in course of sanguinary suppression
by Austria and Russia, sought asylum in the dominions
of the Sultan. Among them were Kossuth, Bem,
Dembinski, and other well-known leaders. The two
emperors demanded their extradition, which was
another word for their slaughter; but the Turks
declared that it was contrary to the Mohammedan
principle of hospitality to give up strangers to their
pursuers, and Sir Stratford Canning supported them
in their honourable resistance. Austria and Russia
broke off relations with Turkey, and matters looked

[1] " Life of Lord Stratford de Redcliffe," by S. Lane-Poole, vol. ii.,
ch xvii.

serious; but the appearance of the English and French fleets at the entrance of the Hellespont showed that there were more Powers to be reckoned with than Turkey; the crisis passed, and the refugees were saved. The fame of the Great Elchi and the honour of the Sultan never stood higher than when they thus upheld the sacred right of asylum.

The second interruption was more serious. It began in a mere trifle. There were monks of different sorts at Jerusalem,—Latin Church, Greek Church, and Armenian Church,—and the two former were perpetually quarrelling over ridiculous details of ritual at the Holy Places where their common Master suffered and was buried. France protected the Latin variety of monk, Russia the Greek; and whether, as has been asserted, the Emperor Louis Napoleon thought it necessary to distract his subjects with a warlike diversion, or whether it merely happened that the quarrels of the monks came to a crisis just then, it is certain that in 1852 the French grew exceedingly imperious in their demands, and Turkey was at her wits' ends to satisfy both complainants. With the help of Stratford Canning, who had now been raised to the peerage as Viscount Stratford de Redcliffe, the dispute was happily arranged in April 1853 : but Russia then insisted on an additional Convention which would have given her a protectorate over all the 12,000,000 subjects of the Sultan who professed the Greek or " Orthodox " religion. This could not be admitted, and though for many months the statesmen of Europe vied with one another in evolving schemes of pacification, it was evident from the first that the

half-crazy Tsar would not be satisfied with less than
war. The Russians marched into Wallachia, without
a tittle of excuse, in June 1853 : but the Turks, guided
by Lord Stratford, contented themselves with a pro-
test, and negotiations were continued at Vienna and
elsewhere. England and France sent their fleets
through the Dardanelles in October ; but still it was
not precisely war. But when, after distinct warning
from the Western Powers, Russia entered the Turkish
harbour of Sinope, and sent a Turkish fleet to the
bottom, and massacred the helpless drowning crews
almost under the eyes of the English and French
Admirals, who were then stationed in the Bosphorus, the fighting spirit of John Bull fired up,
and the Crimean War ensued (March 28, 1854).

The war was made with the object of compelling
Russia to withdraw her army from the Principalities.
But the allied forces of France and England, under
Marshal St. Arnaud and Lord Raglan, had not arrived
at the scene of operations when the menaces of
Austria and the magnificent pluck displayed by the
Turks, under the leadership of Butler and Nasmyth,
in the defence of Silistria, forced the Russians to fall
back. They crossed the Danube in June pursued by
the Turks, and the object of the war was practically
attained.

But there was a general feeling that Russia would
not be reduced to her proper position until the frowning forts of Sevastopol in the Crimea had been razed.
Accordingly in September the Allies embarked on
one of the craziest expeditions that any army ever
attempted. Ignorant of the country, the fortifications,

and the strength of the enemy, they landed on a desolate peninsula with a comparatively small force, no base, and scanty means of provisioning. They found the enemy ready for them in superior numbers and in a strong position on the heights behind the Alma river, and (the French having missed their part of the manœuvre) the English fought their way up the hill in face of a tremendous cannonade, and sent the Russians flying (20 Sept.). Had the Allies been strong enough to push on in pursuit, Sevastopol might have been taken by assault the next day ; but inadequate numbers, the care of the wounded, the caution of some, and the jealousy of others, obliged Lord Raglan to pause ; and, feeling the paramount need of a harbour for commissariat, the Allies made a flank march, seized the port of Balaklava, and prepared to lay siege to Sevastopol from the south side. The Russians made several diversions. One was an attack on the right flank of the British force on 18 October, which provoked the splendid and effectual onslaught of the Heavies under General Scarlett, and the equally brilliant but mistaken charge of the Light Brigade, which has been the theme of poets and patriots for a generation. Those who, like the writer, have seen with their own eyes the fatal " Valley of Death " can alone realize in any degree the " mouth of hell " into which, in perfect calm and with well-dressed ranks, rode " the noble Six Hundred." The terrible loss suffered on that famous day left the English less able to meet fresh emergencies : but on 5 November, surprised in a fog, 8,000 Englishmen, consisting of the Guards and the 20th Regiment, kept a

Russian army of 40,000 men at bay for several hours at one spot on the slopes of Inkerman, until the French came up and helped them to drive the enemy back in confusion.

Meanwhile the siege of Sevastopol progressed slowly. The defence, conducted by Todleben, was alike skilful and indefatigable. The attack was over-deliberate, and, on the part of the · French at least, hampered by interference from home. Several assaults in the spring and summer of 1855 failed to overcome the resistance of the enemy. One French general had died ; the second resigned ; Lord Raglan-borne down with anxiety, and a victim to popular indignation, which in Carthaginian fashion seldom spares unsuccessful generals, succumbed to care and overstrain in June 1855. It was not till September that the Malakov earthwork fell to the vigorous assault of the French, and the city of Sevastopol was at length occupied by the Allies.

Instead of taking advantage of this success, and pushing Russia back to her ancient limits at the Caucasus and the Dniester, and reviving the kingdom of Poland as a watchtower to the west, the Allies made peace, and the Treaty of Paris was signed in March 1856. A trifling rectification of the frontier was made, but the main provisions of the Treaty were the guarantee of the independence and integrity of the Ottoman Empire by the contracting Powers, the abolition of the Russian protectorate over the Danubian principalities and Serbia, the neutralization and opening of the Black Sea to ships of commerce of all nations, and the closing of the Bosphorus and Dardanelles to foreign ships of war while the Porte should be at peace. The Powers pledged themselves not to meddle in the internal affairs of Turkey, and the Sultan promised reforms in his administration and better treatment of his Christian subjects. The principles of this reformation were enunciated in the celebrated *Hatti-Humayūn*, which had been promulgated in the previous February : " brave words " and little more. The vital part of the Treaty, concerning the neutrality of the Black Sea, was repudiated by the Tsar in 1870, when the Franco-German war had deprived England of the only ally who would have joined her in opposing him ; and in January 1871 Mr. Gladstone's government consented to this shameful breach of good faith. The Black Sea is once more a Russian lake, and Sevastopol was taken in vain.

The Treaty of Paris left Turkey practically intact. It did not restore her stolen provinces, but it caused her no fresh losses. The time, however, was not far off when dismemberment would become inevitable. Lord Stratford had long seen that nothing but honest and sweeping reforms could save the Ottoman Empire : but he left the Porte in 1858, and no one who succeeded him was strong enough to enforce those changes which were essential to its preservation. One by one the provinces approached independence. Moldavia and Wallachia, united in 1858, became thenceforward practically an independent state : and the acquisition of a Hohenzollern as hereditary prince in 1866 gave Rumania (as the provinces are now called) a place in European combinations. Troubles broke out in the Lebanon in 1860, a French army was dispatched to restore order, and in the adjustment of rival claims an opportunity was afforded to Lord Dufferin for displaying those diplomatic talents for which he is renowned. In 1861 the Sultan Abd-ul-Mejīd died, and with him passed away the hope of regenerating Turkey. His brother and successor Abd-ul-Azīz was an ignorant bigot, whose extravagance brought his country to avowed insolvency (1875), and thus deprived her of that sympathy which is seldom given to the impecunious. The only remarkable thing he did was to travel. No Ottoman Sultan had ever before left his own dominions, except on the war path, but Abd-ul-Azīz ventured even as far as London, without, however, awakening any enthusiasm on the part of his Allies. In 1876 he was deposed, and—found dead. How he came by his death is a matter of doubt, but his end is said to have turned the brain of his successor Murād V., a son of Abd-ul-Mejīd, who after three months was removed as an imbecile, and succeeded by his brother the reigning Sultan Abd-ul-Hamīd.

This unfortunate prince, who is believed to be endowed with some sagacity, has been compelled to witness the most serious encroachments upon his empire which have yet taken place. Before his accession there had been a revolt among the Christians of the north. Herzegovina rose in 1874–5, and the massacres and brutalities which too often characterize Turkish police-measures ensued. Prompted by Russia, Bulgaria attempted to shake off the yoke in 1876, and some terrible deeds were perpetrated by the Turkish soldiery in suppressing the revolt. Exaggerated as they were by the newspapers, the " Bulgarian Atrocities " at Batak were nevertheless bad enough to rouse a tempest of righteous indignation in England, even without the adroit aid of an inflammatory pamphlet written by Mr. Gladstone. Serbia and Montenegro now joined the rebellion, and the Porte had to exert her strength to meet her numerous foes. The Great Powers used their efforts at mediation in vain. A Conference at Constantinople (Jan. 1877) was met by a rejection of its proposals, and by a melodramatic promulgation of an Ottoman Constitution, of which little more has been heard ; and Russia, separating from the European concert, took the law into her own hands and declared war. (April 1877.) Whether the collective action of the Powers might have attained the desired end without hostilities, and whether the Tsar was really driven onward by the uncontrollable Slav sympathies of his subjects, or was actuated by mere motives of aggrandisement, are questions which must be left unsolved. The war began, and the Turks at first held their own, especially in Asia, where they won the battle of Kizil-tepé, and drove the Russians back from Kars. In Europe, no attempt was made to oppose the passage of the Danube, and the Russians occupied Tirnova and Nicopolis, and even sent a flying detachment under General Gurko over the Balkan. But the great feature of the war was the defence of Plevna by Othmān Pasha. For five months the Russians and Rumanians vainly laid siege to the fortress ; twice they were totally defeated in the field ; till at last in December starvation, aided it is said by bribing the commanders of

the reinforcements who were bringing stores, did the
work which no artillery could accomplish, and Othmān
Pasha, with his army of 32,000 heroes, made a desperate attempt to break through the investing lines, and
was compelled to surrender. The taking of Plevna
cost Russia 50,000 men.

The end was not far off. After Plevna had fallen,
and Mukhtar had been driven back in Armenia with
the loss of Kars, General Gurko again crossed the
Balkan in January, 1878. He cut his upward steps in
the ice, and literally *slid* down the other side. Sofia
was occupied, and, after some gallant fighting in the
Shipka Pass, Radetski forced his way through, and
preliminaries of peace were signed (as in 1829) at the
point of the bayonet at Adrianople. A Treaty was
then concluded at San Stefano, 3 March, in the presence of the Russian army, which was actually encamped on the shore of the Sea of Marmora ; but the
conditions were so damaging to Turkey, that Lord
Beaconsfield interposed, and the Treaty of San Stefano
was abrogated by that of Berlin, June 1878. By this
Treaty, which records the partial dismemberment of
Turkey with the consent of Europe, in spite of all the
pledges of 1856, Servia, Montenegro, and Rumania
were declared independent ; the State of Bulgaria was
created, in two divisions, one of which was to be
autonomous, the other governed by the Porte ; and
Thessaly was apportioned to Greece. Russia regained
the strip of Bessarabia which had been taken from
her in 1856, and retained her conquests in Asia—Kars,
Batūm, and Ardahan. In return for her easy compli-
ance in these arrangements, England accepted a

peculiar position in relation to Turkey: she announced a protectorate over the Asiatic dominions of the Sultan (though to this day no one appears to understand what are the duties and rights involved in the compact), and, in order to have a convenient station whence to observe events in the East, she took possession of the island of Cyprus, which she still holds in fee of the Sultan, to whom she pays tribute.   Lord Beaconsfield (at least ostensibly) took credit for these acquisitions, and considered that the Treaty of Berlin with its accessory conventions formed a satisfactory embodiment of " Peace with Honour."

Thus was Turkey gradually reduced to its present restricted dimensions.   In its old extent, when the Porte ruled not merely the narrow territory now called Turkey in Europe, but Greece, Bulgaria and Eastern Rumelia, Rumania, Serbia, Bosnia, and Herzegovina, with the Crimea and a portion of Southern Russia ; Asia Minor to the borders of Persia ; Egypt, Syria, Tripoli, Tunis, Algiers, and numerous islands in the Mediterranean, — not counting the vast but mainly desert tract of Arabia—the total population (at the present time) would be over fifty millions, and the square mileage over two millions, or nearly twice Europe without Russia.   One by one her provinces have been taken away.   Algiers and Tunis have been incorporated with France, and thus 175,000 square miles and five millions of inhabitants have transferred their allegiance.   Egypt is practically independent, and this means a loss of 500,000 miles and over six millions of inhabitants.   Asiatic Turkey alone has suffered comparatively little diminution.

This forms the bulk of her present dominions, and comprises about 680,000 square miles, and over sixteen millions of population. In Europe her losses have been almost as severe as in Africa, where Tripoli alone remains to her. Serbia and Bosnia are "administered" by Austria, and thereby nearly 40,000 miles and three and a half millions of people have become Austrian subjects. Wallachia and Moldavia are united in the independent kingdom of Rumania, diminishing the extent of Turkey by 46,000 miles and over five millions of inhabitants. Bulgaria is a dependent state, over which the Porte has no real control, and Eastern Rumelia has lately *de facto* become part of Bulgaria, and the two contain nearly 40,000 square miles, and three millions of inhabitants. The kingdom of Greece with its 25,000 miles and two millions of population has long been separated from its parent. In Europe where the Turkish territory once extended to 230,000 square miles, with a population of nearly twenty millions, it now reaches only the total of 66,000 miles and four and a half millions: it has lost nearly three-fourths of its land, and about the same proportion of its people.

Whether what has happened since the famous Congress sat upon the state of Turkey in solemn conclave at Berlin in 1878 can be held to justify the motto of "Peace with Honour" may be decided by the reader on the evidence of facts or the strength of political conviction. One thing seems clear, that, rightly or wrongly, in supporting the Christian provinces against their sovereign, the Powers at Berlin sounded the knell of Turkish domination in Europe. Asiatic Turkey, under the aegis of England's mysterious "protectorate," may still enjoy its ancient barbaric existence, menaced perhaps by Russians in the north-east, by canals in the south, and by advancing civilization everywhere : but in Europe, the Turk will mount guard over the Bosphorus, and sit in the seat of the Caesars only so long as Europe requires him there. Another Power is quite ready to take his place, and even in England the impossibility of permitting a Tsar to reign at Constantinople is no longer quite an undisputed axiom. But whether, with all our prejudice against the "unspeakable" Turk, the Moslem is a worse ruler than the Russian, and ought necessarily to give way to the advancing tide of Slavonic "civilization," is a question too large for this little book. At the best it is a choice of evils.

There are some who believe in a great Mohammedan revival, with the Sultan-Khalif at the head,—a second epoch of Saracen prowess, and a return to the good days when Turks were simple, sober, honest men, who fought like lions. There is plenty of such stuff in the people still : but where are their leaders ? Till Carlyle's great man comes, the hero who can lead a nation back to paths of valour and righteousness, to dream of the regeneration of Turkey is but a bootless speculation.

THE END.

INDEX.

Heroes of the Nations

A SERIES of biographical studies of the lives and work of a number of representative historical characters about whom have gathered the great traditions of the Nations to which they belonged, and who have been accepted, in many instances, as types of the several National ideals. With the life of each typical character is presented a picture of the National conditions surrounding him during his career.

The narratives are the work of writers who are recognized authorities on their several subjects, and while thoroughly trustworthy as history, present picturesque and dramatic " stories " of the Men and of the events connected with them.

To the Life of each " Hero " is given one duodecimo volume, handsomely printed in large type, provided with maps and adequately illustrated according to the special requirements of the several subjects.

For full list of volumes see next page.

The Story of the Nations

IN the story form the current of each National life is distinctly indicated, and its picturesque and note-worthy periods and episodes are presented for the reader in their philosophical relation to each other as well as to universal history.

It is the plan of the writers of the different volumes to enter into the real life of the peoples, and to bring them before the reader as they actually lived, labored, and struggled—as they studied and wrote, and as they amused themselves. In carrying out this plan, the myths, with which the history of all lands begins, will not be overlooked, though these will be carefully distinguished from the actual history, so far as the labors of the accepted historical authorities have resulted in definite conclusions.

The subjects of the different volumes have been planned to cover connecting and, as far as possible, consecutive epochs or periods, so that the set when completed will present in a comprehensive narrative the chief events in the great STORY OF THE NATIONS; but it is, of course, not always practicable to issue the several volumes in their chronological order.

For list of volumes see next page.

HEROES OF THE NATIONS

NELSON. By W. Clark Russell.

GUSTAVUS ADOLPHUS. By C. R. L. Fletcher.

PERICLES. By Evelyn Abbott.

THEODORIC THE GOTH. By Thomas Hodgkin.

SIR PHILIP SIDNEY. By H. R. Fox-Bourne.

JULIUS CÆSAR. By W. Warde Fowler.

WYCLIF. By Lewis Sergeant.

NAPOLEON. By W. O'Connor Morris.

HENRY OF NAVARRE. By P. F. Willert.

CICERO. By J. L. Strachan-Davidson.

ABRAHAM LINCOLN. By Noah Brooks.

PRINCE HENRY (OF PORTUGAL) THE NAVIGATOR. By C. R. Beazley.

JULIAN THE PHILOSOPHER. By Alice Gardner.

LOUIS XIV. By Arthur Hassall.

CHARLES XII. By R. Nisbet Bain.

LORENZO DE' MEDICI. By Edward Armstrong.

JEANNE D'ARC. By Mrs. Oliphant.

CHRISTOPHER COLUMBUS. By Washington Irving.

ROBERT THE BRUCE. By Sir Herbert Maxwell.

HANNIBAL. By W. O'Connor Morris.

ULYSSES S. GRANT. By William Conant Church.

ROBERT E. LEE. By Henry Alexander White.

THE CID CAMPEADOR. By H. Butler Clarke.

SALADIN. By Stanley Lane-Poole.

BISMARCK. By J. W. Headlam.

ALEXANDER THE GREAT. By Benjamin I. Wheeler.

CHARLEMAGNE. By H. W. C. Davis.

OLIVER CROMWELL. By Charles Firth.

RICHELIEU. By James E. Perkins.

DANIEL O'CONNELL. By Robert Dunlop.

SAINT LOUIS (Louis IX. of France). By Frederick Perry.

LORD CHATHAM. By Walford David Green.

OWEN GLYNDWR. By Arthur G. Bradley.

HENRY V. By Charles L. Kingsford.

EDWARD I. By Edward Jenks.

AUGUSTUS CÆSAR. By J. B. Firth.

FREDERICK THE GREAT. By W. F. Reddaway.

WELLINGTON. By W. O'Connor Morris.

CONSTANTINE THE GREAT. By J. B. Firth.

MOHAMMED. D. S. Margoliouth.

GEORGE WASHINGTON. By J. A. Harrison.

CHARLES THE BOLD. By Ruth Putnam.

WILLIAM THE CONQUEROR. By F. B. Stanton.

FERNANDO CORTES. By F. A. MacNutt.

WILLIAM THE SILENT. By R. Putnam.

BLÜCHER. By E. F. Henderson.

ROGER THE GREAT. By E. Curtis.

CANUTE THE GREAT. By L. M. Larson.

CAVOUR. By Pietro Orsi.

DEMOSTHENES. By A. W. Pickard-Cambridge.

THE STORY OF THE NATIONS

GREECE. Prof. Jas. A. Harrison.

ROME. Arthur Gilman.

THE JEWS. Prof. James K. Hosmer.

CHALDEA. Z. A. Ragozin.

GERMANY. S. Baring-Gould.

NORWAY. Hjalmar H. Boyesen.

SPAIN. Rev. E. E. and Susan Hale.

HUNGARY. Prof. A. Vámbéry.

CARTHAGE. Prof. Alfred J. Church.

THE SARACENS. Arthur Gilman.

THE MOORS IN SPAIN. Stanley Lane-Poole.

THE NORMANS. Sarah Orne Jewett.

PERSIA. S. G. W. Benjamin.

ANCIENT EGYPT. Prof. Geo. Rawlinson.

ALEXANDER'S EMPIRE. Prof. J. P. Mahaffy.

ASSYRIA. Z. A. Ragozin.

THE GOTHS. Henry Bradley.

IRELAND. Hon. Emily Lawless.

TURKEY. Stanley Lane-Poole.

MEDIA, BABYLON, AND PERSIA. Z. A. Ragozin.

MEDIÆVAL FRANCE. Prof. Gustave Masson.

HOLLAND. Prof. J. Thorold Rogers.

MEXICO. Susan Hale.

PHŒNICIA. George Rawlinson.

THE HANSA TOWNS. Helen Zimmern.

EARLY BRITAIN Prof. Alfred J. Church.

THE BARBARY CORSAIRS. Stanley Lane-Poole.

RUSSIA. W. R. Morfill.

THE JEWS UNDER ROME. W. D. Morrison.

SCOTLAND. John Mackintosh.

SWITZERLAND. R. Stead and Mrs. A. Hug.

PORTUGAL. H. Morse-Stephens.

THE BYZANTINE EMPIRE. C. W. C. Oman.

SICILY. E. A. Freeman.

THE TUSCAN REPUBLICS Bella Duffy.

POLAND. W. R. Morfill.

PARTHIA. Geo. Rawlinson.

JAPAN. David Murray.

THE CHRISTIAN RECOVERY OF SPAIN. H. E. Watts.

AUSTRALASIA. Greville Tregarthen.

SOUTHERN AFRICA. Geo. M. Theal.

VENICE. Alethea Wiel.

THE CRUSADES. T. S. Archer and C. L. Kingsford.

VEDIC INDIA. Z. A. Ragozin.

BOHEMIA. C. E. Maurice.

CANADA. J. G. Bourinot.

THE BALKAN STATES. William Miller.

BRITISH RULE IN INDIA. R. W. Frazer.

MODERN FRANCE. André Le Bon.

THE BRITISH EMPIRE. Alfred T. Story. Two vols.

THE FRANKS. Lewis Sergeant.

THE WEST INDIES. Amos K. Fiske.

THE PEOPLE OF ENGLAND. Justin McCarthy, M.P. Two vols.

AUSTRIA. Sidney Whitman.

CHINA. Robt. K. Douglass.

MODERN SPAIN. Major Martin A. S. Hume.

MODERN ITALY. Pietro Orsi.

THE THIRTEEN COLONIES. Helen A. Smith. Two vols.

WALES AND CORNWALL. Owen M. Edwards.

MEDIÆVAL ROME. Wm. Miller

THE PAPAL MONARCHY Wm Barry.

MEDIÆVAL INDIA. Stanley Lane-Poole.

BUDDHIST INDIA. T. W. Rhys Davids.

THE SOUTH AMERICAN REPUBLICS. Thomas C. Dawson. Two vols.

PARLIAMENTARY ENGLAND. Edward Jenks.

MEDIÆVAL ENGLAND. Mary Bateson.

THE UNITED STATES. Edward Earle Sparks. Two vols.

ENGLAND. THE COMING OF PARLIAMENT. L. Cecil Jane

GREECE TO A. D. 14. E. S. Shuckburgh.

ROMAN EMPIRE. Stuart Jones.